GREY CUP 100

Graham Kelly

FULL
COURT
PRESS

GREY CUP
100

© 2012 by Full Court Press
First printed in 2012 10 9 8 7 6 5 4 3 2 1
Printed in Canada

All rights reserved. No part of this work covered by the copyrights hereon may be reproduced or used in any form or by any means—graphic, electronic or mechanical—without the prior written permission of the publisher, except for reviewers, who may quote brief passages. Any request for photocopying, recording, taping or storage on information retrieval systems of any part of this work shall be directed in writing to the publisher.

Full Court Press is an imprint of Folklore Publishing Ltd.

Library and Archives Canada Cataloguing in Publication

Kelly, Graham, 1942–
Grey Cup 100 / Graham Kelly.

Includes bibliographical references.
ISBN 978-1-926677-85-9

Kelly, Graham, 1942–
History of the Grey Cup / Graham Kelly.

Includes bibliographical references.
ISBN 978-1-926677-87-3

1. Grey Cup (Football)—History. 2. Canadian Football League—History. 3. Canadian football—History. I. Title.

GV948.K443 2012   796.335'648   C2012-906274-X

Project Director: Faye Boer
Project Editor: Kathy van Denderen
Photo Credits: Every effort has been made to accurately credit the sources of photographs. Any errors or omissions should be reported directly to the publisher for correction in future editions. Photographs on pages 82–83 courtesy of the City of Regina Archives. All other photographs courtesy of the Canadian Football Hall of Fame.
Cover Image: Grey Cup courtesy of the Canadian Football Hall of Fame and Museum; football game in background - Dennis Ku/Shutterstock.com

We gratefully acknowledge the financial support of the Government of Alberta for our publishing program through the Alberta Multimedia Development Program

Government of Alberta

We acknowledge the financial support of the Government of Canada through the Canada Book Fund (CBF) for our publishing activities.

 Canadian Heritage   Patrimoine canadien

PC: 1

Dedication

To my dear wife Lorena, my companion at 24 Grey Cups, for making it possible in so many ways for me to indulge my love of Canadian football. We've made this journey together.

Contents

Introduction 9
Chapter 1: Grey Cup Dawn, 1909-19 11
Chapter 2: East Versus West, 1920-34 16
Chapter 3: The Whirlwind from the West,
*   1935-39* 32
Chapter 4: The End of the Beginning, 1940-47 42
Chapter 5: Eastward Ho the Wagons! 1948-49 53
Chapter 6: Gridiron Greats, 1950-56 77
Chapter 7: Lions, Tigers and Bombers, Oh My!
*   1957-65* 105
Chapter 8: The Riders, 1966-72 and 1976 140
Chapter 9: Dynasty—The Edmonton Eskimos,
*   1973-75 and 1977-82* 186
Chapter 10: Feline Frenzy, 1983-88 218
Chapter 11: The Greatest Grey Cup of Them
*   All, 1989* 249
Chapter 12: Yankee Doodle Dandy, 1990-97 262
Chapter 13: Go Stamps Go! 1998-2001 313
Chapter 14: Saint Anthony and Ben, 2002-12 335
Notes on Sources 383

Acknowledgements

I would like to thank the many past and present CFL players, coaches and executives that I interviewed for this history of the Grey Cup.

I would also like to thank the Calgary Stampeders for making the man from Medicine Hat so welcome at McMahon Stadium over the last 40 years.

I am deeply indebted to Stan Schwartz, the executive vice-president of the Calgary Stampeders, for his constant friendship, input and support.

I want to thank my publisher and especially my editor Kathy van Denderen.

Introduction

The first Grey Cup game was played on December 4, 1909, at Rosedale Field between the Toronto Parkdales and the University of Toronto Varsity Blues, the students winning 26–6 before 3807 fans. Varsity's Hugh Gall's touchdown were the first points scored in Grey Cup history.

Truly Canada's greatest sports spectacle, the Grey Cup unites Canadians from coast-to-coast-to-coast in a celebration that transcends football. Everyone from corporate presidents to prime ministers to school children revel in the excitement and anticipation of the great event. Whether watching at home or attending in person, on Grey Cup Sunday, millions take in the big game.

The Grey Cup isn't about money. And, unless you're from Saskatchewan, it's not a matter of life and death. It is a celebration, a time to party, the only occasion when Canadians from all corners of the country assemble to enjoy a distinctively Canadian sporting event.

In 1921, the Grey Cup went national when the Edmonton Eskimos challenged for the good Earl's trophy. Winnipeg won the West's first Grey Cup in 1935. In 1948, Calgarians invented the Grey Cup festival when they descended on Toronto flipping flapjacks, riding horses, square dancing in front of City Hall and turning staid old Hogtown on its ear.

Throughout the decades, the Grey Cup has showcased some of the most entertaining football ever played in any league. When the Canadian Football League fell on desperate times during the 1980s and '90s, the Grey Cup was the CFL's salvation. The first major crisis came when the Montréal Alouettes folded on June 24, 1987. That year's Grey Cup, as well as those of 1988–89, were marvellous contests decided in the last minute. Those Grey Cups brought the CFL through its darkest hour.

The same was true in the mid-1990s, when expansion to the United States failed in early 1996 and the storied Ottawa Rough Riders ceased operations, giving the CFL another black eye. When fans gathered in Hamilton that year to watch the Argos and Eskimos contest the 84th Grey Cup, many thought it would be the last.

But the venerable old league refused to die. The CFL has proven to be the little engine that could. It has not only endured but has also been restored to health and approaches the future with confidence.

The Grey Cup remains Canada's most cherished sporting tradition and an integral part of our nation's culture.

chapter one

Grey Cup Dawn, 1909–19

Had Governor General Earl Albert Henry George Grey foreseen the place the trophy bearing his name would come to occupy in the hearts of Canadians, he might have shown more enthusiasm for the game of football. Apparently the Earl wanted the trophy to go to the Canadian senior hockey champions, but Montréal entrepreneur Sir Hugh Montagu Allan beat him to the punch and put up a mug himself. Quite likely an aide suggested that the trophy be awarded to the amateur football champion instead, and Grey agreed.

Including 2012, Toronto has played host to the Grey Cup 47 times, the first at Rosedale Field on December 4, 1909, a game between the Toronto Parkdale Canoe Club and the University of Toronto Varsity Blues. The temperature at game time was 2°C, and gate receipts totalled $2616.40. The Varsity Blues won 26–6 before 3807 spectators. Hugh Gall kicked a still-standing record of eight singles in the game.

Albert Earl Grey, 1909

However, the University of Toronto was not presented with the Cup after their victory because Grey's staff forgot to have the $48 trophy made. The oversight was corrected, Birks Jewellers performed their task and the Cup was finally presented to the winners the following March.

One of the great rivalries in Canadian football history has been between teams from Toronto and Hamilton. After the 1987 season, when the league decided to expand the base of the Grey Cup to accommodate more champions' names, they discovered that the University of Toronto's plaque from 1909 was mysteriously missing, replaced by one recognizing the 1908 victory of the Hamilton Tigers over the University of Toronto.

November 27, 1909, game between the University of Toronto Varsity Blues and the Ottawa Rough Riders. Ottawa is wearing the dark and white stockings.

The Varsity Blues repeated as champions in 1910, beating the Tigers 16–7 at the Hamilton Cricket Grounds in a game that drew considerable interest, with 12,000 fans paying $9500 to take in the event—Hamilton's population was only 70,221, whereas Toronto's was three times greater. Red Dixon, Jack Maynard and Hugh Gall starred for the students while Kid Smith led the way for Hamilton.

In 1911, Varsity won their third straight title, defeating their hometown rival Toronto Argonauts 14–7. That year, Lord Grey returned to England. He died on August 29, 1917, and is best remembered for that off-hand gesture of donating a trophy that bears his name to a game he found strange and hard to understand.

Teams from Hamilton won three of the next four Grey Cups, beginning in 1912 when the Alerts, coached by Liz

Marriott, defeated the Argos at Cricket Field by a score of 11–4. After winning three in a row, the University of Toronto had become so attached to the trophy that they refused to turn it over to the new champions. They didn't think it was fair to surrender the Cup without having lost it on the field of battle.

In 1913, Liz Marriott moved over to coach the Tigers, who thrashed Parkdale 44–2. The Argos won the title the next year, downing Varsity 14–2, after which the scholars, being the gentlemen sportsmen they were, promptly turned the Cup over to the victors.

The Hamilton Tigers finally got their hands on the Cup again when they trimmed Parkdale 13–7 in 1915.

Hugh Gall of Toronto kicking the football during the 1910 Grey Cup

With most young men serving their country in World War I, challenges for the Grey Cup were suspended for four years. The stars of those early years included Hugh Gall and Smirle Lawson of the University of Toronto, Jack Newton who starred for U of T and coached the Argonauts, and Ross Craig who played with the Hamilton Alerts and Hamilton Tigers. All are in the Canadian Football Hall of Fame. Honourable mention goes to Varsity's Jack Maynard.

The worst time in Canadian history was from 1914 to 1919. Canada sent an expeditionary force of around 620,000 young men to fight in World War I, a horrific conflict that accomplished nothing except sending millions of soldiers to their premature deaths and setting the stage for World War II. Over 67,000 Canadians died and 173,000 were wounded, many of whom never really recovered. The honour roll of war dead included many football players.

Although the war ended at the 11th hour on the 11th day of the 11th month of 1918, demobilization took over two years. If recovering from the most devastating war in human history wasn't enough, between 50,000 and 60,000 Canadians died during the Spanish influenza epidemic that struck in 1918. It is estimated that over 20 million died of the flu worldwide, more than the number of casualties in World War I.

chapter two

East Versus West, 1920–34

Grey Cups 1920–28

By 1920, Canada was beginning to return to normal, which included all of its sports. The University of Toronto defeated the Argonauts 16–2 to win the 1920 Grey Cup, bringing an end to the early years of Canadian football.

Rule changes in 1921 established many aspects of the game that is still played today. The number of starters was reduced from 14 to 12, and rosters were set at 18 per team, with substitutions allowed. The quarterback was permitted to cross the line of scrimmage. The scoring system was simplified, with a field goal equalling three points, a touchdown five, a single (a punt or kick through the end zone) and a rouge—scored when the return man was tackled in the end zone—also worth one point.

The Grey Cup became a truly national event in 1921 when the Edmonton Eskimos became the first team from the

West to challenge for the trophy. Although the Eskimos became the most successful franchise in Canadian Football League history, their Grey Cup story began rather inauspiciously, losing to the Argonauts 23–0. The westerners had several American college players on their team who had difficulty with the rules of the Canadian game and were repeatedly penalized for interference (blocking). If that wasn't enough, Lionel Conacher, later to be named Canada's athlete of the half century, scored 15 points before retiring from the field of play at the end of the third quarter in order to play hockey that night for the Toronto Maple Leafs.

The following year, the Eskimos, renamed the Elks, returned to the Grey Cup, losing to the Queen's University Golden Gaels 13–1. Thirty years passed before another Edmonton team competed for the national symbol of football supremacy.

Queen's repeated as Grey Cup champions in 1923, humiliating the Regina Rugby Club 54–0. The dominant team in the West at that time, the Rugby Club was simply no match for the Golden Gaels, even though Regina coach Jack Eadie said before boarding the eastbound train, "If Queen's can show any marked superiority over the Regina club, they will be hailed as a team of supermen. Our Regina club is without flaw or blemish so far as I can see…"

In their first attempt to win the Grey Cup, the Regina boys were given a football lesson by one of the finest teams of the pre-forward pass era. Queen's Frank "Pep" Leadlay, Harry Batstone and Billy Hughes are all members of the Canadian Football Hall of Fame. Their devastating use of blocking and end runs changed the game, and they went on to win 26 games in a row, including three Grey Cups.

An important ritual following gridiron contests today is the awarding of the game ball to the most deserving individual on the winning team. In 1923, in a manner similar to a bride throwing her bouquet, the winning captain tossed the game ball in the air and the players fought for possession. Regina's Bill Creighton fought off all challengers to come up with the ball that he proudly brought back to Saskatchewan. In those days, the game ball was actually the real game ball because usually only one football was used for the whole contest.

Because the Canadian Rugby Union (CRU) was controlled by the Ontario and Québec rugby unions, the Grey Cup was played in the East, often at the home of the Eastern champion. This placed the Western champion at a disadvantage, not only from a home-field perspective but also because the trip was quite expensive. Then, as now, Regina was the smallest city to compete for the national crown.

A committee made up of leading Regina citizens was struck to help raise funds for the trip. If the Grey Cup gate receipts were big enough, all team expenses would be covered, but that depended on the weather, which unfortunately was rather nasty on December 1 when Regina met Queen's. For that 1923 game, gate receipts only came to $8746.65, leaving a shortfall. The hat was passed back home, and the bills were paid. Saskatchewan football still operates that way.

Queen's made their final appearance in the Grey Cup in 1924, winning the coveted trophy for the third straight year with an 11–3 win over Toronto Balmy Beach. It was the last Grey Cup victory for intercollegiate football.

In 1924, the Winnipeg Victorias won the West by defeating Regina and Calgary and prepared to go down east. But the executive was split between one group that wanted the team to travel by CPR and the other that favoured the CNR. Rather than compromise, they decided to forego a Grey Cup challenge. The angry players said they would pay their own way, but the executive refused to let them use the team name. Finally, saner heads prevailed, and they decided to go, but the CRU said it was too late and rejected their challenge.

In 1925, two new teams played for the national championship—the Winnipeg Tammany Tigers and the Ottawa Senators—and Ottawa won 24–1 in a sea of mud at Lansdowne Park. The Senators successfully defended their title 12 months later at Varsity Stadium by downing the University of Toronto 10–7, the last time a university team competed for the Grey Cup.

The Western champion in 1926 and 1927 was the Regina Roughriders (their name was changed in 1924), but they declined to challenge for the Cup. The Ontario Rugby Football Union (ORFU) champion Toronto Balmy Beach beat the Hamilton Tigers 9–6 in 1927 to claim the Cup.

From 1928 through 1934, Regina represented the West in the big game six times, including five straight appearances. During that span, Regina only lost four regular-season games. The Roughriders of that era were one of the greatest organizations in Canadian football history. Coach Al Ritchie, Piffles Taylor and Clair Warner made it to the CFL Hall of Fame, all as builders. "Dynamite" Eddie James made the Hall but spent most of his career in Winnipeg. Perhaps losing all six Grey

Cup appearances was the reason why more Roughriders didn't make it into the CFL Hall of Fame.

The 1928 Roughriders, coached by Howie Milne, went undefeated during the regular season before defeating the Winnipeg St. John's Saints in the Western final at Park de Young in Regina, 12–1. Regina's opponent in the Grey Cup was the Hamilton Tigers, hailed as the "most formidable machine ever turned out by the Bengal breed under the mountain." Their leader was none other than Frank "Pep" Leadlay, who had finally graduated from Queen's and was playing senior ball for the Tabbies.

Hamilton officials insisted the Grey Cup be played on their home field, even though Toronto's Varsity Stadium could accommodate 17,000 fans. The Hamilton Amateur Athletic Association grounds were enlarged to hold 12,000. Tiger officials were willing to sacrifice the difference in gate receipts to give their fans a chance to witness the title game.

Accompanying the Riders to Hamilton were the Regina Junior Pats, coached by Al Ritchie. Just before the train left the station, coach Howie Milne resigned for business reasons. Ritchie took over the Riders and stayed over an extra week to coach the Pats in their quest for the Leader Trophy, which was presented to the Canadian junior football champions.

The Roughriders' major concern was their star halfback Fred Wilson, whose left ankle was "slightly" fractured in a game against Calgary a month earlier. Although the great veteran could walk without any trouble, running was another matter, and kicking was out of the question.

The Tigers were undefeated in 1928, outscoring their opponents 146–20. They outweighed the Roughriders by 11 pounds per man. Their stars were future Hall of Famers Huck Welch, Pep Leadlay, Alfred "Cap" Fear, Jimmy Simpson, Ernie Cox and Mike Rodden.

Hamilton opened the scoring in the first quarter with a touchdown by former Regina star Bryan Timmis, followed by a Huck Welch single. It was 6–0 at the half. The third quarter proved disastrous for the visitors. Welch nailed Desmond Grubb for a single. Simpson recovered a Fritz Sandstrom fumble in the end zone for a touchdown, converted by Leadlay. Minutes later, Welch caught Leadlay's onside kick and raced to the Regina one-yard line. Ken Walker scored on a quarterback sneak, again converted by Leadlay. Hamilton led 25–0 after 45 minutes. Timmis added an unconverted touchdown in the fourth quarter, making the score Hamilton Tigers 30, Regina Roughriders 0. A week later, Ritchie's Pats won the junior title, so at least they didn't return home empty-handed.

Grey Cup 1929

Hamilton and Regina met again for the national championship in 1929. To get there, Hamilton beat Sarnia 14–2 and Queen's 14–3. Regina played the first of many Western finals against Calgary. The black-and-gold clad Calgary Tigers were thought to have the best chance at dethroning the perennial champion Roughriders. Former great Fritz Sandstrom coached the Tigers. Their quarterback was the master passer Gerry Seiberling from Drake University.

Yes, passer! In 1929, the forward pass came to Canadian football, although it wouldn't revolutionize the game for another 20 years. Perhaps that was because of the early rules. The passer had to be five yards back of the line of scrimmage when he threw the ball. The pass could not be completed within the opponent's 25-yard line. If the pass went incomplete, punting rules came into in effect, and the opponent could pick up the ball and run. Seiberling completed the first-ever forward pass to Ralph Losie on September 21 at Edmonton.

Playing on a frozen Regina field on November 11—both Remembrance and Thanksgiving Day that year—the Roughriders defeated Calgary 15–8, winning the right to contest the Grey Cup. Once again, the game was played in Hamilton.

Hamilton opened the scoring by tackling Saul Bloomfield for a rouge in the end zone. Bloomfield replied with a single. The Tigers added a point in the second quarter to lead 2–1 at the half. After exchanging rouges, the Tigers took advantage of a break in the third quarter to score the first touchdown. Huck Welch boomed a kick into Regina's end. When Bloomfield couldn't handle it, Jimmy Simpson swooped in, picked up the ball and ran to the end zone, making the score 9–2. With a strong wind at their back, Pep Leadlay and Welch kicked five singles in the fourth period, making the final score 14–3.

The reason the Roughies gave the Easterners all they could handle was their passing attack. Regina completed 8 of 11 passes. Southpaw snapback Jersey Jack Campbell threw nine of them and Angus Mitchell two. There was no attempt to fool the opposition. When they wanted to pass, Campbell had a teammate assume his centring duties, and he took the snap and threw it. The Tigers didn't know how to stop it.

Grey Cup 1930

To return to the Grey Cup in 1930, the Roughriders knocked off the Winnipeg St. John's, Calgary Altomah-Tigers and Vancouver Meralomas. Regina's Grey Cup opponent was Toronto Balmy Beach, who had defeated Hamilton 8–5.

While the Westerners were travelling to Toronto, the CRU issued a statement that the forward pass would not be permitted in the big game because both teams had not been using it during the season. While the Western Interprovincial Football Union (WIFU) and Big Four teams (Toronto, Montréal, Hamilton and Ottawa) employed the forward pass, the ORFU did not, and Balmy Beach was the champion of the ORFU.

Apparently that rule had been on the books all year, but for some reason, the executive in Toronto "forgot" to let the WIFU know about it. This was an example of the many shenanigans that the West believed the East pulled on them, so determined were the Easterners to prevent their country cousins from winning the Grey Cup.

Regina was the heavy favourite to win their first Dominion championship because the Balmy Beachers had been badly battered by the Tiger-Cats in the Eastern final. Ted Reeve had a dislocated shoulder, and Claude Harris and several other stars of the old gold-and-blue were on the limp.

The Riders pulled out of Regina's Union Station full of confidence, unlike their previous eastern pilgrimages where they didn't know what to expect and were in awe of the entire experience. This time, Regina thought they had a good chance to win the championship. Balmy Beach was considered an inferior team to the Tiger-Cats, who had outscored the opposition 295–35.

In the first Grey Cup that the Roughriders played in Toronto, Balmy Beach opened the scoring when Ab Box kicked to the dead-ball line for a point. Balmy Beach tallied their second score when Box converted a Saul Bloomfield fumble into another point. Box had a great day kicking for the Beachers while Bloomfield struggled in a sea of mud six inches deep.

In the second quarter, Claude Harris kicked three singles for Toronto, and Bobby Reid plunged into the end zone from the one on the third down, giving Balmy Beach a 10–0 lead at the half.

The Roughriders got on the scoreboard with a rouge in the third quarter. They made history when Fred Brown scored the West's first touchdown in Grey Cup competition. The tally was the result of an onside kick. Bloomfield closed out third-quarter scoring with a single. Regina had a chance to win the game in the final frame when they had the ball on the enemy one-yard line. On third down, Angus Mitchell called for an onside kick that failed. Later, Ted Reeve struggled in the contest and led his team down the field where Harris kicked for the last points of the game. Before 3914 spectators, Balmy Beach won their second and last Grey Cup, 11–6.

For the first time, Regina football fans were able to follow the game on radio. Through a special hook-up between CKCK Regina and CHWC Toronto, the game was broadcast from Varsity Stadium by Foster Hewitt of the *Toronto Star* and relayed over telephone hook-up.

According to a report in the December 8, 1930, edition of the *Leader-Post*, "The reception from Varsity Stadium was of the best, and the attendant clamour could be heard behind the voice of the announcer. For clarity and coherence, the broadcast could not have been improved upon. A special treat was provided the fans who gathered outside the *Leader-Post* building by the installation of a loud-speaker in a window on the first floor. The CKCK-Toronto hook-up enabled the fans in the street to follow the game play-by-play."

Grey Cup 1931

In 1931, the CRU approved the use the forward pass for all rugby unions whether they wanted to use it or not, with the rule that if a team threw two consecutive incomplete passes, they would receive a 10-yard penalty. Also, if a pass went incomplete within the opponent's 25-yard line, the offensive team lost possession.

Another rule change affected touchdown conversions. The scrimmage line for converts was changed from the 35-yard line to the five-yard line. In addition, a place kick, drop kick, run or pass could be used. Before 1931, a converted touchdown was a rarity. From 1931 to present day, a miss is highly unusual.

The 1931 Roughriders went 5–0 during the regular season. Expecting a close semifinal tussle in Winnipeg, they walloped the St. John's 47–5 at Wesley Park. In a glimpse of things to come, the Riders wore green-and-white uniforms, borrowed from the Winnipeg team because their red-and-black outfits were left behind in Regina.

After dispatching Calgary in the Western final, the Riders prepared to face the Montréal Amateur Athletic Association Winged Wheelers in the Québec metropolis on December 5. Making their first Grey Cup appearance, Montréal were 6–0 in Big Four play and defeated the University of Western Ontario in the Eastern showdown. Montréal had adopted the forward pass in a big way, bringing in quarterback Warren Stevens from Syracuse. He threw to Frank Robinson for the first touchdown pass ever recorded in the Big Four.

The field was frozen on Grey Cup day and snow was gently falling down, adding to the drifts already on the gridiron. It was –12°C at the kickoff. Some players resorted to wearing coonskin coats over their uniforms.

Montréal opened the scoring with a Huck Welch single. The first break came just before the end of the first quarter when Dynamite Eddie James fumbled a lateral from Angus Mitchell. Pete Jotkus kicked the ball into the end zone and fell on it. Welch added the convert to make the score Montréal 7, Regina 0.

There was no further scoring until the third quarter when Welch punted for a single. Shortly after, Montréal made history when Stevens completed the first Grey Cup touchdown pass, a 24-yard toss to Kenny Grant. As the quarter ended with the Wheelers leading 13–0, the Montréalers went into a huddle. Were they planning a sneak play on the ensuing kickoff? (In those days, the team that scored received the kickoff.) Actually, no. Warren Stevens had somehow lost his pants, and a new pair had to be rushed in from the bench.

In the final 15 minutes, Welch added a field goal, and Stevens passed to Wally Whitty for another touchdown. Stevens ran for the convert. Montréal won its first Grey Cup, 22–0, handing Regina its fourth consecutive defeat.

In another less impressive first, Wheeler Edward "Red" Tellier was suspended from football for life for punching George Gilhooley during the game. Tellier was reinstated three years later but never played in Canada again.

With two outstanding passing quarterbacks, pundits had predicted an aerial circus. They were disappointed as Warren Stevens only went 3 for 11, and Curt Schave 3 for 12.

Grey Cup 1932

Regina returned to the big game for a fifth straight year in 1932 after winning the right to represent the West by defeating the Winnipeg St. John's and Calgary Altomahs. The Hamilton Tigers got there by wins over the ORFU Sarnia Imperials and the University of Toronto.

Hamilton was rated no better than even money to win the Cup because their star halfback Frank Turville had a twisted ankle and would be wearing a special brace. Their quarterback, Dr. Ike Sutton, was also nursing an injury. In addition, the Roughriders were considered the finest football team to ever come out of the West.

Said coach Al Ritchie, "This is the best conditioned squad I have ever led east. Every lad is in the pink of condition, and while we have a healthy respect for these Tigers, none of the boys are suffering an inferiority complex."

The weather was unseasonably warm in Hamilton on December 3. The game was played under almost perfect conditions—a warm sun, no wind and a fast track.

After taking the opening kickoff, Regina fumbled three straight times, the last recovered by Hamilton on the Rider 13-yard line. Turville took the snap and lateralled to Donny "Dinny" Gardner, who went over for the touchdown. Turville added the convert.

Following the kickoff, Hamilton marched 50 yards to the Rider 40, where Turville launched a 75-yard single to the dead-ball line. Near the end of the opening quarter, with a third down on their six-yard line, Rider Jack Campbell snapped the ball over punter Charlie Harrison's head. Harrison alertly conceded a safety touch. After 15 minutes of play, the score was Hamilton 9, Regina 0.

After punting and running beautifully, Turville's ankle gave out. Rider hopes rose when they saw him carried to the sidelines. Ray Boadway assumed the kicking duties, adding a single to make the score 10–0 for the home team.

Regina went to the air in the second stanza. Austin De Frate dropped back into the end zone and threw 15 yards to Curt Schave. De Frate put it up again, but this time the ball was picked off by Beano Wright, who ran 20 yards to the end zone. Gardner converted.

The score at the half was 16–0 for Hamilton. Regina was playing well, but a fumble, a bad snap and an interception led to 14 points for their opponents. Another promising drive was killed when De Frate was intercepted by Glen Small.

The pattern continued in the third quarter when Schave fumbled at his own 35. Three plays later, Gardner kicked a 35-yard field goal, making the score 19–0.

The ensuing kickoff saw Hamilton with the ball on their 50-yard line. The Riders forced them to punt. Harrison fumbled the kick right into the arms of Jimmy Simpson, who picked up the pigskin on the dead run and went unmolested to pay dirt. He became only the second player to score four Grey Cup touchdowns, the first being Ross Craig. (Damon Allen currently holds the record with six.) Hamilton led 25–0 after three quarters.

De Frate scored a touchdown in the final 15 minutes, converted by Schave. Final score: Banged-up Bengals 25, Best Team to Ever Represent the West 6.

Grey Cups 1933–34

In 1933, the Winnipeg Rugby Club and St. John's joined forces, calling themselves the Winnipegs. The amalgamated team ended Regina's Western champion monopoly by downing them 11–1. The Winnipegs then defeated Calgary 15–1. The ORFU champions already had a berth in the Grey Cup. To qualify to meet them, Winnipeg was ordered to play the Big Four champion Argonauts. Toronto won 13–0, then went on to win the Grey Cup 4–3 over Sarnia.

The year 1934 offered a special incentive to Western football. The CRU had decided that the Grey Cup game that year would be played at the home of the Western champions for the first time ever. Determined to be the hosts, Regina went 6–0 during the regular season, outscoring the opposition 156–25. They defeated the Winnipegs and Vancouver in the playoffs. Would Regina be the first Western Canadian team to host the Grey Cup?

Of course not. The CRU reneged on their promise, so the Roughriders headed to Toronto to take on the Sarnia Imperials, who had defeated Hamilton 11–4 in the Eastern final.

As usual, the Westerners got off to a shaky start when Ralph Pearce fumbled the first punt of the game, leading to the first of five Hugh "Bummer" Stirling singles. The ball went out of the end zone, and the game was delayed while the police recovered it. Taking advantage of a brisk wind, Sarnia's Alex Hayes dropkicked a field goal, and Stirling added a single. Imperials 5, Roughriders 0.

Early in the second quarter, a mishandled snap led to a turnover on downs to Sarnia. Stirling threw to Orm Beach at the five-yard line. Norm Perry passed to Gord Paterson for the touchdown, which Stirling converted, stretching their lead to 11–0.

Rider luck finally turned when they rose to the occasion defensively and blocked a punt at the Imperial five. Ted Olson then scored from the one. Regina trailed 11–5 at the half. In the third quarter, the Riders stopped a long Sarnia march on their three-yard line. Olson and Stirling exchanged punts. On Stirling's third kick of the series, Andy Young fumbled the punt on his goal line. Johnny Manore fell on the ball in the end zone. The convert was good, and the Rider goose seemed cooked, trailing 17–5.

The never-say-die Riders fought back with Johnny Achtzener recovering a fumble at the Sarnia 23. But they couldn't capitalize, settling for a single point off a wide field-goal attempt. Another opportunity arose seconds into the fourth quarter when a Sarnia third-down gamble on their own 17-yard line failed. Olson threw to Steve Adkins for the touchdown, and Paul Kirk converted, bringing Regina as close as they would come at 17–12. Stirling closed out the scoring with three singles, and Sarnia won their first Grey Cup 20–12.

chapter three

The Whirlwind from the West, 1935–39

Between 1921 and 1934, the West challenged the mighty East for Canadian football supremacy 10 times: Regina seven times, Edmonton twice and Winnipeg once. The Eastern champions outscored their opponents 216 to 29.

Winnipeg's general manager Joe Ryan concluded that the only way the West would win the Grey Cup was by importing American players. He looked south of the border to the neighbouring states of Minnesota and North Dakota. By 1935, Winnipeg had nine American imports: Russ Rebholz, Greg Kabat, player/coach Bob Fritz, Bud Marquardt, Bert Oja, Nick Pagones, Joe Perpich, Herb Peschel and Fritz Hanson.

It was Joe Ryan who established the basic character of the CFL, a hybrid of Canadian and American players. It is an ill wind that blows no good. Because of the Depression, Ryan was able to sign all his nine imports for a total of $7500.

He could do that because he offered that rare commodity in the Dirty Thirties—a job. Most of the Americans he brought to Manitoba became Canadian citizens and lived the rest of their lives in this country.

The greatest of them all was the Whirlwind from the West, Fritzie Hanson. He explained how he came to Canada:

> *In 1935, the best job I could get coaching and teaching in the Dirty Thirties was 90 bucks a month. At the same time, Bob Fritz who was at Concordia College in Minnesota, just across the river from me, had been asked by Winnipeg to find some football players. People from Winnipeg came down to my hometown, Fargo, North Dakota, and they talked to me and some other fellows as well, and we all went up to Winnipeg.*

Grey Cup 1935

The game of football changed dramatically in 1935. Because of the presence of so many imports on Western teams, the Western Interprovincial Football Union (WIFU) adopted some American features. Under the new rules, teams could use the forward pass anywhere on the field, eliminating restrictions within the opponent's 25-yard line. They didn't completely clear the way in what is now called the "red zone." If a pass on third down went incomplete in that area of the field, the opposing team took possession at their 25.

The kicking game was modified by disallowing points for punting the ball beyond the end zone. Western Canadian punters would have to drop their kicks between the goal line and dead-ball lines.

The blocking (called interference then) rules were changed, allowing back fielders five yards past the line of scrimmage. Penalties to prevent a defensive player from interfering with a receiver in the end zone were established. If the defending team interfered with the receiver when a pass was thrown to the end zone, the attacking team was awarded a first down for the first offence. For the second offence, the attacking team would be awarded the ball half the distance to the goal as well as a first down.

While the Canadian Rugby Union (CRU) eventually adopted most of the WIFU's rule changes, the old order of the day prevailed for the 1935 Grey Cup.

Although the Roughriders went undefeated during the 1935 regular season, they lost the semifinal to the Winnipegs who, after eking out a 7–0 win over the Calgary Bronks, prepared to face a tough team of Hamilton Tigers with an array of Hall of Famers such as Seymour Wilson, Jimmy Simpson, Brian Timmis and Huck Welch. Hamilton got to the big game by trouncing Queen's 44–4 and Sarnia 22–0.

Hamilton fully expected to win their sixth Grey Cup against the usual inferior opponent from the Western Canadian boondocks. However, playing for Winnipeg was one of the greatest football players to grace a Canadian gridiron, Fritzie Hanson. Easterners had never heard of him. That was about to change.

It was a miserable day in Hamilton on December 7. With a kickoff temperature of 3°C and rain, the field for the 23rd Grey Cup was a sea of mud, hardly conducive to a great performance by a running back.

Winnipeg opened the scoring with a Bud Marquardt touchdown in the first quarter, coming on a pass from Russ Rebholz. The Tigers responded with a field goal, and Bob Fritz lateralled to Rebholz who then threw to Greg Kabat, who trundled in for a major. At the half, the Westerners led 12–3.

In the third quarter, Hamilton charged back with a touchdown by Wilf Patterson, but Fritzie Hanson put the game on ice with a spectacular 78-yard punt return for a touchdown in the third quarter. Rebholz converted; Kabat added a single. Frank Turville had two singles, and Winnipeg conceded a safety touch. The final score was Winnipeg 18, Hamilton 12. The West had won its first Grey Cup.

Hanson overcame the treacherous field conditions, returning seven punts for more than 300 yards, including the 78-yard touchdown. Because official statistics weren't kept back then, Hanson is not credited with any Grey Cup records.

Did he receive a bonus for winning the Grey Cup?

"Oh, no," Hanson said. "My first year, 1935, I got a straight 125 bucks a game. The next year, I signed up for 1500 dollars a season. It doesn't sound like much, but everything is relative. I was able to get a pretty decent job at the same time, and, you know, $2000 a year was pretty good pay in the Dirty Thirties."

Grey Cup 1936

In 1936, reporter Vince Leah observed that the Winnipeg players were the "Blue Bombers" of Western football. He was borrowing from the great American sportswriter Grantland Rice, who had nicknamed world heavyweight boxing champion Joe Louis the "Brown Bomber."

The newly named Winnipeg Blue Bombers finished first that year with a mark of 5–2–1 but lost the two-game total-point semifinal 24–12 to second-place Regina, who won their 16th Western championship by dispatching the stubborn Calgary Bronks 3–1.

St. George, Kansas, native Dean Griffing arrived on the Canadian football scene in 1936 as coach of the Regina Roughriders. When accused of biting an opponent, the big barrel-chested man pointed to his bridgework and denied the charge, allowing that "I might have gummed him up a little bit." Griffing was with the Riders until 1943. In 1945, he moved West and founded the Calgary Stampeders. He returned as the GM of the Saskatchewan Roughriders in the mid-1950s.

The East was not amused when Winnipeg won the Grey Cup in 1935. Believing the balance of power was shifting because of the widespread use of American imports in western Canada, the eastern-dominated CRU, in a roundabout way, banned them. They ruled that no player could compete unless he had lived in Canada for a year. He could play only if he had taken up residence in the team's city before October 1 of that season. The Western Canadian Rugby Union (WCRU) ignored the rule.

Regina's five imports, including player/coach Dean Griffing, were declared ineligible for Grey Cup play. The Roughriders refused to make the trip east without them. Western officials announced Winnipeg would take Regina's place. "No way!" said Griffing. "We'll play the Grey Cup without our Americans." They sent a telegram to CRU president Bobby Hewitson to that effect, only to be notified that the WCRU had withdrawn their challenge and no western team would play for the dominion title. Two BC executives, as well as WCRU president A.M. Naismith and Alberta Union president A.W. Matthews, resigned in protest. No matter. Sarnia won their second (and final) Grey Cup, defeating the Ottawa Rough Riders 26–20.

Grey Cup 1937

In 1937, the Blue Bombers were living proof of Murphy's Law that "Whatever can go wrong, will." Toronto beat the Blue Bombers 4–3 in the Grey Cup that year, but many observers believed they were just plain lucky. It is said in sports and in life that sometimes it is better to be lucky than good. The Toronto Argonauts of 1937 and beyond were both. Wearing the double blue were the likes of Alvin "Red" Storey, the Stukus brothers (Annis, Bill and Frank), Bob Isbister and Teddy Morris.

In the first quarter, Bill Stukus fumbled on his seven-yard line. According to CFL historian, the late Gordon Walker, who was there that day, referee Hec Crighton was unable to determine who had recovered the ball and gave it to Toronto, reasoning they would be in dire straits if he didn't. Soon after, Bill Stukus fumbled a punt in the end zone, which Winnipeg recovered. The Bombers were called for no yards.

When Bud Marquardt blocked a kick, the ball bounced into the arms of Teddy Morris. When Fritzie Hanson fumbled a punt, the ball bounced directly to Boatman Bill Bryers. The term "Argo Bounce" originated with that game, signifying a lucky break. The Bombers should have stood in bed.

Grey Cup 1938

Winnipeg and Toronto met again for the championship in 1938, which had one of the greatest individual performances in Grey Cup history, authored by Toronto's redheaded whirlwind, Alvin "Red" Storey. Trailing the Blue Bombers 7–6 in the fourth quarter, Red Storey came off the bench and scored three touchdowns in less than 12 minutes.

The Bombers led 4–0 after the first quarter on a field goal by Greg Kabat and an Art Stevenson single. In the second frame, Annis Stukus teamed up with Art West on a 56-yard pass and run for a touchdown, converted by Annis' brother, Bill. Kabat kicked Winnipeg into a 7–6 lead at the half. Early in the fourth quarter, the Argo coach sent Red Storey into the fray.

Storey's first touchdown came on a 38-yard run from scrimmage, the second on a short run set up by his own 37-yard interception return and the third major came on a 12-yard run from scrimmage. He wasn't done, though, setting up another touchdown by running 102 yards to the Winnipeg four-yard line. Bernie Tornton took it in. The final score was Red Storey 30, Winnipeg 7.

Fritzie Hanson remembered that day all too well.

"We were badly hurt," he explained. "Greg Kabat was supposed to cover Red, but he was injured. Our coach Reg Threlfall wanted to take him out, but he wouldn't go. So they gave him a shot of novocaine in his leg. But he still couldn't move, and I couldn't get over there in time to stop Storey. Old Red had a great day, didn't he? But that was it for him. I see Red occasionally and he says, 'That was my day. I never had one before nor have I had one since.'"

The Whirlwind from the West, 1935–39

Annis Stukus remembered that day differently.

We were down 7–6 with 12 minutes to go, but we knew that the game was over. It was just going to be a question of how many points.

We gave them a lesson in Canadian football. They outweighed us by about 20 to 40 pounds up front. So we ran a three-man end run to one side of the field, then back to the other side, kicked, got the ball back and ran it and ran it. We ran Winnipeg right into the ground. We were greyhounds. We could run all day. In fact, we were running better in the fourth quarter than we were in the first. As a result, we just wore those guys out.

We scored four touchdowns in the last 12 minutes. Red got three of them. We gave them an example of Canadian football, how it can be played and used to score points by being in better shape than the other guy.

So it wasn't a case of Red Storey coming off the bench when all was lost and heroically saving the day? Annis Stukus replied:

Oh, no, Red was just the guy who was fresh.

I started at quarterback and called a play, and for some reason Red froze. I waved to the bench and had him sent off and the coach, Lew Hayman, as usual, forgot he wasn't in there. Hayman was a great guy to get you ready for a game. But the day of the game, if we could have locked him up in a hotel room, we'd have won four or five straight Grey Cups.

Anyway, I got winded, and when I was about to go back in for the last 12 minutes, I asked Lew if I could take Red with me. Lew said that Red was already out there. I told him he had been sitting beside him on the bench all day.

So Red went out there pissed off and fresh and tore them apart. He should have had four or five touchdowns!

Grey Cup 1939

Winnipeg returned to the Grey Cup for the third straight time in 1939 and the fourth in five years. The Argos finished one point behind the 5–1 Ottawa Rough Riders, who crushed them 39–6 in the two-game total-point final. The Bombers were first in the West with a mark of 10–2. Calgary vanquished Regina in the semifinal before losing the total-point round to Winnipeg 35–20.

The teams exchanged touchdowns and were tied 6–6. The Bombers drew first blood when Ottawa's Orville Burke fumbled on his 10-yard line. Andy Beiber took it in from the seven. Ottawa replied when Burke completed a pass to Rick Perley, who lateralled to Andy Tommy who scored, a play covering 52 yards. The 6–6 tie held until the fourth quarter when Les Lear blocked an Ottawa punt. Greg Kabat missed the ensuing field-goal try but scored a single.

The unfortunate Mr. Burke coughed up the ball, recovered by Jeff Nicklin who ran to the Ottawa 30. Kabat punted it into the end zone. Burke tried to kick it back, but the ball dribbled off his foot and went out of bounds on the Rider nine. Art Stevenson then booted the ball over the end zone for the win. Winnipeg had won their second Grey Cup, 8–7.

Looking back on his career, Fritzie Hanson said:

The 1935 Grey Cup was the greatest, I guess, because it was the first. But I think back to 1939 when we beat Ottawa 8–7. We played with only 13 players. A couple were declared ineligible, several were hurt. Our punter couldn't lift his leg to kick the ball, so we gambled on third downs. I carried the ball 13 times in a row during that game.

During the course of a game, regular season or playoff, Hanson carried the ball 30 to 40 times, as well as doing a full shift on defence and returning punts and kickoffs. Hanson didn't like the move to specialists nor did he care for the passing game that characterized CFL football from the 1970s on.

"I think football is going downhill," Hanson said in 1980. "I think the hitting was a lot better in my day, they were more tenacious, there were much tougher linemen. We didn't have any blocking, so the onus was on the backs themselves. We ran with a lot of power. They don't do that now. But this crap now…golly, a guy runs 20 yards and they have to give him oxygen."

chapter four

The End of the Beginning, 1940–47

Come September 10, 1939, Canada was at war with Germany for the second time in a generation. Football players such as Fritzie Hanson, Jeff Nicklin, Paul Rowe and many others traded in their moleskins for khaki. Until the end of hostilities in 1945, football continued to be played, primarily by service teams.

The decade of the 1940s opened on a familiar note, with the East and West squabbling over the number and eligibility of imports. Winnipeg won the West handily, and they were prepared to defend their title against Ottawa. Typically, the Canadian Rugby Union (CRU), tired of the upstarts from the West, declared Winnipeg ineligible because they had not played under CRU rules. The president of the CRU, Jack Bannerman of Calgary, wanted the residence rule done away with so teams could sign more Americans. When his executive would not agree and instead sanctioned a two-game Grey Cup between Ontario Rugby Football Union (ORFU) champion

Toronto Balmy Beach and Ottawa, Bannerman resigned, and the West withdrew from the CRU.

When the Sports Service League, an organization devoted to raising money for the armed forces, tried to arrange an East–West Grey Cup sponsored by George McCullagh, the owner of the Toronto *Globe and Mail*, the CRU would have none of it. There was a general feeling in Western Canada that the East would do anything to prevent the West from winning the Grey Cup. Westerners also believed the Easterners looked down their noses at them and regarded any Western win as a fluke.

Grey Cups 1940–41

In 1940, the Ottawa Rough Riders won the only two-game total-point series Grey Cup ever played, beating Balmy Beach in Ottawa 8–2 in front of 4998 spectators on December 7. Only 1700 showed up for the earlier game in Toronto on November 30, won by the Rough Riders 12–5.

The CRU soon realized the Grey Cup without the East versus West element didn't excite people, so everyone concerned kissed and made up. A Winnipeg team represented the West six of the next seven years. The Blue Bombers took on the Ottawa Rough Riders in 1941.

After Winnipeg opened with a Ches McCance field goal, Ottawa struck back with one of the most memorable plays in Grey Cup history. Hall of Famer Tony Golab's punt was high but short. It bounced back into his arms, and he ran 45 yards to the end zone. George Fraser converted and later added the first of three field goals.

Winnipeg celebrating their win after the 1941 Grey Cup

In the second quarter, Winnipeg was set to punt. When Wayne Sheley saw all the Rough Riders up on the line, he told Bud Marquardt to drift off to the side. Sheley took the snap and threw to Marquardt, who ran to the five and lateralled to Mel Wilson who scored. It was 9–9 at the half.

Marquardt got his major in the third stanza when Bernie Thornton hit Rider quarterback Orville Burke. The ball flew out of his hands into Marquardt's waiting grasp. It was clear sailing to pay dirt. McCance converted and scored a fourth-quarter field goal. Fraser replied for Ottawa. The final score was Winnipeg 18, Ottawa 16. Although he scored no points, Fritzie Hanson was the star of the game, carrying the ball 25 times for 66 yards, an impressive performance at that time.

Grey Cups 1942–44

By 1942, the demands of war were making it hard for teams to find players. The Western Interprovincial Football Union (WIFU) and Big Four suspended play until 1945. Service teams contested the next three Grey Cups. The Toronto RCAF Hurricanes, coached by Lew Hayman, beat the Winnipeg RCAF Bombers 8–5 in 1942. It was the Hamilton Flying Wildcats over the Winnipeg RCAF Bombers 23–14 in 1943. No games were played in the West the following year.

The 1944 Grey Cup was won by St. Hyacinthe–HMCS Donnacona Navy over the Hamilton Wildcats 7–6. After the victory, Royal Canadian Navy officials tried to forfeit the game and return the Cup on the grounds that Donnacona had broken a rule forbidding service teams to play against civilian teams. Believing the bosuns had won it fair and square, the CRU refused to strip them of their title.

Although Donnacona won the Grey Cup, they weren't the navy champions. HMCS York, coached by Ted Morris, defeated Donnacona for that title. When the war ended, Morris took over the helm of the Good Ship Argonaut, bringing stars like Frank Morris (no relation) and Royal Copeland with him.

Also piped aboard was Windsor, Ontario, native Joe Krol. One of the all-time greats of the game, Krol arrived on the scene in 1943 from the 1939 Intercollegiate Champion University of Western Ontario Mustangs, joining the Hamilton Flying Wildcats and leading them to a Grey Cup in his rookie year.

Unlike their opponents, the Wildcats weren't a service team and therefore had somewhat of an advantage. "We didn't have any problems keeping a team together," Krol explained. "We were all working in the wartime plants and we were playing mostly service teams. The calibre of play wasn't as good because most of the good ballplayers were in the service all over the country and overseas."

Grey Cup 1945

Early in 1945, Joe Krol, after being cut by the Detroit Lions, signed a contract with Toronto. On October 27, Krol made his Argo debut in Montréal. He threw five touchdown passes, kicked two singles and two converts in a 31–6 victory. Four of the five TD passes were to Royal Copeland. As a result of that performance, writer Jim Coleman dubbed Copeland and Krol the "Gold Dust Twins."

Offensive guard Frank Morris blocked for Krol that day. Toronto-native Morris was a member of the Argo team, comprised entirely of Canadians, that won three straight Cups (1945, 1946, 1947), and he also played with the three-peat Edmonton Eskimos of the mid-1950s. Morris later became Edmonton's super scout, playing a major role in building the great Eskimo teams of the '70s and '80s.

> *I joined the navy out of high school. I had never played football before. I played soccer and hockey and fastball and baseball, everything but football.*
>
> *I joined the navy in 1942 and played fastball. We represented Canada at the world championships in Detroit. A number of guys on that fastball team had played with the Argos. They decided they were going to put a navy football team*

together. They felt I was big enough to come out and give it a shot. That was my introduction to football.

Morris raved about Copeland and Krol.

They were great. They complemented one another really well. Copeland was a tremendous football player. He was a running back and a dandy.

Cope was a Toronto kid. He should have been in Hollywood. He was one of the best-looking kids you'd ever seen. The women used to chase him all over the place. He looked like an Adonis. He used to winter in California at Muscle Beach. He had that kind of a body. He was just a real good-looking athlete, a great football player and a heckuva guy!

Copeland and Krol's impact on the Grey Cup was immediate. In their first of three straight wins over Winnipeg, the Argos crushed the Bombers 35–0. Krol and Copeland each scored a touchdown, with Krol's the result of a 50-yard interception return. Krol also threw two TD passes.

Grey Cup 1946

In 1946, the CRU instituted blocking up to 10 yards from the line of scrimmage. They also ruled that each team, East and West, could carry five American imports.

The Montréal Alouettes were born in 1946. Torontonians Lew Hayman and financial backer Eric Cradock started the Als with the help of Leo Dandurand and Joe Ryan.

They finished first with a record of 7–3–2 in their inaugural season but lost to Hayman's former team, the Argonauts, 12–6 in the Eastern final.

The Gold Dust Twins were at it again in the Grey Cup that year. Although Winnipeg had a statistical edge, Krol and Copeland did them in. Krol threw a touchdown pass to Copeland, who later returned the favour after Krol had intercepted a pass on the Bomber 45-yard line. Krol also connected in the end zone with Rod Smylie and Boris Tipoff. The fifth Argo major, a one-yard plunge by Byron Karrys, was set up by one of the most spectacular plays in Grey Cup history.

In those days, teams often put a speedy receiver out in the flank and slightly behind the punter. Just as today, a player behind a kicker is eligible to recover the ball. Joe Krol punted toward the sideline. Royal Copeland raced down the field and caught it over the heads of the Blue Bomber defenders and made it to the one-yard line. Toronto beat Winnipeg by a score of 28–6.

The 1946 game was the last Grey Cup played by teams made up totally of Canadians. The following year, Winnipeg added five imports, including their Minnesota quarterback Bob Sandberg, but the Argos held out for another year.

Grey Cup 1947

The Grey Cup of 1947 saw the third straight match-up between Toronto and Winnipeg. Just as Regina had dominated Western football from 1911 to the early 1930s, Winnipeg was the team to beat from 1935 through 1947, appearing in 10 Grey Cups in 13 years. In the other three years, the WIFU didn't compete for the Cup.

Winnipeg won three championships during those years, but none at the expense of the Argos, to whom they lost six times. Toronto has never lost a Grey Cup to Winnipeg, though they came close in 1947.

Bob Sandberg almost beat Toronto single-handedly, leading the Bombers to a 9–1 lead at the half. But the Gold Dust Twins sang their old familiar song when Frankie Morris recovered a fumble (the Argo Bounce?), and Joe Krol promptly hit Royal Copeland with a pass for a touchdown. Near the end of the game, Krol scored a single on a missed field goal. With less than two minutes to go, Krol booted a single to tie, 9–9. With seconds remaining, Winnipeg wanted to retain possession of the ball so Bomber coach Jack West elected to gamble on third-and-two. They got nowhere.

"It was third down, and they had the ball on the 30-yard line, and they lined up in punt formation," recalled Frankie Morris.

> I knew that at times, instead of centring the ball back to the punter, they would give it to Bert Iannoni, a guard. They had a guard sneak play.
>
> When the centre turned the ball, I knew he wasn't going to make the long snap, and I damn near took the handoff myself when I made the tackle. We took possession of the ball because they lost yards on the play.
>
> The funny part of it is, we got into the huddle and Joe Krol started to call a play, and our team captain Steve Levantis, one of the really great old Argos, said, "To hell with the running play,

kick it." Krol kicked it into the end zone for the winning point. If we had run a play, we would have been in overtime.

Toronto won 10–9. It was the last time a completely Canadian team won the Grey Cup. Truly, 1947 marked the end of an era.

For the greatest referee in Canadian football history, the game marked the beginning of a distinguished career. Paul Dojack was involved as an official in 15 Grey Cups before retiring in 1970. The Regina native was elected to the Canadian Football Hall of Fame in 1978.

"My first Grey Cup was in 1947 after I came out of the service. We worked with four officials. I was an umpire. I got my expenses plus $15."

For Joe Krol, 1947 was the most memorable Grey Cup. "That was quite a game. We beat the Bombers on the last play. I kicked a single on a quick kick to tie the game and another one to win it. That one took a bounce over the goal line and rolled out of bounds. I kicked it away from the receiver."

That's not all Krol remembered about that day in 1947.

"I personally think the greatest game I ever saw a man play was that very same game we won 10–9. Bob Sandberg was a team in himself. We knew he was going to carry the ball, and we still couldn't stop him."

Because Krol was such a great passer, it is only natural to assume he was, along with Don Getty and Russ Jackson, one of the last of the great Canadian quarterbacks. Not so.

"That's a mistake everybody makes, thinking I played quarterback," chuckled Krol. "I never played quarterback, to be honest with you, I played halfback. But I know why people make that mistake. We had an odd sort of formation where I got quite a few direct snaps and threw passes off it, more or less a single wing. I would line up almost directly behind the snap, four or five yards deep."

Quarterbacks were interchangeable. There have only been two occasions in Canadian professional football history where three brothers played on the same team at the same time: the Stukus brothers in the late 1930s, and Tom, Joe and John Forzani in Calgary, 1973–75. Playing against the Montréal Cubs in the second last game of the 1938 regular season, Bill, Frank and Annis Stukus put on a display the likes of which was never seen before or since.

"There never has been three brothers who were quarterbacks who played in the same backfield," Annis explained.

All three of us were quarterbacks. When I played quarterback, my brother Bill played left halfback and Frank was the fullback. When Bill went in at quarterback, I went over to wingback from where I moved out one day and invented the position of slotback. Frank stayed at fullback. When Frank went in at quarterback, I played fullback and Bill the left half.

We had a play where you handed off to the running back who threw a lateral to another running back who threw a forward pass to the quarterback who had snuck down the sidelines. We wound up with five touchdowns that day in Montréal.

Each of us scored a touchdown. We were down 13–0 at the end of the first quarter and finally won the game 58–13, which was a high score in the days of two bucks and a kick.

In those days, just because you had the ball didn't mean you were going to keep it.

Through 1947, the Grey Cup was just a football game, albeit since 1921, for a national championship. In 1948, a bunch of wild westerners changed all that.

chapter five

Eastward Ho the Wagons! 1948–49

At every Grey Cup since 1948, chuckwagons, country bands, white Stetsons and pancake breakfasts have been a familiar sight. Calgarians invented the Grey Cup festival.

Hootin', hollerin' and flipping flapjacks in front of Toronto's City Hall, the wild Westerners went east in 1948 to show support for their beloved Stampeders in their first-ever Grey Cup appearance.

Dean Griffing founded the Calgary Stampeders in 1945, although senior football had been played in Calgary since the late 19th century. He was the team's first coach. Under his direction, the Stamps finished first in 1946, second in 1947, both times losing in the Western final to Winnipeg. Griffing was succeeded by Les Lear.

Born on August 22, 1918, in Grafton, North Dakota, Lear grew up in Winnipeg and began his Bomber career in

1937, playing in four Grey Cups with two victories. In 1944, he became the first Canadian-trained player in the National Football League (NFL) when he signed with the Cleveland Rams. He also starred for the Detroit Lions during his four-year stint south of the border.

Stampeder president Tom Brook was looking for someone with Canadian football experience as well as a pipeline to American imports when, in 1948, he recommended Lear to the Board of Directors. As soon as they agreed, Brook opened the door in his hotel suite and proclaimed, "Gentlemen, here is our new coach!" Lear signed a two-year deal at $8000 per season.

Rather than fill his import quota with collegians, Lear chose gnarly old pros: quarterback Keith Spaith, centre Chuck Anderson, receiver Woody Strode and tackle Joe Aguirre. Lear kept the fifth spot open for himself.

Although the Americans were important, 31 of the 36 players were Canadians who, while underpaid, were essential to success. Lear picked up home-brew Winnipeg veterans Bert Iannone, Norm Hill, Harry Hood and Fritzie Hanson and a quartet of Canucks from the West Coast—running backs Cedric Gyles, Jim Mitchener, Rod Pantages and Pete Thodas.

"I grew up in Vancouver," Pantages reminisced.

I played at King Edward High School and for the junior Blue Bombers. I was approached by Les Lear and asked if I would like to play for the Stampeders. And, of course, I was excited as hell and said, "Sure, I'd love to." So when I went out

> *there to spring training, Doug Rawls came with me. He played centre, but he wasn't very big and he got cut. Les then asked me if there were any other players that could make the team. And I said, "Sure, there's Thodas, Ced Gyles and Jim Mitchener," and they all played for the Stampeders. I was 19 when I joined the Stampeders in 1948.*

"It so happened I was on my way to go to a logging camp," recalled Thodas, "but I went out with the boys the night before so I missed the boat. Then this fellow called me and said they wanted me to come to Calgary to try out. I said, 'Fine.' If I hadn't missed the boat, I would have missed football. Strange, isn't it?"

Another young Canadian to join the team was Norm Hill, a key figure in the 1948 Grey Cup.

> *I grew up in Winnipeg and played on a really good high school team, provincial champions. I played my first two years on the University of Manitoba team, but my family was in Calgary. Late in August, I heard about a practice the Stampeders were having, so I went down there, just to stay in shape until I got back to Winnipeg. But I made the team. I told Les Lear I was thrilled to make the team, but I was going to school. I can't play football in Calgary and go to school in Winnipeg. Lear said, "We'll fix that up." So from the very first, once university started in early September, they flew me to all the games, all the time I played for the Stampeders, 1948 to 1950.*

With a succession of great quarterbacks, the Stampeders have always been known as a passing team. And the Stampeders were the first team to complete a forward pass. Lear brought in Keith Spaith and Woody Strode. While other teams ran twice as much, Calgary favoured a passing attack. The ratio between passing and running was 60–40. The other teams really hadn't seen a passing game like Spaith and Strode put on. Soon after, the other Western teams hired passing specialists to counteract Calgary's considerable success.

Grey Cup 1948

In 1948, the Stampeders went undefeated. No other CFL team has managed to accomplish that. In going 12–0, the Stamps outscored Saskatchewan and Winnipeg 218–61. Their only close calls came in three games against Saskatchewan, all won by a single point.

In the two-game Western final, the stubborn Roughriders battled the Stamps to a 4–4 tie in Regina. Calgary won the home-field rematch at Mewata Stadium 17–6. Then it was on to Toronto and a Grey Cup date with the Ottawa Rough Riders.

The Western champions were a mixture of veterans and youngsters of every race and religion, unusual for 1948. In a conversation at the Stamps' eastern Grey Cup headquarters with the great sportswriter Jim Coleman, the scribe said Lear had the disposition of an arthritic grizzly bear, and Lear described his team: "Take a look at my cowboys. We have Jewish cowboys, Negro cowboys, Chinese cowboys, Greek cowboys, you name it, we got 'em." These "cowboys" were

Rub Ludwig, Woody Strode and Chuck Anderson, Normie Kwong, Pete Thodas and Rod Pantages.

Jim Mitchener played with or against all the great quarterbacks of that era, and he described Keith Spaith as a "great quarterback."

"He was a drop back passer," said Mitchener. "Sam Etcheverry, Bernie Faloney and Jackie Parker could run. But Keith could throw the ball anywhere, and he was a great punter. He was certainly one of the best who ever played in Canada in my mind. Parker had speed none of the others had. I think Sam was the toughest of them all."

In 1948, Spaith completed 75 of 151 passes for 1246 yards, 13 TDs and 10 interceptions. His punting average was 42.5 yards. Fritzie Hanson appeared in five Grey Cups with Winnipeg, winning in 1935, '39 and '41, and losing to Toronto in 1937 and '38.

Although he almost had a leg blown off by an errant grenade on a military range, Hanson returned to the gridiron wars with Calgary in 1947. His presence elicited mixed emotions.

"Fritzie Hanson was the greatest ballplayer this country has ever seen," declared Stampeder Dave Berry.

Pantages was less impressed with Hanson.

He was fast, alright, but he sort of lost a lot, and it was the end of his career in 1948. I had a big argument with Lear in Winnipeg. We were playing our second game. Us young guys had run the ball down to about the 20-yard line. And then, Lear would take us out and put Fritzie Hanson,

Paul Rowe and Harry Hood in and they'd score. I said to Lear, "C'mon, Les, us guys are running the ball down there and then you put the old buggers in and they score. We want to score, too, you know."

Shortly after the war, African Americans made their appearance in Canadian football. Always referred to as "negroes" at that time, their experience north of the 49th Parallel ranged from dismal in Regina to welcoming in Edmonton and Montréal. Calgary was somewhere in between.

The first blacks to play for the Stampeders were centre Chuck Anderson and receiver Woody Strode, both former teammates of Les Lear with the L.A. (nee Cleveland) Rams.

Woodrow Wilson Woolvine Strode was born in 1914 in Los Angeles, the son of a Blackfoot mother and a black father. After serving in the Pacific during World War II, Strode attended UCLA where he made All-American while starring with Jackie Robinson. He took cinema and theatre classes and was soon working as a stuntman and bit part actor.

Like Robinson in baseball, Strode endured racial slurs and deliberate attempts to injure. After two years in hell, Strode was happy to answer Lear's call and head north. He was 34 when he became a Stampeder in 1948.

Strode retired after the 1950 season to pursue a movie career, appearing in over 70 films, including *Spartacus*, *The Ten Commandments*, *The Man Who Short Liberty Valence*, *The Cotton Club* and *The Quick and the Dead*, which was released in 1995 after his death at 80 and dedicated to him.

As a Stampeder, Strode picked up 964 yards on 44 receptions, nine TDs. The two-time All-Star was instrumental to both Calgary majors in the 1948 Grey Cup.

The "wagon train" that would transform a football game into Canada's greatest sporting festival pulled out of the station at 9:45 PM. Tuesday, November 23. Over 1000 Calgarians came down to look at the 15-car train. A baggage car had been converted into a barn for 12 horses that would ride in the Grey Cup parade. Another baggage car was transformed into a dance hall and barn.

Dave Berry described the trip to Toronto. "Every time we stopped, we got off the train and did calisthenics. I remember we stopped at one town and there must have been four feet of snow—it was snowing like hell—and we'd run from the end of the train to the engine and back and then do exercises until the old guys said, 'All aboard.'"

While the players arrived a week ahead of time, the train Stampede Special pulled into Toronto's Front Street Union Station on Friday morning, November 26. Decked out in cowboy outfits, whoopin' and hollerin', the fans immediately made their presence felt, square dancing in the train station.

Les Lear, in the meantime, had scouted Ottawa thoroughly, who along with Keith Spaith had watched the Eastern final. Said Lear, "I don't think they'll be able change their tactics with only a week between the Eastern and Canadian finals. We came east to win the Grey Cup, and that's what we're trying to do. The boys are in great mental and physical condition, and there will be no alibis if we don't take the Cup."

Ottawa coach Wall Masters commented, "I don't know a thing about Calgary, but I know we're ready. We haven't any injuries worthy of note, and I am more than pleased with the way the boys trained this week. I can't recall one game over the season where the mental attitude has been as good as for this one."

The oddsmakers favoured Ottawa 8–5.

The Stampeders arrived at Oakville's Pig and Whistle Inn on Sunday, November 21. They trained at nearby Appleby College. Lear took nothing for granted in preparing the team.

Pete Thodas got a kick out of his coach's paranoia. "God, it was funny. Les Lear wouldn't allow planes to fly over our practice. And he took us down to the basement in this school and he closed all the doors. The team's down there and he brought film of an Ottawa game and we watched it…in particular we watched how they liked to pull that sleeper play. Of course, we pulled it on them."

The cuisine left much to be desired. "And then eating cheese sandwiches every day. I can recall the guys all getting teed off with their cheese sandwiches. Chuck Anderson just said to hell with it, took off and left camp. They sent Bert Iannone after him, and he brought him back. We would have been without a centre. It was funny."

The Stampeders certainly weren't down east on a holiday. "We were on the field at 8:30 in the morning," said Thodas, "and we worked out until about 11 o'clock. Then we went for lunch, back on the field at 1:30 and off by four. Friday afternoon we bussed in and stayed at the Royal York Hotel."

Varsity Stadium could accommodate just over 20,000 spectators. No previous Grey Cup had attracted such widespread interest as this one, which was remarkable considering the Argonauts weren't in it.

On Saturday morning, Grey Cup day, the Calgarians saddled their horses, got the chuckwagons ready and staged the first Grey Cup parade. Leading the parade was former Calgarian, now mayor of Toronto, Hiram McCallum, decked out in gabardine, plaid shirt and Stetson, astride a handsome black mustang. Right behind in full dress were Sarcee chiefs George Ryder and Dave Crowchild, followed by the rest of the men and women on horseback, performing for an enthusiastic crowd.

The 1948 Grey Cup game was held three years after the end of World War II when demobilization was complete. It was the first celebration since the war where Canadians from all regions of the country came together to have fun around a football game and reminisce about the incredible national sacrifice and undertaking that was World War II.

Before and after the parade, flapjacks were flipped, bacon fried, coffee poured and Western songs played and sung at City Hall.

Legend has it that a member of the group rode a horse into the lobby of the Royal York Hotel, prompting management to post a sign, "No Horses Allowed in the Lobby." However, no accounts mention such an event, and if it actually happened, the rider has never been identified. Over 50 years later, Rod Pantages said, "We stayed at the Royal York, horses in the lobby and everything."

Horses were in the lobby? "I think so, yeah. Oh, I don't know, maybe not then."

Pete Thodas said, "There was nothing in the lobby because they cleared all the furniture out after they were riding their horses in there."

Equestrian Marmie Hess told the *Calgary Herald* on November 24, 2001, that she didn't think it happened because the cowboys wouldn't want to endanger their horses by riding them on the marble floors.

According to Frank Dabbs' biography of rancher Bill Herron, Calgary's cowboys and Indians rode their horses through the great hall of Union Station. Herron, one of the organizers of the trip, planned to ride his horse into the Royal York but was persuaded not to by his friend, the hotel manager.

The football game and its accompanying festivities were covered extensively by the *Herald* and *The Albertan*, but no story makes mention of a horse in the hotel. The coverage indicates the celebrations were boisterous but fairly harmless.

Grey Cup day dawned overcast and cool with the temperature at game time around 7°C. Radios were set up in offices all over Calgary and in retail stores so customers could follow the action as they shopped. Patients at Colonel Belcher Hospital all had earphones and radios. Meanwhile, the police court session was one of the shortest in memory as legal officials rushed through in order to get home and listen to the game.

Before the Stampeders took to the field, Dave Berry said, "Les Lear told us to play our game, play our position and don't get too many stupid penalties. That's all. Do it right, and you'll win; do it wrong, and you'll lose."

At 1:00 PM EST, Governor General Viscount Alexander performed the ceremonial kickoff. The Stampeders wore their dark red and white striped uniforms, and Ottawa wore white, black and red.

Wilf Tremblay kicked off to Jim Mitchener at the 34. The teams battled back and forth through the first quarter, near the end of which Tony Golab punted for a single from the Calgary 45. Ottawa 1, Calgary 0.

The first of two strange plays saw the Stampeders take the lead in the second frame. With Ottawa at third-and-one on the Calgary 44, Howie Turner faked the punt and took off. Strode nailed him for a two-yard loss. Spaith hit Harry Hood on the Rider 48 and then found Woody Strode at the 13. With everyone regrouping after that big catch, Norm Hill drifted over to the other side of the field and lay down on the enemy 20-yard line. Ottawa fans yelled themselves silly and pointed at the crafty Hill, to no avail. It seemed everybody in the stadium except the Ottawa Rough Riders (and some Stampeders) knew he was there. Time was whistled in, Spaith dropped back to pass and threw to Hill in the end zone. The ball hit Hill's hands and bounced up in the air. A defender knocked him flat on his back. The ball fell into his lap for a touchdown. Calgary 6, Ottawa 1.

Hill, now a retired Winnipeg neurosurgeon, said he probably got a big assist from Canada's figure-skating star Barbara Ann Scott. "Apparently right before that play, Barbara Ann Scott was coming into the stands in that area.

Everyone, including the Ottawa players, wanted to get a glimpse of her, so they weren't paying any attention to me."

Recalled Pete Thodas:

Where I was positioned in the huddle, I was left halfback, and Normie was left end. He'd be right beside me, and Johnny Aguirre, who was playing left tackle, was opposite me. We got back into the huddle and I said, "Where the hell's Norm Hill?" And Aguirre grabbed me and said, "Get your ass in the end position." He pulled me where Normie would normally be standing. I said, "What's going on?" and he said, "He's out there sleeping it." And I said, "You've got to be joking."

Keith threw the ball and there he was. Aguirre knew it and nobody else.

I think there was mud on the ball. It squirted, and he popped it up and it finally fell into his arms and he sat down in the end zone.

Hill said, "It was my idea. Lear had decided before the game there would be none of that trick-play stuff, but he forgot to tell the players. So, I just did it. John Aguirre went into the huddle and told them I was out there. It bobbled up in the air and I had to catch it again."

In the third quarter, Ottawa quarterback Bob Paffrath directed a powerful attack with Tony Golab and Howie Turner. Starting at the Stampeder 46, where the westerners had lost possession because of illegal blocking on a punt, the Riders marched all the way to the one. Paffrath plunged into the end zone, and Eric Chipper converted. Ottawa 7, Calgary 6.

The second strange play occurred in the fourth quarter. Still ahead by one, Ottawa had the ball on their own 37-yard line. Paffrath threw an overhand pass back to Pete Karpuk, thus making it a lateral. The ball was wide of the mark and hit the ground. Karpuk thought it was an incomplete pass, but Woody Strode picked it up. "I looked up," said Strode, "and there was a referee standing right in front of me. I looked right into his eyes. He didn't nod his head or blow a whistle or even blink. I didn't wait to ask the man any questions. I just thought I'd better take the ball away from there and talk afterwards."

When he was about to be tackled at the 25, Woody Strode lateralled to Jim Mitchener, who took it to the 10.

"If I had had any speed," said Mitchener, "I would have scored. It was a pitch-out and turned out to be a lateral and Karpuk dropped it."

Thodas also looked back at that big Grey Cup moment:

Bob Paffrath threw the ball to Pete Karpuk. He thought it was a forward pass, which it wasn't. It was a lateral pass even though he threw it overhand. And so the ball was still alive. Woody picked it up and started running and lateralled to Mitchener, and I'm right beside Mitchener and I'm telling him to lateral it to me, but he swallowed it at the 10-yard line.

Then they called an off-tackle play and I went across. I met Karpuk on the goal line with the best straight-arm I ever made.

That was the first touchdown Thodas scored that season. Rod Pantages laughed. "In 1948, I had scored, Ced had scored, Jim Mitchener had scored and, you know, afterwards we used to drink beer and have a good time. Pete said, 'Don't worry, when I score, there'll be a half-day holiday.' The little fart scored the winning touchdown in the Grey Cup, and they had a half-day holiday in Calgary when we got back from down east. Unbelievable!"

But Ottawa wasn't done. With less than two minutes remaining, Paffrath drove his team deep into enemy territory. He dropped back and threw the ball toward the end zone. Harry Hood leapt in front of the receiver and made the interception. That was it. The Calgary Stampeders had won their first Grey Cup 12–7.

The Stampeder fans whooped it up in downtown Toronto. As per the custom of the day, when the game ended, fans poured onto the field and tore down the goal posts. They set them up in the lobby of the Royal York Hotel around which they had a rousing Western hoedown. In the entrepreneurial spirit of the west, one individual sawed slices off the goal posts and sold them for a buck a piece. The next day, the Stampede Special pulled out of Union Station at 1:45 PM.

The man who would win three more Grey Cups in six tries, setting several records on his way to the Hall of Fame, saw little action that day in 1948. Alberta's future lieutenant governor Normie Kwong was a wide-eyed rookie that year.

The Calgary native played junior football with the North Hill Blizzard:

> *I knew I wasn't going to start, but it was still an exciting time to be there. You hoped against all odds that you would play a lot. Of course, there were other veterans ahead of me at the time. I went in for about four plays. That was just because Les Lear made sure everybody got into the game so they could say they played in the Grey Cup. The following year, though, I started the game and played most of it.*

Kwong, who was instrumental decades later in saving the Stampeders and the CFL, was the team's leading rusher in 1949. He was proud to be part of the first Grey Cup festival:

> *Yes, I was part of the original start-up of Grey Cup week. We went down to Toronto ahead of the fans, of course, but we came back with them on the train.*
>
> *It really was a spontaneous time, everything happened because someone thought of it at the time, nothing was planned. On the way back, people met us at every little whistle stop along the way, and the coach made sure that one or two players were always there to greet the people no matter what time of night. There were people there right across Canada.*

The Victory Special pulled into the CPR station in Calgary at noon on December 1, 1948. Before that, the wives and girlfriends of the players were given corsages and boarded

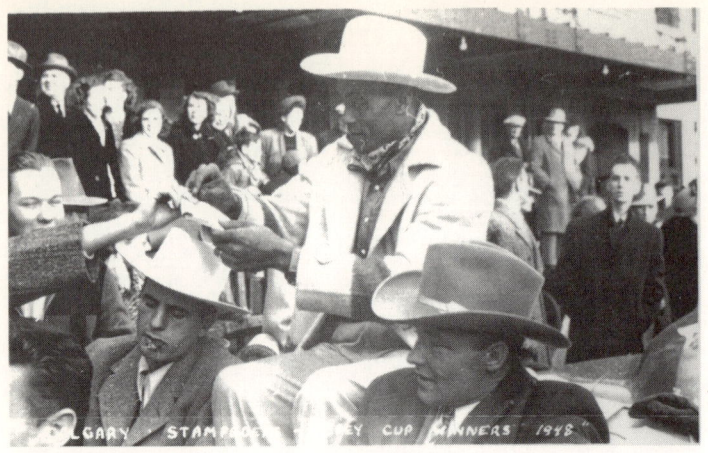

Woody Strode in white Stetson signing autographs after the Stampeders 1948 Grey Cup victory

the train just west of Calgary, along with the hero of the 36th Grey Cup, Norm Hill. Greeting the conquering heroes were Mayor J.C. Watson, the Calgary Tank Regiment Band and cheerleaders from the city's high schools.

The players were escorted through the train station between lines of boy scouts. The Grey Cup was carried in a Jeep specially fitted with a saddle. After parading through the downtown, dignitaries welcomed the team from a stage in front of the Palliser Hotel.

Among the over 30,000 people who were in attendance was a little boy named Murray Gibbs. His mother took him to the celebration, and 60 years later, in 2008, he was in the crowd welcoming the team back from Montréal when the Stampeders won their sixth Grey Cup.

Nineteen members of the Grey Cup champions did not return for the next season. New to the team was Sugarfoot Anderson, who began his 61-plus-year career with the club. Ezzert Anderson Jr., son of a slave, explained how he became a Stampeder:

> *Woody Strode and Les Lear came down and got me. They were looking for another end. I had been in the Pacific Coast League with the Los Angeles Dons. I played against Johnny Unitas, Y.A. Tittle and Otto Graham. I had retired after playing 10 years.*
>
> *I played end on both sides of the ball. I'm the first guy who made All-Pro both ways. When we started the game, Les Lear would kiss us goodbye and say "I'll see you at the end of the game, if they don't take you out on crutches." Lear was a top-notch coach. I call him Canada's Vince Lombardi, a no-nonsense guy.*

Grey Cup 1949

Led by Keith Spaith, Woody Strode, Sugarfoot Anderson and Normie Kwong, the Stampeders in 1949 picked up where they left off, winning 10 straight. Through September 1949, they outscored Edmonton 66–11 (the Eskimos returned to the WIFU to stay in 1949) and thrashed Winnipeg 52–8. The Roughriders were a horse of a different colour, succumbing 22–19 and 13–1.

October was a lot tougher for the Stampeders. On October 1, they came from behind to beat the Eskimos 12–8. They squeaked by the Bombers 3–0 in Winnipeg and

Saskatchewan 10–3 in Regina. Calgary ran their winning streak to 22 games by knocking off Edmonton 31–6.

The Stamps hosted Saskatchewan on October 22 in a snowstorm. The Riders outplayed Calgary from start to finish, with ex-Stampeder Del Wardien kicking a field goal for the 9–6 Rider victory. It could have been worse—twice the visitors were held on the one-yard line.

Including postseason play, the Stampeders had gone 25 games without a loss. They won the rest of their 1949 regular-season games, finishing the two years with a mark of 25–1. The record of 22 straight victories still stands.

In the playoffs, the Stampeders opened with a two-game total-point series against Saskatchewan, with the first game in Regina. Rod Pantages scored two touchdowns in the first quarter to lead the Stampeders to an 18–12 win.

Hostilities with Ottawa were resumed in Calgary on Remembrance Day in front of more than 14,500 fans, the biggest crowd in western Canadian football history at that time. The outcome would be decided by who could kick and who couldn't.

With under three minutes left, the Riders led the game 8–4, but the Stamps led the series 22–20. That's when the fun began.

The Riders went to work from deep in their own end, marching to the Stampeder 18-yard line. The visitors lined up to kick themselves into the Grey Cup, but the Buck Rogers' 25-yard attempt from in front of the goal posts was wide.

But wait. Calgary was offside! Del Wardien, cut by Lear the year before, was sent in to do the deed five yards closer. Same result. Pete Thodas conceded a harmless single. Calgary lost the battle 9–4 but won the war 22–21.

The Calgary culprit who was offside was none other than coach Les Lear. But nonetheless, Calgary was on to Toronto to defend the Cup.

While Calgary was putting together their winning streak, Hamilton had gone 1–10–1 in 1948 and 0–10 in 1949, the longest losing streak in the modern era. Ottawa finished first in the east with a mark of 11–1, bringing their two-season regular-season record to 21–3. Montréal finished second, six points behind the Rough Riders. The Als won the Eastern two-game final 36–20.

The 1949 Alouettes, coached by four-time Grey Cup winning coach Lew Hayman, included future Hall of Famers Eagle Keys, Ches McCance, Virgil Wagner, Herb Trawick and Bruce Coulter. Hayman picked up Stampeder Chuck Anderson and Hamilton quarterback Frank Filchock, who were signed to a two-year deal for $18,000 and given an offseason job.

A former star with the New York Giants, Filchock was banned from the NFL for failing to report a bribe attempt. He went to Hamilton, and when they couldn't afford to pay him, to Montréal.

Opposing Filchock that 1949 Grey Cup was Keith Spaith, the WIFU MVP two years running. The California native attended Southern Cal and was drafted by the L.A. Rams, but when he failed to make the team, Spaith signed with the Hawaiian Warriors of the Pacific Coast League. In 1947, the team was suspended for betting on themselves to win by a certain number of points. They won the game in question but not by enough points to win their bet.

Spaith was suspended indefinitely from playing professional football in the United States.

Spaith certainly earned his keep as a Stampeder. In the 1948 Grey Cup, he had been on the field for the full 60 minutes, at quarterback making interceptions and punting. After the 1954 season, he retired to the construction business in California, where he died in 1976 at age 52.

The Stampeders practiced at Appleby College to get ready for Montréal. Lear's preparation included having his team run through Alouette plays. Although every team now uses a scout team to prepare for an opponent, Lear originated the practice, once again being years ahead of his time.

After several days of rigorous workouts, Sugarfoot Anderson proclaimed, "We'll prove we're mighty men!"

Lear declared, "The boys are perfect, both physically and mentally. All that can be done, has been done."

When asked about the field, Lear said, "Well, I would like a dry field, of course, but even on a snow-covered field, it will be a passer's battle if the footing is good for the receivers."

It wasn't. The grounds crew at Varsity Stadium scraped the snow and ice off the field Friday morning, but the CRU stubbornly refused requests to provide a tarpaulin until they were shamed into it by the infamous "Mud Bowl" of 1950.

It was snowing and −8°C at 2:00 PM on November 26, 1949, when mayors Hiram McCallum of Toronto and Don MacKay of Calgary handled the ceremonial kickoff. The field was charitably described as "muddy," with 20,087 spectators looking on.

It appeared the gridiron gods were favouring Calgary when, on the opening kickoff, Virgil Wagner bobbled the ball at his 40-yard line and Woody Strode recovered. Paul Rowe got the ball to the Montréal 18. A penalty and an incomplete pass snuffed out the drive. After the teams exchanged punts, the Alouettes got rolling.

Starting at his 25, Filchock tossed a 40-yarder to Bob Cunningham and then hit Ralph Toohy for 22. Two plays later, Wagner ran in for the touchdown, converted by Ches McCance.

Minutes later, Norm Hill fumbled a punt, recovered by Herb Trawick at his 46. After a penalty, Montréal started at the 31. Three plays later, Cunningham scored. The convert was nullified by an offside.

At the end of the first quarter, it was Montréal 11, Calgary 0.

After picking up a single on a missed field goal, the Stamps forced the Als to punt. Fielding the ball at his 40, Thodas ran 18 yards to the 52. It was Spaith to Strode for five yards, and then Harry Hood, Thodas and Pantages took it the rest of the way, with Hood doing the honours from two yards out. The convert was good, making the score Montréal 11, Calgary 7.

Then disaster struck. It was two-and-out for the Als. Spaith dropped back to pass on his 38-yard lime, when Herb Trawick beat his block and knocked the ball from his hand. Trawick picked up the ball, cast Norm Hill aside and ran for the touchdown. The convert was good. At halftime, Montréal led 17–7.

In the third quarter, a long drive was snuffed out when Filchock intercepted Spaith at the Lark 25. Keith English and Filchock took off up the field lateralling the ball back and forth until Filchock dropped it on the Calgary 28, with the Stampeders recovering. Spaith was sacked for a 10-yard loss, so Pantages quick-kicked. Filchock threw a pass from the 55 to Wagner at the 20. Pantages intercepted but was called for interference. Three plays later, Wagner scored. After three quarters, Montréal led 23–7.

The Als picked up a field goal, a rouge and a single in the final 15 minutes, Calgary tallied a safety touch and a Sugarfoot Anderson touchdown when he picked up a Filchock fumble and took the ball in. The final score was Montréal 28, Calgary 15.

The playing field "was a mess," according to Dave Berry:

> *It was muddy, it was really bad-slippin' and slidin' and goodness knows what.*
>
> *We were on their 10-yard line and Harry Hood ran it right down to the two. Riley Matheson had blocked a guy about eight yards down the field, and it was so bad they slid together another five yards and the referee called him for blocking over the 10 yards.*
>
> *Starting the second half, they kicked to us. It was a short kick, and Normie Hill went for the ball. One of their players tripped him, and another fell*

> *on the ball. That's interference. You can't do that. But the referee let it go.*
>
> *We argued like hell so we got a 15-yard unsportsmanlike conduct tacked on us. That was the winning touchdown by the way. If you look it up, you'll find the same guy made both calls and never umpired again. I'm not saying for one second that we should have won that game. I'm just saying the referee shouldn't have won it. You can't take anything away from them as a team. Virgil Wagner was a great player, so was Herb Trawick.*

After the game, Lear had to be restrained from going after line judge Jimmy Simpson.

Frank Filchock put on one of the greatest performances in Grey Cup history, completing 12 of 20 passes for 210 yards and making three interceptions, two of which ended Calgary scoring drives.

Sugarfoot Anderson described the train trip back to Calgary:

> *We had a bar car and a dance car. On our way back, we stopped in Medicine Hat and some fans let all the horses and cows out. We were delayed three or four hours while they rounded them up and got them back on the train.*
>
> *We had a great time. I'll never forget it. There were thousands of people at the station when we got back to Calgary. You'd think we had won the game. It really shook me up. They closed the schools and the town down.*

When asked what kind of bonus he got for playing in the Grey Cup, Sugarfoot Anderson said:

> *Do you remember those old Hudson Bay coats? His and hers? The ones with the red, black and yellow stripes? That's what we got. And we got a little bitty old ring from Peoples Credit Jewellers. Wasn't nothing to write home and tell nobody about. I think it had a 15-points diamond on it.*

After the game, Les Lear said, "We'll be back next season with the greatest team ever to come east."

Montréal could also look forward to the years ahead with confidence. But 31 years would pass before the Alouettes drank from the Cup again, and 32 years for Calgary.

chapter six

Gridiron Greats, 1950–56

The 1950s and 1960s in many ways represented the CFL's golden age, dominated by great rivalries: Edmonton versus Montréal, Winnipeg versus Hamilton, Saskatchewan versus Ottawa.

Winnipeg and Toronto resumed their Grey Cup rivalry in 1950. The Blue Bombers, coached by Frank Larson and starring quarterback "Indian" Jack Jacobs and halfback Tom "Citation" Casey, dominated the Western Interprovincial Football Union (WIFU) with a mark of 10–4 and eliminated the Eskimos in the final. The Big Four race was close with Hamilton on top with 14 points, Toronto 13 and Montréal 12. The Argos won the two-game total-point Big Four final 35–19.

The Argos sailed in rough seas in 1950. Coach Ted Morris had been fired for refusing to sign American imports. Joe Krol sided with Morris, believing the Canadian game would be just as good without Americans:

I said that in 1960. I got in Dutch with some of the people when I said I thought they should do one of two things: either throw the game entirely wide open to Americans and have no limits on it or start to reduce the number of Americans down to none after initially getting them to come up here and show us how to block and so forth. If we had done that, I think we would have ended up with as good a quality of football as we have now.

That year, the number of imports allowed increased from five to seven players.

Several players deserted the ship for Edmonton, including former Argos Annis Stukus and Frankie Morris. The American Football Conference folded that year, and Toronto signed quarterback Al Dekdebrun from Buffalo, along with Buckets Hirsch and John Kerns. The Argos' new coach was Frank Clair, who chalked up the third most wins in CFL history behind Wally Buono and Don Matthews.

Grey Cup 1950

Despite the field fiasco of the 1949 Grey Cup, the Canadian Rugby Union (CRU) still stubbornly refused to order a tarpaulin for Varsity Stadium in Toronto. The worst conditions of all-time occurred in 1950 when a heavy snowfall overnight melted the next day. A snow removal truck was mired in the muck and had to be towed by a semi-trailer unit. How bad was it? The 1950 Grey Cup was called the "Mud Bowl."

Gridiron Greats, 1950–56

Game action from the 1950 Grey Cup game (also known as the "Mud Bowl") between the Toronto Argonauts and the Winnipeg Blue Bombers

The hometown Argos won 13–0. Nick Volpe kicked two field goals, Joe Krol had two singles and Al Dekdebrun scored a touchdown on a one-yard quarterback sneak.

Winnipeg couldn't run in the slop, and Jack Jacobs, a superb passer on a dry day, couldn't handle the slippery pigskin. Onlookers were surprised Toronto didn't have the same problem. Joe Krol explained why.

"Our quarterback Al Dekdebrun had thumbtacks taped to his fingers with just enough of the points sticking out to grip the ball. It turned out to be a heckuva gimmick."

When asked about the thumbtacks, Argo coach Frank Clair feigned ignorance about the tactic but then changed his tune.

"Well, I was only told about it afterwards," he said carefully, "and all I can say is, I don't know. But if he did, it was a good idea."

Clair paused for a few seconds and then said, "Actually, they were cut down to about a 32nd of an inch so they wouldn't hurt anybody. It was a pretty good idea on that day because really it was so muddy you could barely hold the ball at all."

Pundits claim the field conditions were so bad that Bomber Hall of Fame lineman Buddy Tinsley would have drowned had it not been for the quick thinking of referee Hec Crighton, who noticed Tinsley laying facedown in the field. Whether Tinsley could have drowned escaped Krol's notice, although, he said, "I suppose it was possible because I know the slush was ankle deep, over the tops of my shoes. It is quite possible if he was laying there for any length of time that he could have hurt himself."

Even Tinsley gets a kick out of the story. But it wasn't true. "No, I wasn't drowning," he said.

> *I had hurt my knee in the playoffs. When I went down east, they taped my knee and quadriceps so tight, the muscles wouldn't move. I happened to get hit right on the thigh real hard. That paralyzed my leg and I fell forward.*
>
> *The conditions were atrocious that day. There was water floating on the field and pieces of ice.*

A lot of our guys fell down, but I fell forward. I was lying there with my head on my arm very unhappy because I got hurt.

I was just laying there because I couldn't move my leg. A couple of guys came over and helped me up.

I don't know how that story got started. I think people in the stands thought I was drowning because of the conditions.

Grey Cup 1951

Neither Toronto nor Winnipeg made it back to the Grey Cup in 1951. In the East, Ottawa finished in a three-way tie for first with Hamilton and Toronto. The teams tossed a coin to determine the finish, with Ottawa coming out in first, followed by the Tiger-Cats, who won the two-game total-point semifinal 31–28 before losing to Ottawa in the final, 17–7 and 11–9.

There was also a three-way tie for first in the West, with Calgary the odd cowboy out. A tie-breaking formula gave top spot to Saskatchewan. Eskimo coach Annis Stukus kicked a field goal to eliminate third place Winnipeg 4–1. In an exciting best-of-three Western final, Eskimo Jim Chambers ran for 95 yards along a fan-laden sideline to score the winning touchdown in game one at Regina. The Riders won the next two games, 12–5 on the road and 19–18 at home. Excitement was the word of the season in the Saskatchewan capital, which was renamed "Dobberville" in honour of the greatest sports phenomenon to ever hit the prairie province.

In the 1940s, the Roughriders fell on hard times with only two winning seasons. In 1948, when Moose Jaw and

Saskatoon dropped out of the CFL, the Regina Roughriders became the Saskatchewan Roughriders. The legendary love affair between fans and football team began in 1951 when a tall Tulsan, Glenn Dobbs, former quarterback of the Los Angeles Dons, arrived in Regina to quarterback the Roughriders. Dobbs took Saskatchewan by storm.

Licence plates with "Dobberville" adorned cars from one end of the province to the other. At recess, Dobbs' son was followed around the school grounds by children anxious to bask in his reflected glory. Everywhere he went, Glenn Dobbs was mobbed by adoring fans.

Little Bobby Kramer in Winnipeg greeting the Roughriders enroute to the 1951 Grey Cup in Toronto

Miss Grey Cup 1951, Myrtle Bainbridge (bottom centre with white hat) at the Grey Cup celebration in Toronto. Saskatchewan lost to Ottawa 21–14.

Two days after winning the West, the Roughriders embarked by train for Toronto. Aboard were Mr. and Mrs. Ken Charlton. Charlton was a Regina native who began his career with the Riders in 1941. After stays with service teams during the war and a stint with Ottawa after, Charlton returned to Regina where he played until his retirement in 1954. Charlton was inducted into the Canadian Football Hall of Fame in 1992.

He loved the train trip to Toronto. "It was super. It was like a big party all the way down."

Mrs. Charlton agreed. "It was absolutely beautiful but the players didn't party. A porter came through the car and said, 'Shhh, these are all the players' wives. They're a bunch of nuns.' The players were in another car. We were all at the back, and it was just a ball. I rode on the bread truck in the parade." Those on the Saskatchewan float in the Grey Cup parade threw little loaves of bread to the crowd.

Dobbs described the 1951 Roughriders.

We were not an overwhelming team and darn, Jack Russell, the big end got hurt, and we had trouble at centre when Red Ettinger got hurt. Some of our Canadians were older. Toar Springstein was in his second-last year. Ken Charlton, the perennial halfback, was close to the end of the line, just like a lot of us were. Kenny was a hard-working dude. We were all the same kind of guys. We knew we didn't have all the ability, so we worked hard.

Charlton said going into the Grey Cup, "We had a lot of injuries, but except for Jack Russell, they all played, but not as well as they could have."

Getting ready to meet the Western invasion was Ottawa receiver Bob Simpson, a native of Windsor who had played one year of high school ball and one year with the hometown Rockets of the Ontario Rugby Football Union (ORFU) before joining the Ottawa Rough Riders in 1950.

"Mr. Versatility," Simpson was an All-Star end in 1951, '56 and '59, flying wing in '52 and '53, running back in '57 and defensive back in '57 and '58.

Simpson's coach in 1951 was Clem Crowe. "Clem didn't think Canadians could play football, so he didn't give much credit to them. If you weren't an American, you couldn't play well, which was really the way he expressed it. Obviously, he and I didn't get along too well," said Simpson.

Come Grey Cup week, the Ottawa Rough Riders were all business.

Simpson said:

We arrived in Toronto on Tuesday and stayed at the King Edward Hotel. We didn't really want to be part of the festivities. We had a job to do. You have to trust your athlete. He knows the job that's

The 1951 Grey Cup game in Toronto between the Ottawa Rough Riders and the Saskatchewan Roughriders

at hand. Sure, he'll go out and have a couple of beers on Wednesday and Thursday night, but he is certainly not going to be walking the streets looking for trouble or anything.

Grey Cup day was windy. Near the end of the first quarter, Dobbs put Saskatchewan into the lead with two singles. Simpson was still in awe of the punting prowess of the Tulsa All-American 40 years later. "I was catching punts at the time. There was quite a wind that day. On Dobbs' first punt, he was standing on his own 40-yard line. I was standing on my 15-yard line. It went through the end zone and landed 12 rows up in the bleachers. I had never seen a kick like that before in my life."

That's all the scoring the Westerners could muster until the fourth quarter. Ottawa scored three touchdowns and a single, leading 19–2 after 45 minutes.

Benny MacDonnell, Alton Baldwin and Pete Karpuk scored Ottawa's three TDs.

"The most important catch was Pete's. It was a streak pattern. Pete had good speed, and he headed down the sideline," recalled Simpson. "He outran their defensive back who was a little banged up. Tom O'Malley threw an absolutely perfect pass. Pete caught up with it about the 12-yard line and went in for the touchdown."

The Green Riders didn't give up. Dobbs completed a touchdown pass to Jack Nix while fullback Sully Glasser scored another. But that was it. Ottawa added a couple of singles to win 21–14.

After the game, Saskatchewan's coach Harry "Blackjack" Smith was fired and replaced by Dobbs, who had no coaching experience.

Grey Cup 1952

The Saskatchewan Roughriders finished last in 1952 with a 3–13 record. The 1952 Grey Cup marked the beginning of the Edmonton Eskimos' sojourn with greatness and the Toronto Argonauts' last hurrah before setting sail on the Sea of Futility.

The Eskimos had reorganized in 1949, adopted green and gold as their colours and joined the WIFU. They soon became the flagship team of the CFL and were one of the most successful organizations in all of sport.

Since their return to the grid wars that year, the Eskimos and Argos have had an interesting relationship, be it trading Jackie Parker to Toronto in 1963 or Ricky Ray in 2012. In 1993, the Eskimos swung the biggest trade in CFL history with Toronto and promptly won the Grey Cup—the Argos finished last. When Edmonton joined the Western Conference in 1949, they hired ex-Argo Annis Stukus as coach to put the team together.

Upon arriving in Edmonton, Stukus wondered what he had gotten into:

> *I get out to Clarke Stadium and they've got 2700 bleacher seats there, and we're going to play pro football. They condemned the stands at the race track, and one of our directors had the job of tearing them down. I asked him to take them down*

> *piecemeal and move them over to the east side of Clarke Stadium so we had at least 7700 seats.*

On a budget of $45,000, Stukus went hunting for football players and found them in Toronto. Frank Morris was one of them:

> *In 1949, my last year with Argos, I was selling beer for Labatt Breweries, and I was in the Town tavern on one of my calls and Stuke was there recruiting Dougie Pyzer and Don Durno. There were four or five guys at the table. I sat down and joined them and set up a round of Labatts for them and got talking and somebody casually said, "Why don't you come out west and play football?"*
>
> *I had some reasons for doing that. Stuke made me an offer, and he was supposed to have a job for me out there. I moved to Edmonton, and my wife and two kids joined me about a month later.*

Stukus compiled a record of 19 wins and 23 losses. He made the playoffs in 1950, ousting Saskatchewan in the semifinal 24–1 before losing the final to the Bombers. The Eskimos made it to the final the next year, losing to Saskatchewan. At the end of that season, his contract up, Stukus returned to the Toronto Star as a sportswriter. His successor as coach was Frank Filchock.

With Claude Arnold at quarterback and Rollie Miles and Norm Kwong in the backfield, Edmonton finished second to the Blue Bombers with a record of 9–6–1. The third-place Stampeders went to Edmonton and won the first of the two-game total-point semifinal 31–12. Filchock rallied the troops, taking the second game in Calgary 30–7 and the round 42–38, before beating the Bombers in the final.

After winning the right to represent the West in the Grey Cup for the first time in 30 years, Filchock said he wouldn't accompany the team to Toronto because the team had not honoured his contract, which he said called for a Grey Cup bonus. It didn't. Filchock said he wouldn't go unless he had a new contract covering 1953 and 1954. The contract he was under, which would expire on December 31, 1952, paid him $8500 plus bonuses and travel expenses, adding up to $11,000. Executives Ken Montgomery and Frank Anderson offered Filchock $31,000 over two seasons. Filchock agreed if the club also paid his income tax and gave him a $1000 signing bonus. He said he was prepared to accept the signing bonus over two years.

Montgomery told Filchock that the Board of Directors were very upset about the bonus. Filchock said if he didn't get the bonus with $500 paid up front immediately, he would not go to Toronto. The club caved in and said they would have the contract drawn up upon the team's return from the Grey Cup.

In December 1952, Filchock demanded the right to take on another job as a car salesman. But because the club wanted him to make community appearances and promote high school, junior and university football, they said no, pointing out that he was already going to be the highest paid coach in Canada. Filchock made a counter-offer, but the club had had enough and let his contract lapse on December 31, 1952.

Down east, the first-place Argos beat out Hamilton and the Sarnia Imperials, and Frank Clair prepared his team to meet Edmonton.

It would be the devil-may-care Filchock against the "Professor" Frank Clair, who believed in meticulous preparation. Not so Frank Filchock. According to Morris, "Frank would ad lib plays. That was the way he functioned. We'd come off the field and he'd get down and diagram plays and away we'd go."

This strategy didn't work against Toronto.

Poor play selection cost Edmonton dearly. The Eskimos unleashed a powerful running attack with Kwong, Miles and Rod Pantages. In the first quarter, Pantages fumbled out of bounds on the Argo one-yard line, resulting in a 10-yard penalty, but Kwong ran the ball into the end zone two plays later. Wilbur Snyder failed to convert.

Nobby Wirkowski scored on a quarterback sneak. With the convert, it was Toronto 6, Edmonton 5. Red Ettinger kicked a field goal and converted Bill Bass' touchdown, giving the Easterners a 15–5 lead. A converted TD by Kwong narrowed the gap to 15–11, with six minutes left in the fourth quarter.

Scrimmaging from the enemy 54, the Eskimos marched relentlessly down the field. Miles picked up 14 yards, Pantages 11 and Miles for another 13, bringing the ball to the Argo 16-yard line. Despite this success on the ground, Filchock and Claude Arnold opted to go to the air. On first down, Arnold couldn't find an open receiver so he threw the ball into the ground, an incomplete pass under U.S. rules but a fumble in Canada. Argo Art Scullion jumped on it.

The Eskimo defence got the ball back with three minutes left, but Arnold was intercepted by Ed Sergel. In the dying minutes, Wirkowski put the icing on the cake with a touchdown pass to Zeke O'Conner. The final score, Toronto 21, Edmonton 11.

While the Eskimos returned to the big game in two years, Toronto didn't make it back for 19 years and wouldn't win another Grey Cup for 31.

Grey Cup 1953

In 1950, the ORFU Tigers and the Big Four Wildcats amalgamated as the Hamilton Tiger-Cats. Between 1953 and 1965, the Winnipeg Blue Bombers and Hamilton Tiger-Cats clashed in the Grey Cup seven times, the Westerners winning four times. There are 21 players and coaches from those two teams of that era enshrined in the Canadian Football Hall of Fame.

Carl Voyles laid the foundation for a Hamilton franchise that finished first in the East 13 times in 22 years and appeared in the Grey Cup 11 times, winning six of them. Hired as coach and general manager in 1950, Voyles signed Ralph Sazio and Jake Gaudaur, who both became giants of the CFL.

Starting at end for the Blue Bombers in '53 was Harry Peter "Bud" Grant, up from the NFL Philadelphia Eagles, and Neil Armstrong. Gerry James, son of Dynamite Eddie, shared the backfield with Tom "Citation" Casey and Lorne Benson.

Buddy Tinsley, Dean Bandiera and Dick Huffman anchored the line. Bud Korchak did the kicking.

The 8–8 Bombers finished third behind Edmonton and Saskatchewan. They walloped the Riders 43–17 in Regina when Benson scored six touchdowns, a record that still stands. Winnipeg lost the second game 18–17 but won the round 60–23. In the final, Edmonton took the opener 25–7 at Winnipeg but lost the next two at home.

The Tiger-Cats finished in a first-place tie with Montréal, each with 8–6 records, two points ahead of Ottawa. Hamilton rolled over the Alouettes 37–12 and 22–11. With players like Lou Kusserow, Vince Scott, Cam Fraser, Bernie Custis and Ed Bevan, the Tiger-Cats were a team as tough as the city they represented.

The 1953 Grey Cup matched the brilliant passing of Jack Jacobs against Hamilton's tenacious defence. Jacobs set a record by completing 31 of 48 passes. He threw for 357 yards. The only scoring in the first half came on an Ed Songin quarterback sneak that capped a long Hamilton drive featuring passes to Vito Regazzo and Lou Kusserow. Gerry James opened the third quarter with a long kickoff return, giving his team excellent field position. Catching and running, Tom Casey took the ball to the one. James carried it over.

Ed Songin struck back, hitting Regazzo on a 50-yard pass and run for the touchdown. Hamilton led 12–6. The game appeared to be wrapped up when Cam Fraser kicked the Bombers in deep, pinning them on their five-yard line. But the remarkable Jacobs wasn't done yet. With passes to

Andy Sokol, Neil Armstrong, Keith Pearce and Tom Casey, he marched the Bombers to the Ti-Cats' 15.

Dick Huffman then executed the tackle-eligible play, running the ball to the five. Casey carried to the three. On the last play of the game, Jacobs dropped back for his 48th pass and threw to Casey on the goal line. But Lou Kusserow timed his tackle perfectly, dislodging the ball from the startled receiver's hands and giving Hamilton the win.

When the big moment came, the Ti-Cats were ready. Jake Gaudaur explained:

> *I give Carl Voyles an awful lot of credit. Films weren't very prominent in those days, even for coaching. Whatever ones we had were so grey and foggy you could hardly get any benefit from them. But the one thing that seemed to be apparent on the film was that any time Winnipeg got inside the 25-yard line, they would go to Tom Casey. So we had a "Casey" to practice against all week.*

The Bombers insisted Kusserow should have been called for interference. Gaudaur was ambivalent about that:

"Coach Voyles said, 'Risk a penalty if you have to, but get to this guy.' Lou Kusserow may have got there a little ahead of time, I don't know. It was a very close play. But he was coached to err on the side of committing a penalty."

As impressive as Jacobs' stats were, the Bombers only scored one touchdown. With their running backs, some wondered why Winnipeg passed so much. Buddy Tinsley had a theory.

"Psychologically, I thought the whole thing was that in the 1950 Grey Cup, Jacobs couldn't throw, and he wanted to show everybody he could throw. We were throwing the ball down on the goal line. We shouldn't have been doing that."

Grey Cup 1954

One of the greatest teams in the history of Canadian football was the Edmonton Eskimos between 1954 and 1960. Overall, the Eskimos have been the dominant force in Canadian football, appearing in the Grey Cup 24 times with 13 wins. There are 43 Eskimo players, coaches and builders in the Canadian Football Hall of Fame.

Eleven of Edmonton's Grey Cup appearances were against Montréal. Fans in the 1950s were thrilled by the escapades of some of the greatest players the game has ever known, such as Eskimo stars Jackie Parker, Normie Kwong, Rollie Miles, Johnny Bright, Frank Anderson and Ted Tully, and Lark stars Sam Etcheverry, Red O'Quinn, Hal Patterson, Alex Webster, Pat Abruzzi, Tex Coulter, Herb Trawick and Joey Pal.

In 1954, the Eskimos, coached by Frank "Pop" Ivy and quarterbacked by Bernie Faloney, finished in a first-place tie with Saskatchewan, getting the bye on the basis of having more wins. The Conference final against the Blue Bombers featured three bitterly fought games. Edmonton won the opener 9–3, lost in Winnipeg 12–6 and won the West by winning at home 10–5. They defeated the ORFU Kitchener Waterloo Dutchmen 38–6 for the right to go to the Grey Cup, the last time the ORFU participated in the Grey Cup sweepstakes.

Montréal, at 11–3 under the direction of Douglas "Peahead" Walker, dominated the Big Four and easily dispatched Hamilton in the Eastern final. The Alouettes were heavily favoured to beat the upstarts Eskimos from the West.

The 1954 Grey Cup was a tremendous offensive game. Montréal set the still-standing record of 656 yards total offence. Montréal and Edmonton ran up 1090 yards between them, second only to their total in 1955. The two teams also racked up the third-highest yard total in 1956.

Edmonton opened the scoring when Rollie Miles, chased from the Alouette three-yard line back to the 25, threw to halfback Earl Lindley in the end zone. Bob Dean converted.

Montréal struck back in dramatic fashion. With the ball on the Als' 20, "Sam called an audible," said Red O'Quinn.

> We had what was called a fire pass where he would take the ball from the centre and jump up in the air and throw it to me on a quick slant across the middle. Pop Ivy had been working with Rollie Miles and Jackie Parker to intercept it. They had seen the films.

> We threw it a lot, a quick pass between the linebackers. They thought they were going to come up and intercept it, but they overshot me, and I went through there and put a hand out and the ball stuck. I was off and running. I managed to make it to the goal line before Miles and Parker could catch me.

The 90-yard reception is still the second longest ever in a Grey Cup game.

Jackie Parker (left) and Normie Kwong of the Edmonton Eskimos with the Grey Cup in 1954

Again Edmonton came right back, with Bernie Faloney capping off a long march with a one-yard quarterback sneak for a touchdown, making it 14–6 for the Eskimos. Then Montréal tallied touchdowns by Red O'Quinn and Chuck Hunsinger to lead 18–14 at the half.

The only scoring in the third quarter was a Montréal single, kicked by Jim Poole. In the final quarter, Sam Etcheverry connected with Joey Pal on a 14-yard touchdown. Glenn Lippman replied for the West. Etcheverry proceeded to move his club to the Eskimo 11 with just under four minutes to go. Leading 25–20, a touchdown or field goal would put the game out of reach.

Over the years, a few great or controversial plays stand out that were crucial in determining the outcome of the game. The 1954 Grey Cup was decided by the Hunsinger play.

Chuck Hunsinger was a halfback. On the fateful play, he took the ball from Etcheverry and tried to pass (his version) or fumbled (the official version). Jackie Parker scooped up the ball and ran 90 yards for a touchdown, a still-standing record. That tied the game.

"I've got the film here," said Frankie Morris. "They still show stop-action of Hunsinger with the ball up. The Alouettes made the point it was a pass, that it should have been ruled an incomplete pass, not a fumble. But he was carrying the ball. He kind of jumped up in the air. I think it was Ted Tully who hit him. In the stop-action shot, it looks like he's going to push the ball with his right hand on a lateral pass. But he got hit. The ball came free, Jackie picked the ball up and ran the rest of the way for the touchdown."

Jackie Parker, one of the greatest offensive performers in U.S. college and Canadian football history, is best remembered for that defensive play in the 1954 Grey Cup:

> *They were trying an end-run, and Ted Tully got through and hit Hunsinger simultaneously. The ball popped out and I happened to be there. I picked it up and started running with it.*
>
> *I don't think it was an attempted forward pass, but I don't know that. It looked like our players*

got through quickly and stopped the end-run and kind of stripped the ball.

Hunsinger got hit behind the line of scrimmage, but one of the offensive linemen was in the vicinity. Being a very astute football player, Hunsinger might have tried to pitch it back to him, but he didn't really have a chance.

Red O'Quinn also looked back on that fateful day:

I was on the bus going from the Royal York out to the stadium and I was sitting beside Chuck Hunsinger. Everyone was so keyed up about the game. Chuck said, "The only thing I don't want is to be a goat. I don't want to mess up." It turned out that it was the biggest mess-up of his career. He had a wonderful basketball and football career. Today he laughs about it and says, "If it hadn't been for that play, I'd have been long forgotten."

It really was a forward pass. Chuck tried to push the ball forward to Ray Cicia, a guard pulling around. Jim Staton had missed his block on the tackle, and the tackle came through and was right in Chuck's face from the time he got the ball.

He did the wrong thing. He panicked and tried to throw it forward to Cicia. It didn't work out; the ball was on the ground. Parker came through like a shot, picked it up and was gone. Etcheverry couldn't catch him.

Parker's 90-yard run tied it up, but it was up to kicker Bob Dean to win the game by kicking the extra point.

He hadn't missed all year, but even the convert attempt was dramatic because centre Eagle Keys was out of the game. Keys was a study in courage. Despite an injury, he limped onto the field to snap the ball for a Bob Dean field goal and two converts. By the time Parker made his dramatic run, Keys could not continue.

"Eagle was the starting centre," said Johnny Bright, "but he had a broken leg and couldn't continue. So here we are changing the centre. When the snap count was being called, someone said, 'Let's not mess it up, fellows. No mistakes. Let's block.'"

The myth that Keys snapped that ball lives on it. Who did snap it?

Bright didn't say.

Rollie Miles: "I think it was Eagle Keys."

Eagle Keys: "I didn't do it."

Bill Briggs snapped the ball, the convert was good and Edmonton won their first Grey Cup. The final score was 26–25.

Receiver Red O'Quinn was magnificent for Montréal, catching 12 passes for 290 yards, including the longest 90-yarder for a touchdown, both of which are records that have yet to be broken. O'Quinn was inducted into the Canadian Football Hall of Fame on January 6, 1981.

Grey Cup 1955

In 1955, the Eskimos and Alouettes met again in Western Canada's inaugural Grey Cup at Empire Stadium, Vancouver. Montréal was 9–3 and barely edged out Toronto in the Eastern final 38–36.

Although the Alouettes were a marvellous passing team, fullback Pat Abruzzi had won the Schenley Outstanding Player Award as a rookie. The award to honour the CFL's best was established in 1953. The first winner was Eskimo fullback Billy Vessels. Sam Etcheverry won in 1954. In Abruzzi's four seasons as an Alouette, he picked up 3749 yards and scored 39 touchdowns, including 20 in 1956, a record that stood until 1994.

The Eskimos breezed through the regular season, running up a record-setting 14 wins against two losses. They beat the Bombers two straight in the final. As Bright explained, they were a team on a mission. "Come hell or high water, there was no way we were going to lose the playoffs to Winnipeg because we had to go back and thrash Montréal.

"Montréal had made comments that the Grey Cup game was a million-dollar classic, but this was the first time a nickel-and-dime team had shown up. They said we had no business even being in the same ball park with them, that we had won on a fluke the year before."

Rollie Miles agreed. "We didn't get much respect. Even after we won in 1954, we still didn't get much respect."

Said Parker, "We'd been the team that went down and won a Grey Cup in '54 and everybody thought we weren't very good. But we were a good team. We had a lot of really excellent players who gave it all they had.... When we beat Montréal again in 1955, that was the best one for me because we kind of said, 'Hey, we're not that bad.'"

The 1955 Grey Cup match-up was the army versus the air force. Johnny Bright and Normie Kwong rolled over the Alouettes like Sherman tanks, Kwong running for 145 yards and Bright for 82. Both scored two touchdowns. Edmonton set a single-game rushing record of 438 yards, which they broke the following year. Sam Etcheverry threw for an incredible 508 yards, a record that still stands.

Abruzzi scored a touchdown for the Alouettes. Hal Patterson got the other two, although he didn't play the last quarter and a half because, as he said, he "got hit in the head and was a little woozy." Kwong, Bright and Bob Heydenfeldt matched with majors for the West, making the score 19–18 for Montréal at the half.

The Alouettes didn't score another point. Bright broke the game open in the third quarter. "There hadn't been very many long gains made running," he recalled.

> *We were 42 yards out, and we ran what we called a 41-counter. I broke it the 42 yards for a touchdown, which put us up to stay.*
>
> *Later in the game we were on the eight-yard line and Jackie called a 38 pitchout. Montréal had a mouthy back by the name of J.C. Caroline who later became an All-Pro defensive back with the Chicago Bears. He had been stating what he would do to me.*
>
> *I turned the corner on the pitch. I ran over J.C. and knocked him out and scored a touchdown. From then on, nobody challenged me very much in that game.*

Bob Dean converted all five TDs and added a field goal and convert, making the final score Edmonton 34, Montréal 19.

Kwong's record 30 carries in the 1955 game still stand. His 145 yards is the third best in Grey Cup history, and he is fourth all-time for Grey Cup rushing yardage behind Mike Pringle, Leo Lewis and George Reed.

Despite his tremendous performance, Kwong's fondest memory is of the win over Montréal the year earlier. "The 1954 game was most satisfying because we were such underdogs, and we won the thing. It was more fun to win because we were so downgraded, and we showed them."

Grey Cup 1956

The Eskimos also showed the Alouettes in the 1956 Grey Cup. Tied 20–20 in the third quarter, the Eskimos went on to win 50–27. A touchdown became worth six points in 1956. Jackie Parker scored three of them and a single. Johnny Bright was magnificent, rushing for a still-standing record of 171 yards. It was the greatest game he ever played and the greatest individual performance in Grey Cup history.

"With Rollie Miles hurt, Norm and I carried almost all the offensive load. I caught nine passes. I had two touchdowns," said Bright. "I went in and played one quarter of defensive ball, recovered a fumble, knocked a pass down and intercepted one. In 1956, I made more of a contribution to the overall success of the team than at any other time. That was the greatest satisfaction I had."

The Eskimo quarterback in that game was Don Getty.

"One thing I was very pleased about as a Canadian quarterback," said Alberta's future premier, "was that in the Western final and the Grey Cup, we scored over 100 points. I was very proud of that. I think that's the real measure of a quarterback. Can you get the ball in the end zone?"

How was Edmonton able to thrash Montréal so thoroughly? "They were a tremendous club," conceded Getty.

> *But we won because the week we were practicing in London, Ivy put in a system we hadn't used all year. We were going to go at the touch of the guard's hands to the ground, and the ends and tackles had to race up there. I was going to call for the ball the instant I got behind the centre. So we had kind of a rolling start. We were by the big, heavy guys like Doug McNichol, Tex Coulter and Jim Staton before they had a chance to exercise their weight advantage against us. That was very effective. We just wore them down.*
>
> *They were ahead in the third quarter, but by then they were running out of steam and we were going faster and faster. Ivy didn't put in the system to blow them away but because we were stale. He thought we needed to work on something new.*

Said Red O'Quinn, "They outsmarted us. They came out almost on the dead run and never did stop. They snapped the ball while everybody was moving. They had it timed perfectly. Everything was a quick count."

Frankie Morris believed Montréal's lack of strategy was crucial to Edmonton's success in the 1955 and '56 Cups.

"We played them three years in a row, and every year we set our offence to go against the defence that they had run the year before. We thought they would make some changes, but three years in a row, they never changed a damn thing."

"Our biggest mistake was not changing our defence," admitted Sam Etcheverry. "We held to the same defence in all three Grey Cup games against them. We just came out on the field and tried to outscore them and not worry about defence."

"They weren't a better team," lamented Alouette Hal Patterson. "They just out-coached us. We had only two defences, a 5–4 and a 5–2. We didn't have anything else, and we pretty well got picked apart."

The losses were a bitter disappointment for Etcheverry. The University of Denver product passed for 35,582 yards in seven years of recorded statistics, completing 1630 passes for 174 touchdowns and a 57 percent average. No statistics were kept in 1952 and '53, his first two seasons in the league.

Etcheverry described his feelings about the big game. "When you haven't won the Grey Cup, it is something that sticks with you the rest of your life. It's something that always comes up. People remember it. It comes up in my business. Some people are very critical that I never won the Grey Cup as a player. You know, every person in your home stands is not automatically on your side."

chapter seven

Lions, Tigers and Bombers, Oh My! 1957–65

T he great rivalry in the CFL began in 1956 between Winnipeg and Hamilton.

In 1956, Ti-Cat GM Jake Gaudaur hired 1955's NFL Coach of the Year, Jim Trimble, who had been fired by the Philadelphia Eagles. Trimble, a robust barrel-chested man with wavy grey hair and twinkling blue eyes, was bombastic, charming and fun. His players loved him. "Jim was a colourful guy," recalled Ti-Cat legend Angelo Mosca. "He wasn't a great X's and O's man, but he could coordinate and motivate. He had the people in place to do the coaching. I respected him then and still do today."

Bud Grant took over the reins of the Winnipeg Blue Bombers in 1957.

In 1957, Gaudaur signed future Hall of Famers John Barrow and Bernie Faloney, as well as fullback Gerry McDougall and one of the toughest men to ever grace a gridiron,

Ralph Goldston. The year before, Gaudaur had brought in Tommy Grant and Chester "Cookie" Gilchrist.

The man who led the Ti-Cat offence from 1957 to 1964 was University of Maryland All-American Bernie Faloney, who ranks third all-time behind Anthony Calvillo and Doug Flutie for Grey Cup pass completions and yardage, and second in touchdown passes. Originally an Eskimo, Faloney came to Canada because of economics. "I was drafted by the San Francisco 49ers to play defensive back and backup quarterback," he explained.

> *They offered me $9000. Maryland was number one in the country. Edmonton had hired Pop Ivy who was with Oklahoma. We had played them in the Orange Bowl game.*
>
> *Pop Ivy wanted to take his Split-T offence to Edmonton. He called me and said they would like to have me up there, and the contract was much better. It was for $12,500. The Canadian dollar had a 10-percent premium at that time. For a kid getting out of university, that was a lot of money to start out with.*

Faloney ended up in Hamilton three years later because Edmonton made an uncharacteristic mistake. After his first season in green and gold, Faloney had to return to the U.S. to fulfill his two-year military commitment. In 1957, when negotiation lists were instituted in the CFL, Faloney was ready to return, but Edmonton didn't have him on their list. Jim Trimble did.

Faloney made the Eastern All-Star team five times and won the Schenley Award for Most Outstanding Player in 1961. He was elected to the Hall of Fame in 1974.

"He wasn't the greatest quarterback in the world," said Mosca, "but I'll tell you one thing, when you got to the five-yard line, you thought you were on the one because he was a believer in what he did, and he had the confidence of his players and their respect."

Much the same could be said for Faloney's Winnipeg rival, Ken Ploen, who had been named the Rose Bowl Player of the Game after leading Iowa State to a 35–19 win over Oregon State. In his inaugural CFL season, Ploen led the Bombers to a 12–4 second-place finish and made the Western Conference All-Star team. He went on to win four Grey Cups for the Bombers.

"I attribute a lot of that success not only to the Canadian game but to bringing up the Iowa offence," Ploen said. "Because of the wingbacks that were available here in Canada, we played the Wing-T with the roll-out options, the bootlegs and different things. It seemed to fit the Canadian game, particularly the wide field. No one had seen it up here too much, and it worked very effectively."

When asked about great Grey Cup performers, Bud Grant replied, "Kenny Ploen would be number one. He always had great games. Many times we used him both ways as a defensive back and a quarterback."

Kenny Ploen set no records and won no awards. All he did was win.

Grey Cup 1957

Edmonton finished first in the West in 1957 with a record of 14–2, Winnipeg second at 12–4. After eliminating Calgary in the semifinal round, the Blue Bombers faced the three-time champion Eskimos, winning the opener 19–7 at home. Winnipeg lost a 5–4 nail-biter in Edmonton and then won the West by defeating the Eskies 17–2.

Hamilton finished first in the Big Four. The Alouettes got by Ottawa 24–15 in the semifinal, but Hamilton ended their Eastern domination by winning the two-game total-point final 56–11. It was a powerful, talent-laden, injury-free team that took on the Blue Bombers in the 1957 Grey Cup.

Beat up when the game began, things got worse for Winnipeg when Ken Ploen hurt his knee and Gerry James sustained a broken hand when he was stepped on. Another back, Dennis Mendyk, wore a cast to protect a broken wrist.

In the first quarter, Mendyk was hit hard by Cookie Gilchrist and coughed up the ball. Ray "Bibbles" Bawel picked it up and ran 53 yards for a touchdown. A little later, Hamilton capitalized on the first of James' four fumbles and went 46 yards in four plays, the last one a six-yard run for the score by Bernie Faloney. Gilchrist scored two touchdowns, Gerry McDougall, one.

An otherwise dull game was made memorable by one of the strangest plays in Grey Cup history—the Bibbles Bawel incident. About 10 minutes into the fourth quarter, Bawel, a defensive back from Indiana, picked off a Winnipeg pass and had clear sailing down the sideline to the end zone. He didn't get very far before a fan near the Bomber bench stuck out his foot and tripped him. Bawel fell at the enemy 42-yard line. Referee Paul Dojack marched the ball half the distance to the goal line. A couple of plays later, Gilchrist carried it in.

"We didn't have a rule covering such an event so I made a judgement call," explained Dojack. "Bawel was pretty well on his way, there was no doubt about it. We had a little consultation and decided he could have very well gone in. But you couldn't give any particular penalty because you couldn't penalize a spectator.

"We said half the distance to the goal line and time enough for three plays, which gave Hamilton ample opportunity to go in. The game was pretty much in hand at that time. The Tiger-Cats had a good lead."

"The guy who tripped him was a lawyer from Toronto," reminisced the late Ralph Sazio. "For years after, he corresponded with Bibbles, and I believe he sent him a watch one year."

Bomber defensive back Norm Rauhaus couldn't believe his eyes. "That guy ran right by me to get him.... Our trainer, Jim Ausley, almost nabbed him, but the guy got by him. There was no question Bibbles would have gone all the way."

The final score of 32–7 indicated that Hamilton dominated that day, but the Bombers had more yards and first downs, and the Cats were only ahead 13–7 after three quarters. However, Hamilton's unanswered fourth-quarter points represents the second-highest tally in Grey Cup history.

"We wore them down," said Faloney. "We would pound and pound, and in the fourth quarter, everything came to fruition."

Rauhaus said, "We were a very beat-up team. We probably surprised everybody, including ourselves, by beating Edmonton to make it to the Grey Cup."

Bud Grant agreed. "In 1957, after we'd beaten the Eskimos, we went to Toronto, but we only had half a team. We had fellows that couldn't play or only played a few plays. We were just lucky and happy to be there."

"The score wasn't indicative of the game," argued Kenny Ploen, "because I think we were down deep in their end about four times, and Gerry James fumbled every time we were ready to score. We found out afterward he was playing with a broken hand."

A star of that Hamilton team was John Barrow, who made the All-Star team on both offence and defence, something never accomplished before or since. Although regarded as one of the best defensive tackles of all time, Barrow played five different positions, making All-Star at every one of them. An All-American from the University of Florida, he was the greatest defensive lineman ever to play in the CFL. He was an All-Star 12 straight years, four times on both sides of the ball. He was runner up for the Outstanding Lineman Award five times. He won it in 1962.

"My first Grey Cup was in 1957, and it was the biggest thrill of my life, and, of course, we won. We had a very strong team," said Barrow.

Barrow's opponent for most of his Grey Cup years was another Hall of Famer, offensive tackle Frank Rigney, who remembered Barrow's talents.

"I played against John Barrow in all five Grey Cups I was in. John was a great football player and not just physically. He was a smart player, too. When you were playing against a fellow the calibre of Barrow, you had to figure out different ways to block him because you certainly couldn't block him one way regardless of what the play was."

A number three draft choice of the Philadelphia Eagles, Rigney was no slouch himself. A Rose Bowl teammate of Ploen, Rigney came north a year later.

Rigney explained why he signed with Winnipeg. "First of all, the money was better in Canada. Secondly you could also have a job and do better financially, which I did for 10 years.

"So it was a combination of things that brought me to Winnipeg. I certainly never regretted it."

If the money was better than in the States, Rigney recalled it still wasn't that good. "I got a contract my rookie year in 1958 for $8500—$8000 plus a signing bonus of $500.

"The next year, even after we had won the Grey Cup, they wouldn't give me the 500 bucks they gave me for a signing bonus. I actually played my second year for less money than my first."

Although the imports were paid better, American Buddy Tinsley felt Canadians were the strength of the ball club. "Fellows I played with like Cornell Piper and Ed Kotowich could have made any NFL team. They were as good a pair of running guards as there were. That's what made Winnipeg strong in those years. We had so many good Canadians that played first-string. We not only had those two boys, there were others like Gordie Rowland and George Druxman."

Hamilton also had outstanding Canadians. Ralph Sazio thought he had assembled such a strong team that they would win many Grey Cups in the years to come. Instead, they lost four straight to Winnipeg, beginning in 1958, which was one of the greatest Grey Cup games ever played.

Grey Cup 1958

In 1958, the Bombers were healthy and raring to go after rolling over the West at 13–3. The Ti-Cats were 10–3–1 as champions of the Big Four. As if avenging their previous year's loss wasn't incentive enough, Hamilton head coach Jim Trimble added fuel to the fire by declaring "We'll waffle them!"

Although Kenny Ploen had been the all-star quarterback in 1957, rookie Jim Van Pelt from Michigan was at the controls in the 1958 Grey Cup.

"I started the season at quarterback, but about the sixth game, I separated my shoulder in Calgary," said Ploen. "I sat out for six games, and Jim, who was playing safety at the time, took over. When I got healthy, I came back and played both ways. Jim stayed at quarterback. I played offensive halfback and safety."

Vancouver hosted the Grey Cup for the second time on November 29, 1958, on a balmy fall afternoon. Hamilton did look like they might waffle Winnipeg, jumping into an early

14-point lead when Gerry McDougall capped off a long drive with a touchdown. Minutes later, Van Pelt fumbled, and Ralph Goldston recovered and ran 75 yards to the end zone.

The Bombers replied when Van Pelt capped a 90-yard drive by sneaking over from the one. In the second quarter, he closed the gap by kicking two field goals.

Then Jim Trimble made a decision that defies explanation. On the last play of the first half, with the ball on his 13-yard line, he decided to punt! Norm Rauhaus broke through, blocked it and recovered the ball in the end zone. The Blue Bombers went into the dressing room with a 20–14 lead.

"You could call it a coaching error," said Bernie Faloney charitably. "Cam Fraser was our punter at the time, and I was doing some of the kicking as well. We were in a spread punt, supposedly, and Cam was in a tight punt. In the spread, the punter is 15 yards back, in the tight, 12. Cam didn't get back where he was supposed to be, so he didn't have enough time to get the ball off."

Angelo Mosca was characteristically blunt. "We should have won that Grey Cup, but there was a bad coaching error before half time, punting the ball instead of grounding it."

Rauhaus described what happened. "I was fortunate enough to get through unscathed, block the punt and fall on it in the end zone. For a young Canadian kid like me, doing something like that was very exciting."

Can one play make or break a Grey Cup? "We were winning the ball game prior to half time," explained Faloney. "When the punt was blocked and Winnipeg scored a touchdown, we went into the dressing room down points. That hurt us. We just didn't come back."

Losing Ralph Goldston didn't help matters either. He was thrown out in the second quarter for punching Leo Lewis. Ralph Sazio thought the ejection was too severe. "That was ridiculous. It might have been a late hit…maybe. You'd have to question that. If you want to penalize him, fine, but you don't get rid of an American when you only have 11 or 12. And when you lose a guy of his ability, you're not just losing a defensive back. He was a backup fullback and a receiver. That was an absolute crime."

Commented Jake Gaudaur, "To me, the toughest player who ever played in this league was Ralph Goldston. But Ralph was capable of taking his aggressiveness beyond the point he should have."

Referee Paul Dojack explained the call. "He punched Leo Lewis. It was just a regular punch, but we were pretty rigid on punches, forearms, kicking and that type of thing. That was the call by the sideline official, which meant a disqualification. And that was it. If an official said he used his fists, that was good enough for me."

In the third quarter, fullback Charlie Shepard and Jim Van Pelt scored majors for Winnipeg while Faloney stormed back with two touchdown passes to Ron Howell. Because of a missed Bomber convert, when the third quarter drew to a close, Hamilton led 28–27. Early in the fourth, Shepard tied it up with a single.

The outcome was decided by a little razzle-dazzle. Scrimmaging from the Ti-Cat 25-yard line, Van Pelt threw to

Kenny Ploen at the one. Van Pelt then took the ball into the end zone. The final score was 35–28. Van Pelt's contributing 22 points is still second best in Grey Cup history.

After winning the Grey Cup and playing two seasons with the Bombers, Van Pelt was drafted into the U.S. Air Force, never to play football again.

Of the four Grey Cups the Bombers won, 1958 was the most memorable because, as coach Bud Grant explained, "Winnipeg hadn't won a Grey Cup in 17 years. After what we had gone through the year before, and then playing Hamilton again, and Jim Trimble who'd been my coach in Philadelphia saying they were going to waffle us, 1958 was the most satisfying."

Grey Cup 1959

In the 1959 season, Hamilton won 10 games for the third year in a row. In the Eastern semifinal, a rookie quarterback named Russ Jackson led Ottawa to a 43–0 rout of the Alouettes. His magic continued with a 17–5 win over Hamilton in the first of the two-game total-point final, but the Ti-Cats rebounded to win the round 26–24.

Winnipeg finished first with a record of 12–4 and beat the Eskimos two straight in the final. The 1959 Grey Cup was played at Toronto's brand new CNE Stadium by the shore of Lake Ontario.

Typical of Toronto Grey Cups, the field was a soggy mess, but not because of the lack of a tarpaulin. After it rained, the tarp was put down, which prevented the turf from drying out. The play matched the weather—dull, uninspiring.

The only scoring in the first quarter of the third straight meeting of the teams was a Bomber field goal by Gerry James.

In the second quarter, Vince Scott broke through to block a Winnipeg punt. The ball squirted away from Scott in the end zone. Winnipeg recovered, surrendering only one point.

In the third quarter, Steve Oneschuk kicked Hamilton into the lead with two field goals. The Bombers replied in the final quarter with a touchdown and four singles by Charlie Shepard and a major by end Ernie Pitts. The final score was 21–7, not a great day for Hamilton.

"To be honest," recalled Bernie Faloney, "Winnipeg had the better team that year. They just bottled us up. We couldn't do anything right."

"It was pretty sloppy out there," said Ploen. "We were in control of that game from start to finish. The score wasn't indicative of our domination, but that's the way it goes sometimes."

Grey Cup 1960

The rivalry between Winnipeg and Hamilton was put on hold for a year. The Blue Bombers finished first in 1960 but lost to Edmonton in the Western final.

Bud Grant said, "I think our '60 team was the best team we had, the most dominant. But the third game of the final, we couldn't do anything. Kenny Ploen fumbled on a quarterback sneak when we were ahead 2–1. All we had to do was run the clock out, but he fumbled. He had broken a bone in his left hand in the second game in Edmonton. I remember standing on the sidelines thinking that my friends in the States are never going to understand a 2–1 football game. The score ended up 4–2, and Edmonton won. But that was probably our best team."

In 1960, the Tiger-Cats ended an 11-year playoff run by tumbling into the Eastern cellar with a 4–10 record. Toronto finished first but lost the final to second-place Ottawa, led by former Argo coach Frank Clair.

Facing Edmonton in the 1960 Grey Cup was a strong Ottawa squad. "We had Dave Thelan and Ronnie Stewart," said Bob Simpson. "We also had a very strong offensive line: Kaye Vaughn, Fred Robinson, Bruno Bitkowski, Milt Graham and Tom Jones. I was on the left end, Billy Sowalski was on the right. We ran the ball and controlled the ball."

Instead of Bright, Kwong and Parker dominating the ground game, Ottawa's diminutive running back Ronny Stewart led the Rough Riders to victory. The three Eskimo stars combined for a grand total of 22 yards.

Edmonton coach Eagle Keys observed, "Ottawa played a man-to-man defence, which we really hadn't seen in the West. We weren't really prepared."

Ottawa out-rushed Edmonton 247 to 49 yards. Stewart had 99 of them. Russ Jackson said the ground game was Ottawa's style. "We did not have a team that was geared to throw the ball a great deal. We felt it was important to control the ball and not give the Eskimos a chance to score a lot of points."

They didn't. The Westerners' sole touchdown came on a 63-yard pass from Jackie Parker to Jim Letcavits.

Ottawa scored two majors, the first by Bill Sowalski. "That was a fake off a reverse we had run throughout the season," said Jackson. "It was the first time we ran it that game. It should have been a running play, but I decided we were going to fake it. Bill was all alone in the end zone. I recall him saying that the ball took so long to get there he was afraid he was going to drop it.

"Our second touchdown was scored by lineman Kaye Vaughn, the only touchdown of his college and professional career. He recovered a fumble in the end zone."

Gary Schreider added a field goal and convert. Final score: Ottawa 16, Edmonton 6.

The Eskimos were certainly hurting, although Jackie Parker said they lost to a better team.

"That's very kind of him," said Bobby Simpson. "That day they had to actually pick Johnny Bright up and carry him off the bus. I know they shot him up. When I saw him on the field, he was running, but he was hurting. Parker was hurting. They had a couple of linemen hurt. You could have tossed a coin on who would win if we were all healthy."

The big news of 1960 was one of the most sensational trades in Canadian sports history: the Sam Etcheverry and Hal Patterson trade. Jake Gaudaur masterminded the deal.

"Montréal had lost the playoff to Ottawa. I had read in the morning paper that [Montréal owner] Ted Workman was blaming Etcheverry.

"We had finished last that year. I picked up the phone and said to Workman, 'How about doing a straight trade: Etcheverry for Faloney.' And he said, 'That's great. Are you interested in Patterson as well?' I just about dropped off my chair.

"I said, 'Tell you what, Ted. I'll catch the first plane to Montréal. I'll call you from the airport to let you know of my arrival. You can pick me up, and we can talk about it.'

"He picked me up at the airport, and we went to his home. I decided to offer him Don Paquette, a very promising tough youngster I really liked because at age 17, when he came to us, I could see him as a replacement for defensive end Pete Neumann. He wasn't very big, but he was tough as hell.

"So I said, 'How about Don Paquette?' Workman said, 'That's fine.' That was it. That was the extent of the negotiations."

Gaudaur wanted Etcheverry because he was thinking of attendance. "I was thinking more of a promotional thing at that time," said Gaudaur. "To me, Sam was still a fantastic quarterback. He was deemed at that time to be better than Bernie."

However, Sam Etcheverry refused to report to Hamilton, so the quarterback swap was off. The trade came down to Don Paquette for one of the greatest receivers of all time, Hal Patterson. While the deal certainly helped Hamilton, it was the beginning of the end of football in Montréal, given that Etcheverry and Patterson were nearly as popular as Rocket Richard and Jean Beliveau.

Gaudaur, who had the greatest respect for the Alouette owner, had an explanation for Workman's decision.

"Not too long after he got into the ownership of the Alouettes, he got into something called Moral Re-armament.

He became obsessed with it—I mean absolutely obsessed with it. Players told me he would be in the dressing room preaching it."

Part of Moral Re-armament was a kind of public confessional. The story goes that Mrs. Workman, also a believer, made some remarks that indicated her relationship with Etcheverry and Patterson was more than platonic. "Whether there was any substance to the rumour," Gaudaur concluded, "I guess we'll never know. But very definitely that might have been a factor in wanting to get rid of Etcheverry and Patterson."

For Hamilton, the trade was a success on the field and at the gate. "To demonstrate the irony of the thing," said Gaudaur, "Patterson joined us and sold out our stadium the next year, and Bernie won the Most Outstanding Player Award."

Despite Gaudaur's rejection of him, Faloney was happy to stay in Hamilton. "I didn't want to leave. I was making my home and business there. I had my farm going, my work going. I had two children who were entrenched. Jim Trimble didn't want to make that trade—he told me that."

Grey Cup 1961

In 1961, the Ti-Cats returned to first place with their customary record of 10–4. The Argos had fallen from first to third but hammered the defending champion Ottawa Rough Riders 43–19 in the semifinal. Toronto then routed the Ti-Cats 25–7 at CNE, carrying an 18-point advantage into the second game in Hamilton.

Overtime was the word of the day in 1961 postseason play. Hamilton came back and tied Toronto 27–27 after two games of regulation play. The Ti-Cats then scored four touchdowns in 20 minutes of overtime.

Winnipeg was in first place at 13–3 and earned their fourth Grey Cup appearance in five years against Hamilton by beating Calgary two straight.

The only scoring in the first half of the 1961 Grey Cup came on a Bomber single by Jack Delveaux and a TD pass from Bernie Faloney to Paul Dekker. In the third quarter, Faloney and Ralph Goldston teamed up for a major, answered by two Gerry James field goals. James added a major in the fourth quarter to tie the game at 14 and send it into overtime, the first in Grey Cup history.

For Bud Grant, the day began in a most unusual way.

We were staying at the Westbury Hotel. We went to leave for the game on the bus, and the elevators were all messed up. We were staying on the top floor to kind of get away from everything.

We were always sticklers to leave right on time, and everybody had to be there because we didn't want to be at the stadium too long, sitting in the dressing room. We had it timed out pretty good.

Some of the players got stuck on the top floor. They had to walk down. Others were stuck in the elevator. We left about 15 minutes late, so the ride to the stadium was just like we were in a pressure cooker. The players were just ready to burst.

There wasn't a word spoken when we got off the bus. We had to change and get on the field in about 20 minutes. I thought we were going to explode when we got there.

"By the time we got out there, we were ready," Leo Lewis said with a chuckle.

Both teams played such tenacious defence that the game had to go into a second overtime period. With the ball on the Ti-Cat 18, Kenny Ploen dropped back to pass. The defenders dropped back to cover, so Ploen took advantage of a gaping hole and ran for the winning touchdown. Winnipeg won 21–14.

Ploen explained what happened.

It was a pass play to Farrell Funston, but he got wrapped up and knocked down going over the middle. That kept me chugging around. It was just one of those instinctive things. The pressure starts coming, there's a little opening, you feel something, you start running to the right. The first thing you know, you pick up a couple of good blocks, get a couple of breaks and you're in the end zone.

Scoring the overtime touchdown was a great thrill. It was the way we came back in that game. We were down 14–7 before we tied it up. We almost won it in regulation. We kept on coming in the overtime. That was a tough game. Hamilton and Winnipeg had some great Grey Cups.

Grey Cup 1962

Winnipeg and Hamilton were back at it in 1962 for the famous "Fog Bowl." Visibility was good when the Grey Cup game began at CNE Stadium, but the fog arrived early in the second quarter. Commissioner Sydney Halter went down to

John Diefenbaker performing the opening kickoff at the 1962 Grey Cup, also known as the "Fog Bowl"

the sidelines several times and found that visibility at field level was good. Because the fog seemed to be getting thicker, Halter ordered half time cut by five minutes.

By the fourth quarter, the players could barely see one another, and Halter called the game with 9:29 remaining. Trailing the Bombers 28–27, Hamilton had the ball in Winnipeg territory. Hostilities resumed the following day.

The fog prevented fans from witnessing one of the greatest Grey Cups ever played, featuring brilliant performances by Ti-Cat Garney Henley and Blue Bomber Leo Lewis, the game's Most Valuable Player. Lewis scored two touchdowns, threw for another, rushed 41 yards and caught seven passes for 77 yards. Henley had two majors, 100 yards rushing and 119 yards on pass receptions.

Henley opened the scoring by running 74 yards for a touchdown, the second longest romp in Grey Cup history. Don Sutherin missed the convert. In the second quarter, Henley ran 18 yards to pay dirt. Again, the convert was missed. Bob Kuntz rounded out Ti-Cat scoring in the first half with a two-yard plunge for a touchdown. Lewis replied twice for the Bombers and threw for a third to Charlie Shepard. At halftime, Winnipeg led 21–19.

Scoring was completed in the third quarter when Dave Viti and Shepard exchanged majors, and Sutherin picked up a single on a missed field goal.

The Fog Bowl was the only Grey Cup played over two days, won by Winnipeg 28–27. For the players, it was their strangest football experience.

"At field level, it wasn't that bad," remembered Bernie Faloney. "For 10 or 15 yards you could see very well. It wasn't as bad as a lot of people made it out to be, but it got pretty bad in the fourth quarter."

Said Kenny Ploen, "I think the officials made the right decision. I didn't think so the day they called it, because down on the field at our level, it was still workable to do things. A punt would go out of sight, and if you threw a long, high pass, you might lose it, but otherwise you could still see not too badly. Later when I saw the replay of the game from the fans' viewpoint, I could understand. They couldn't see anything."

Game action at the 1962 Grey Cup ("Fog Bowl") between Hamilton and Winnipeg

Referee Paul Dojack made the decision to halt the game. "We knew ahead of time there was liable to be a fog coming in. Syd Halter kept pushing and pushing and telling me to run the game pretty fast. 'Keep it going, keep it going. We're liable to get fog.' Sure enough, by the fourth quarter, we were having difficulty.

"It was left up to me. We were communicating with the sidelines quite regularly. There were nine minutes to go in the quarter. From the far hash marks, I couldn't see the down markers. The fog was pretty low then. So we had a consultation. We said let's delay for a bit of time. Ultimately, the two managers and Syd Halter got together and put it off for 24 hours. When we came back the next day, there was no further scoring. Strange."

Joe Zuger was a rookie in 1962, participating in the first of 10 Grey Cups as a Ti-Cat player or general manager. "It was awfully strange throwing passes in the fog. I threw a touchdown pass to Dave Viti. I threw it up in the air into the fog. I don't know how he saw it coming down out of the fog.

"I hurt my left ankle during the game. All I did the next day was punt. We didn't get much sleep the night before the second day. We had to go to another hotel. It was an emergency thing. We just went in with our equipment on, took it off, went to bed and put it on again. It wasn't a good night."

Leo Lewis agreed. "That was an experience you wouldn't want to go through again, coming back the next day after playing your heart out.

"Even though there were only 9:29 left, we had to go through the whole thing, getting dressed, getting warmed up and enthused. There were guys who played the day before who could not play the next day. Luckily, we hung on. Hamilton didn't do much, and neither did we."

"There was a lot of pain in the dressing room," said Frank Rigney. "All your bumps and bruises come out the next day. There were a number of people being shot with Novocain so they could go out and play."

Angelo Mosca longed for some action on a Saturday night. "Bob Minihane and I said, 'Shucks, we can play nine minutes standing on our heads.' We went downtown and flagged a cab. There's got to be 10,000 taxis in Toronto, but we flag down one with our assistant coach Ralph Sazio in it."

Play resumed the next day with Hamilton third down at the Bomber 40. Recalled Bernie Faloney, "We had the chance to move the ball in. It was third down, and Joe Zuger threw a real fine pass from punt formation to Dick Easterly, who dropped the ball. That would have put us on about the 20-yard line going in. Even if we didn't score the touchdown, a field goal would have won it."

For Hall of Famer Don Sutherin, the Fog Bowl was a nightmare. Though he holds the record for most Grey Cup converts at 17, he missed two that day and had a disputed field goal. He felt personally responsible for the defeat.

"There was a discrepancy over a field goal I had kicked, and I missed two extra points. As a matter of fact, it boiled down to where those were the points that cost us the ball game. You just don't miss extra points. I did, and that was the deciding factor in that Grey Cup."

As for missing a field goal, Sutherin said, "Wide World of Sports televised the game. It was so foggy that anything with any height—like a punt or a field goal—couldn't be seen at all. But the TV camera showed the ball hitting right in the middle of the top of the maple leaf that was situated in the centre of the end zone. To do that, the ball had to go through the uprights."

Bomber Norm Rauhaus said, "The problems weren't that great for defensive backs. There were more problems for the offence. Say, for example, a guy ran a 15-yard pattern, and the quarterback made an 8–10 yard drop. He would have trouble seeing someone to throw to."

"We stopped throwing at the end of the third quarter," said Ken Ploen.

The Fog Bowl was a great day in a losing cause for Garney Henley. Henley's magnificent career spanned 16 seasons, all with the Tiger-Cats. He appeared in seven Grey Cups, winning four. The diminutive defensive back and receiver from Hayti, South Dakota, was the last of the great two-way players.

Sixth in all-time interceptions with 60 (Sutherin is seventh), Henley caught passes through 16 consecutive seasons, a record that still stands. He was an all-Canadian defensive back nine straight years from 1963 to 1971. In 1972, he made All-Canadian as a receiver. He also won the Schenley Award for Most Outstanding player that year. Three years after retiring, he was inducted into the Canadian Football Hall of Fame. No one was elevated to that select company so soon after leaving the game.

Henley's Grey Cup performances were outstanding. Besides the 74-yard run, he had 15 receptions for 267 yards and three interceptions. His 266 combined yards in the Fog Bowl is the third-best mark in Grey Cup history. He is fifth all-time in career Grey Cup combined yardage.

Henley may have been the most gifted individual to ever play in the CFL. Ironically, basketball was his first love and baseball second. Football was an afterthought.

Despite Henley's impressive performance, he wasn't the Grey Cup MVP. That honour went to one of the greatest running backs in the history of Canadian football, Leo Lewis. A six-time All-Star, the "Lincoln Locomotive" scored 79 touchdowns during his 12-season career and rushed for 8861 yards. He holds the Grey Cup records for combined yards and kickoff return yardage. He was the first member of the Bombers to be inducted into the CFL Hall of Fame.

Yet Lewis never won a rushing title or a Schenley award. Did such lack of recognition bother him? "It did, yes," said Lewis, "but I came up when Edmonton had those great ballplayers. There was no doubt that Jackie Parker and Johnny Bright were outstanding. Any other time, I might have had the opportunity to win an award."

As for being named the 1962 Grey Cup MVP, "That was the only year the MVP didn't get a car," Lewis said with a laugh.

Grey Cup 1963

After their loss in the Fog Bowl, the Hamilton Tiger-Cats regrouped for the 1963 season. Following 13 years as an assistant with Carl Voyles and Jim Trimble, Ralph Sazio became the head coach. Trimble had compiled a record of 60–36–2. His team finished first and went to the Grey Cup five of his seven years. But after winning his Grey Cup debut, he lost four in a row.

Ralph Sazio said it was time for a change. "Sometimes a coach has to move on. Jim was very frustrated because his team had lost four straight Grey Cups.

Prior to the 1962 Grey Cup, Trimble was drinking with a Toronto reporter in the bar of the Royal York Hotel. Taking exception to the reporter's prediction about the upcoming confrontation with the Blue Bombers, Trimble, it was alleged, dragged the scribe from the bar down to the waterfront where he whaled the tar out of him. As Sazio said, "Sometimes a coach has to move on."

Still, Sazio had a tough act to follow. "When I took over from Jim in 1963, it wasn't good enough just to go to the Grey Cup. The pressure was on us to win."

In Sazio's inaugural campaign, the Ti-Cats won their usual 10 games to finish first. They took the opener of the Eastern final 45–0 and won the round 63–35. Winnipeg had fallen on hard times, finishing fourth that year with a record of 7–9. The 1963 Grey Cup was a battle of the Cats in Vancouver.

The British Columbia Lions were admitted to the Western Interprovincial Football Union in 1953, beginning play the following year.

General manager Herb Capozzi hired Bud Grant's assistant, Wayne Robinson, to be his head coach. A no-nonsense, tough taskmaster, Robinson whipped the Lions into the playoffs for the first time in 1959 where they lost the total-point semifinal 61–15 to Edmonton. They slipped back to fourth to begin the new decade.

In 1961, Robinson recruited Minnesota All-American middle linebacker Tom Brown and swung a trade halfway through the season, sending four players to Calgary in exchange for quarterback Joe Kapp. It didn't help. The Lions won only one game that year. Robinson was fired in September, replaced by his assistant Dave Skrein.

Skrein coached the club to 7–9, their second-best record ever, good enough for fourth place. In 1963, the Lions finished first with a mark of 12–4, defeated Saskatchewan in the Western final and prepared to host Hamilton in the Grey Cup.

The Lions fielded an exciting offence led by QB Joe Kapp, RB Willie Fleming and receivers Pat Claridge, Jerry Janes, Mack Burton and Sonny Homer.

Their defence was one of the best ever, featuring Dick Fouts, Mike Cacic, Mike Martin, Greg Findlay, Tom Brown, Norm Fieldgate, Walt Bilicki and By Bailey.

Seven Lions made All-Canadian in 1963. Dave Skrein was Coach of the Year, and Tom Brown won the Schenley Award for Most Outstanding Lineman. Hal Patterson, Angelo Mosca, John Barrow and Garney Henley were Hamilton's All-Canadians.

The field on November 30 was described as "heavy." The sky was clear, and the temperature at game time was 7°C. This was the fourth Grey Cup held in Vancouver, but despite the presence of the hometown team and good weather, it had the smallest crowd at 36,545.

Hamilton opened scoring in the second quarter when Bernie Faloney threw a four-yard touchdown pass to Willie Bethea. Art Baker scored from the one. Peter Kempf replied with a field goal.

Hamilton added to their 14–3 lead in the third quarter when Faloney and Hal Patterson combined on a 70-yard pass and run for a touchdown, making the score 21–3. Mack Burton scored BC's sole major. The final score: Hamilton 21, BC 10.

The 1963 Grey Cup is remembered for the Willie Fleming incident, when Angelo Mosca knocked Fleming unconscious and out of the game. The hit obscured the fact that Hamilton was a fine football team that beat a defence that yielded only 14.5 points a game.

Willie Fleming had picked up 1234 yards for the Lions that year. He averaged 9.7 yards per carry, the best in CFL history. When Fleming was knocked out of the game, he had 12 yards on five carries and no receptions.

At the nine-minute mark of the second quarter, Fleming took the ball from Joe Kapp and headed around the end toward the sideline. Joe Zuger hit him, and Fleming fell forward to the ground. In the meantime, Mosca had been running hard toward the sideline, thinking that if he didn't cut Fleming off, he could score. Mosca hurled himself through the air. A second or two after Fleming hit the turf, Mosca landed on top of him in what was either a later hit (the Lions' story) or an unavoidable accident (the Ti-Cat version). Mosca was penalized, but BC's great star was done for the day.

"The odds were against us after Willie was hurt," observed the great Norm Fieldgate years later.

"I guess the play itself wasn't that bad except he did catch him with his knee. He got a 15-yard penalty, which isn't much to sacrifice for losing a player. I don't think there was intent to harm."

At the time, the Lions were outraged, blaming their defeat on Fleming's absence. Ralph Sazio was unimpressed. "That was a lot of crap. Instead of saying it was a well-played, hard-fought game and we won, BC wanted to make excuses.

"If you look at the film, you'll see that Mosca made a great play. He was playing left tackle, and he came from that position past John Barrow, Eddie Bevan and Pete Neumann, past three or four guys to meet Fleming at that point. He showed great quickness. There was no controversy. As far as I'm concerned, the Lions had their ass beat."

Don Sutherin was nearby and witnessed the incident. "I was about five steps away. What happened was this: Joe Zuger was the guy that hit Fleming first. But he hit him in such a way that he bounced off. Mosca was coming in and thought that Fleming was still going to be standing when he got there. He dove, Joe slid off Fleming, Mosca was still in the air and by the time Angie landed, Fleming was lying flat on his stomach on the ground. I heard the collision and the grunt, and it was history. It's pretty tough to stop a 285-pound man in midair."

Referee Paul Dojack explained the call. "Fleming was out of bounds, Mosca's momentum was there, but there was no effort to let up a bit. On that particular incident, the sideline official called a late hit out of bounds and the penalty was applied."

Bob Ackles commented on the Fleming incident. "It wasn't as bad as it was built up to be. But here's your star player going out—the only hope you thought you had at that time of winning the game—and Mosca puts him out for the remainder of the game.

"Those things happen all the time. It's just that it happened in Vancouver. Here's our best football player being put out of the game by dirty, old Angelo Mosca. At the time, it really got everyone up in arms against the dirty *Easterners*!"

Mosca pleaded innocence. "The situation was this: he was cutting up the sideline. I came from 45 yards away to make that play. I was scared he was going to turn back up into the playing field, so I dove to cut off the angle, and as I did, he put his head down.

"It was one of those things where I went over the top of him and caught the back of his head with my knee. It wasn't intentional. If you see the play, it looks like I deliberately did it, but I had already committed myself."

BC quarterback Joe Kapp saw the situation differently. "Old Angelo was never known as the most disciplined of football players. I told him what I thought when it happened, and I talked to him again after the game."

"Joe refused to shake hands with me after the game," said Mosca.

Mosca and Kapp were still angry 48 years later. At a CFL Alumni luncheon in Vancouver on the Friday of Grey Cup week, 2011, Kapp sarcastically presented Mosca with a bouquet of flowers. Mosca hit Kapp with his cane. Kapp punched him senseless to the floor and kicked him.

Willie Fleming had his own version of the incident on the field: "I'm the last one to know what happened. The Hamilton players saw it one way, Joe Kapp saw it another way, and I was the one on the ground who was out cold and didn't see anything."

Grey Cup 1964

In 1964, the Lions beat Calgary in the Conference final after finishing first again with a record of 11–2–3. Hamilton topped the Big Four at 10–3–1. They lost the first game of the two-game total-point Eastern final in Ottawa 30–13 but bounced back at home to win the game 26–8 and the series by one point.

Six Lions made All-Canadian, with the Ti-Cats getting nine. Ralph Sazio was Coach of the Year. Leo middle linebacker Tom Brown won his second straight Schenley for Outstanding Lineman. Ti-Cat Tommy Grant won the Schenley for best Canadian.

On a drizzly, overcast day in Toronto for the 1964 Grey Cup, Hamilton's offence was purring, running up 436 yards in total offence, compared to BC's 309. The Ti-Cats had 24 first downs, the Lions 16. Yet Hamilton trailed 34–8 at the end of the third quarter.

When the Lions were given a couple of lemons, they made lemonade.

Joe Kapp worked the Lions down the field to the enemy one-yard line early in the first quarter. Bob Swift scored the touchdown. In the second stanza, the Leos lined up at the Ti-Cat 15 to try a field goal. Holder Pete Ohler dropped the ball. He calmly picked it up and threw to Jim Carphin in the end zone. They missed the convert. Before the half ended, Fleming ran 46 yards for BC's third touchdown. The score was 20–1 in favour of the Lions at the half.

The mishandled snap wasn't the only "bad" break BC suffered. Lightning struck twice when the Lions lost their leading rusher (1054 yards that year) in the second quarter; fullback Bob Swift tore up his knee. He was replaced by Bill Munsey, an all-Canadian defensive back with nine interceptions.

Hamilton opened second-half scoring when Bernie Faloney pitched out to Johnny Counts, who ran 58 yards to the end zone.

Then Bill Munsey went to work. In a performance reminiscent of Red Storey, Munsey demolished the Tiger-Cats in a mere three minutes and eight seconds. With the score 20–8, Munsey ran 18 yards for a touchdown. Three minutes later, Bernie Faloney tried the lateral again, but it was low, and Counts couldn't handle it. Munsey picked up the ball and went 71 yards for another major, the third longest in Grey Cup history.

Behind 34–8, a lesser team would have collapsed. Not Hamilton. Faloney threw touchdown passes to Tommy Grant and Stan Crisson. The Cats added a convert, single and safety to make the final score 34–24. The Lions had won their first Grey Cup.

Willie Fleming compared the two Grey Cups. "I didn't finish the game in 1963. I don't know if that would have made a difference. I think it was just a case of growing up in 1964. We were kind of excited the first time in '63. In '64, we knew what to look for. We had a lot of good ballplayers, and nobody on our team really dominated. Everyone contributed; we really pulled together."

Bob Ackles fondly remembered November 29, 1964. "Hamilton had big, tough guys, and they were playing pretty close to home, but we beat their butts pretty good."

Ackles described the scene upon the team's return to Vancouver. "Wild. We arrived home late, about 10 o'clock.

There were about 20,000 people at the airport all standing in the pouring rain. It was quite a sight."

Grey Cup 1965

Of all the forces of nature that can affect the outcome of a football game, none is harder to handle than wind.

Breezy Grey Cups happened in '75, '88 and '95, but only one has been called the "Wind Bowl." That was 1965, the last of the great match-ups between the Bud Grant Blue Bombers and the Trimble-Sazio Tiger-Cats.

The temperature on the day of the 1965 Grey Cup was 4°C, but the wind was gusting to 85 kilometres per hour. Under normal circumstances, the Bombers likely would have won. Winnipeg had 15 first downs to Hamilton's eight. They recovered five Hamilton fumbles. Usually the team that makes the fewest mistakes wins. Not on this day, unless you include errors in judgement by Bud Grant.

Don Sutherin opened the scoring by driving the kick-off into the end zone where Dave Raimey gave up a single. The Bombers could go nowhere on their possession, and the punt barely made it over the line of scrimmage. Dick Cohee ran 32 yards to the Bomber seven and then went over for the touchdown. A couple of minutes later, Hamilton increased their lead to 10–0 when Kenny Ploen conceded the first of three safety touches.

The second quarter, and the wind, belonged to Winnipeg. Art Perkins scored an eight-yard touchdown after being set up by Leo Lewis. Later, halfback Raimey set up Lewis for his five-yard major. One convert was good, so Winnipeg led 13–10 at the half.

Hamilton scored eight points with the wind in the third quarter with a 69-yard Joe Zuger to a Willie Bethea pass-and-run touchdown and a single that Zuger kicked on the run. Winnipeg conceded two more safety touches, confident they could pull the game out of the fire in the fourth quarter when they had the wind.

It was not to be. The staunch Ti-Cat defence held the Bombers to a field goal. Hamilton won 22–16.

Ralph Sazio praised his defenders. "We were leading near the end with two or three minutes left, and Winnipeg had the ball. They must have gambled at least three times on third-and-three or four. Their big fullback Art Perkins hit in there time and time again, and it looked like they might score a touchdown and beat us.

"But Herb Paterra was our linebacker, and on their third gamble, Herb stuck him right in the hole and ran the clock out. We hadn't beaten the Blue Bombers of Bud Grant in four previous tries, so this was a big one."

The Bombers contended that Perkins made that yard, and if referee Paul Dojack had spotted the ball properly, Winnipeg would have gone on to win.

Although Ken Ploen was convinced Perkins made the first down, he wasn't critical of Dojack. "I can appreciate how difficult it is. Let's face it. Over a career or even a game, you get some good spots and some bad ones. I think it all averages out. To blame the official is nothing but an alibi."

Blue Bomber Frank Rigney feigned sympathy. "There is a mass of humanity out there, and it is very difficult to see where the farthest advance did occur. I think officials spot it somewhere within a yard or two of where it should be."

Sazio described what it was like to coach in such windy conditions. "You pretty much throw the game plan out the window and improvise. You play it a little tighter and eliminate as many mistakes as possible. You eliminate mistakes by not making things too difficult."

Did he out-coach Bud Grant in the Wind Bowl? "Yes," Sazio replied. "Bud conceded three safeties to me when the wind was against him, and that was the difference in the ball game. We refused to concede points. I preferred to take our chances rather than give up points."

Rigney conceded that Hamilton handled the wind better than they did. "They shut our running game down. And there wasn't much else we could do. I never really had any regrets or second thoughts about the safeties."

Although John Barrow was the Grey Cup MVP—the only defensive lineman to ever win that award—Angelo Mosca thought Joe Zuger was the unsung hero that day. "Winnipeg gave up three safeties, and we won by six points. We didn't have to concede points because Joe Zuger had a great day punting into the wind. He kicked very low into the wind and then got it up high when he had it at his back."

With the Ti-Cats win in the 1965 Wind Bowl, one of the great rivalries in Canadian sports came to and end. Hamilton and Winnipeg wouldn't contest another Grey Cup until 1984.

chapter eight

The Riders, 1966–72 and 1976

Between 1959 and '61, the Saskatchewan Roughriders won 8 out of 48 games. Between 1962 and 1976, they made the playoffs every year and appeared in the Western final every season between 1966 and 1976. They made it to the Grey Cup five times. Even though they won the championship only once during that decade, it was truly their golden age.

Even in the dark days of the late 1950s, Roughrider general manager Ken Preston was slowly but surely putting together a powerful football team. Already there were linemen Ron Atchison, Bill Clarke, Al Benecick and Reggie Whitehouse. Linebacker Wayne Shaw and lineman Garner Ekstran arrived in 1961 along with perennial All-Star centre Ted Urness.

The nucleus of the offence was assembled in 1963. Along with Ron Lancaster came receiver Hugh Campbell and running backs Ed Buchanan and George Reed. In 1964, tackle

Clyde Brock, flanker Gord Barwell, tight end Jim Worden and defensive back Bob Kosid came aboard. The year 1965 saw the arrival of place-kicker and guard Jack Abendshan, linebacker Wally Dempsey, defensive back Ted Dushinski and receiver/punter Alan Ford. Eagle Keys became the head coach. The team's major acquisition in 1966 was defensive lineman Ed McQuarters.

Abendshan, Atchison, Benecick, Clarke, Lancaster, McQuarters, Reed, Urness, Preston and Keys are in the Canadian Football Hall of Fame.

Grey Cup 1966

As the 1966 season began, the Roughriders' challenge was to accomplish what no other Saskatchewan team had done before: win the Grey Cup. Saskatchewan had topped their division for the first time since 1951, finishing with a mark of 9–6–1.

Hugh Campbell's 102 points on 17 touchdowns led the league in scoring, and he finished second in receiving with 66 catches for 1109 yards. Lancaster and Reed were first in passing and rushing yardage, but Ottawa's Russ Jackson beat out Lancaster for the Most Outstanding Player Award.

Like Saskatchewan, Ottawa finished on top for the first time since 1951. Ottawa won the Grey Cup in 1960 over Edmonton, but for the next five years, they were runners-up to Hamilton. Ottawa finally got the Ti-Cat gorilla off their back in 1966, beating the Bengals 62–17 in the two-game total-point final. The wins were dedicated to their defensive coach Bill Smyth who died a couple of weeks earlier.

The 1966 Grey Cup quarterbacks, Russ Jackson and Ron Lancaster, were old friends and rivals. But Jackson wasn't initially signed as a quarterback. "When I went to Ottawa, I did not make it as a quarterback. I made it as a defensive back in 1958. Only injuries got me into the quarterback role late in 1958." His first contract was for $4700, with a $500 signing bonus and a ticket back and forth to Toronto to go to school. Jackson attended the Ontario College of Education in Toronto and played for Ottawa on the weekends.

Lancaster came into the league with Ottawa from Wittenberg University in 1958. Jackson and Lancaster coexisted for four years, but Ottawa coach Frank Clair wasn't a fan of the two-quarterback system, and both men wanted to start. The "Little General" was sent to the Roughriders in 1963. "I was traded to Saskatchewan for not very much," Lancaster recalled. "I think I went for the waiver price of $500. There were no players involved. I always said I went for a broken helmet with no face mask."

His running mate George Reed came cheaper than Lancaster. "Originally, BC had my rights when I came out of Washington State," Reed said. "They traded my rights to Saskatchewan. In those days, the money was as good as in the NFL, and they offered me more money to come up here, and that's how I got here." Reed and Lancaster's career records stood into the 21st century. Halfback Ed Buchanan was acquired from Calgary for $500.

Assistant coach Jack Gotta described the 1966 Roughriders:

> *That team was pretty solid all the way around. You think about George Reed, Eddie Buchanan,*

Ronnie Lancaster, the corps of receivers we had… those guys were as good as any who ever played in the league.

And then defensively, such guys as Wally Dempsey and Garner Ekstran just played hard all the time. They were tough guys. Everybody picked up on it.

"We had a pretty good crew," said Alan Ford.

We were pretty close-knit. The coach can't do that. It's got to be the guys in the locker room. You need guys who are leaders. There was no "I" in George Reed or Ron Lancaster. Those were the guys who carried the team in terms of the "we" stuff.

George worked harder than anybody else at practice. Ron would never miss practice. Both would play hurt. If you've got leaders, it really makes a big difference. Ron would do what he felt was necessary to get ready to play, and other people would notice that and follow along with him.

Only two Roughriders had any Grey Cup experience—the quarterback and the coach, Eagle Keys, who prepared carefully for the 1966 Grey Cup. "Unless you are prepared to dedicate yourself to the Grey Cup game," Keys said, "you don't deserve to win it. I always felt that there's no sense being there if you don't win it."

While Ottawa was in downtown Vancouver involved with the festivities, Keys had his team isolated in Burnaby. Hugh Campbell believed Eagle Key's experience was important in preparing the team for the Grey Cup. "The important thing in having been to the Grey Cup," he counselled, "is how to cope with the carnival going on around you. That's the advantage. As a player in the Grey Cup, I remember being amazed at the number of photographers. It was beyond the sports media. It was a happening. Everyone was there. Everything was Grey Cup. That was a new thing for us. We were a bunch of wide-eyed guys. Eagle had to cope with that."

Grey Cup week was business as usual for Lancaster. "Eagle would never change the way we did things all year. He was a believer in doing certain things, and we prepared for that game the same as any other.

"Both teams are going to be ready to play. Heck, you can't hardly wait for that day. That's what you're playing for from the start of the season. Man, it's tough getting there. That's the first thing you find out."

The Roughriders' strategy against Ottawa was simple: run, run, run and run some more, not only to advance the ball and score but also to eat up the clock. Ottawa liked to go with a spread line by splitting defenders outside, giving Reed and Buchanan the opportunity to find gaps and capitalize on blocking angles.

Despite Ottawa's explosive offence, Keys felt the opposition's greatest strength was defence. His ace in the hole was Lancaster. Eagle Keys said in the *Regina Leader-Post* the day before the game, "You don't see Canadian quarterbacks using check-off or audibles very much, but that's the device we hope to use to defeat Ottawa.

"Ron Lancaster won't call his plays until he is lined up, ready to receive the snap from centre and has seen the defensive formation. I think it's our only chance against a defence that has no weaknesses as far as I can tell."

Lancaster would play a brilliant game.

When it came time to introduce the Roughriders, the players were uptight and incredibly tense. A timely pratfall may very well have been the turning point in the greatest day in the history of Saskatchewan sports.

When the announcer called out number 53, Jack Abendshan headed out of the tunnel at Empire Stadium. Alan Ford described what happened next.

"Abendshan slipped and fell during the introductions. The track was muddy, so when he got up and ran out, he had this big brown spot on his rear end. Everyone knows when you get down to that last game, it's pretty emotional in the locker room. So that did certainly loosen us up."

"He fell in the mud," Lancaster said. "He was going across those boards through the mud, and his cleats went out from under him. Everybody laughed. You always think of things that can relax you. You can plan things, but they don't really have the effect something like that does. That was funny."

Jack Abendshan kicked off at 2:00 PM under an overcast sky in 10°C weather. Assisted by two Saskatchewan offsides, Russ Jackson marched Ottawa in five plays to their own 49. Making those predicting an Eastern rout look like geniuses, Jackson combined with Whit Tucker on a 61-yard pass and run for a touchdown. Moe Racine missed the convert. The victim on the play was Dale West. He explained what happened.

"I saw Ronnie Stewart going through a three back, and I came up and supported, which I never did for six or seven years of my career, so I don't know why I would do it then. Tucker ran by me and got a touchdown. Larry Dumelie got blamed on television, which was fine with me, but I knew it was me."

Dale West soon atoned for his sin by intercepting at the Ottawa 43.

"The end came out," West said, "and got tangled up with Ted Dushinski and went down. The ball came to me, and I took it to the nine-yard line. Then Ronnie threw to Jim Worden for the touchdown."

Said Alan Ford, "Jim Worden was telling Ronnie all the time that he could beat Gene Gaines. Ronnie threw a pass to him when he was wide open in the end zone. Worden came back saying, 'I told you I could beat him deep.'"

"Basically they won," explained Gene Gaines, "because Ronnie Lancaster was a great actor. We thought he was going to give the ball to George. He stuck the ball in George's gut and pulled it out, and the next thing you know, the tight end Jim Worden is down the field and bang—touchdown. We all took the bait."

In the second stanza, linebacker Wally Dempsey snuffed out an Ottawa drive at his 33 by wrestling the ball away from Jay Roberts. After a successful third-down gamble at the Ottawa 50, Lancaster marched the troops down to the 19-yard line, aided by a spectacular Ed Buchanan catch. Lancaster then threw to Ford in the end zone. Bob O'Billovich deflected the ball into Ford's waiting arms.

"His touching it took a little speed off it, made it like a knuckle ball landing in my lap," Ford said. "It was probably the easiest reception I ever made, the one I'll remember the longest."

O'Billovich also commented on the play:

We were in a three-deep zone, and I was playing deep third to my side. Huey Campbell ran an out on my side. The inside guy ran a corner, where he went in and then came back to the flag on the corner, and I reacted to the throw. If I make the play and hold onto the ball, I'm a hero because that wasn't even my responsibility. I don't think Ford could have got the ball if it hadn't been deflected right into his lap because he slipped and fell down in the end zone.

So it was just the luck of the draw that when I wasn't able to squeeze the ball to hold onto it, that it would fall right in his lap. It could have gone in any direction.

But it didn't. Saskatchewan 14, Ottawa 6.

After the ensuing kickoff, with the ball on Ottawa's 25, Russ Jackson was flushed out of the pocket, running for his life. He rifled the ball down field to a streaking Whit Tucker, who caught up to it at the Saskatchewan 39 and kept going to the end zone. The convert was good.

Once again, Saskatoon-native Dale West was the culprit. "I had Tucker man to man," he explained, "and was okay with him down the field. Jackson came up toward the line of scrimmage, and I thought he was going to run across, so

I came up. He threw it over my head. For six or seven years, CTV had that picture of me chasing Tucker to the end zone in their intro for every CFL game."

So West messed up big time?

"Nah, he didn't," said Russ Jackson. "We just found a little extra time, and when you do that with receivers like Tucker, they're going to find some open space out there."

Bill Kline added a single to make the halftime score 14–14.

Although the stats still favoured Ottawa, momentum was beginning to shift. The Easterners picked up only one first down in the second quarter.

In quarter number three, the Green Riders began to assert themselves on the ground after an anemic two-yards rushing in the first half. Near the end of the quarter, Garner Ekstran threw Jim Dillard for a loss, and Don Gerhardt sacked Jackson, forcing Bill Kline to punt from his end zone. Gene Wlasiuk returned it to Ottawa's 32-yard line, setting up the coup de grace as the third quarter ended with the game still tied at 14.

At the beginning of the final frame, George Reed picked up a first down on three carries. Lancaster threw to Hugh Campbell at the five. On the next play, Campbell out-duelled Joe Poirier for the touchdown. Abendshan converted, giving the underdogs a seven-point lead.

Ottawa went three and out on their ensuing possession. Starting at the Red Riders' 47-yard line, Buchanan ran for six yards and Reed for 10 to the Ottawa 31. Reed then blazed his way to the end zone. The convert made it 28–14.

Three minutes later, Ford completed the scoring with a single. Final score: Saskatchewan 29, Ottawa 14. The longest drought in Grey Cup history was over.

Saskatchewan picked up 169 yards on the ground in the second half. Once Hugh Campbell gave them the lead, their punishing ball-control offence finished Ottawa off. The beginning of the end came earlier, however. The Easterners had only one first down in each of the second and third quarters and two in the fourth.

George Reed explained what happened. "We never got away from our ground game. We kept trying to mix it in. We were able to keep pounding away. Lancaster threw a couple of passes that put us in a position to deliver the knockout punch. I happened to be the knockout punch."

The victory was all the sweeter given that no one gave the Green and White a chance. "Oh, yeah," said Reed, "we had no chance of winning. They had already given the Grey Cup to Ottawa, so it was quite a thrill to go in and show them that we belonged on the same field and then watch everybody's disbelief that we won it."

Dale West said, "The television cameras were in the Ottawa dressing room, so if anybody wanted to get interviewed, they had to walk across to the Ottawa side."

"We never should have been six-point underdogs," said Eagle Keys. "But the publicity sure didn't hurt. The way folks were writing about the game, you'd have thought we didn't belong on the same field as Ottawa. That got to our fellows a bit. They have pride in themselves, and they didn't enjoy being downgraded so much."

What went wrong for Ottawa?

"We were emotionally drained because Bill Smyth, our assistant coach, had died suddenly during the semifinal week," Russ Jackson said.

> *We had won first place. We then had to go and play Hamilton in a two-game total-point final in which we played terrifically.*
>
> *There was an air strike at the time, and we had to go by Chicago and Seattle and bus up to Vancouver. That's not an excuse because certainly Saskatchewan was full value for their win.*
>
> *At halftime, the score was 14–14, and our whole offence consisted of scrambling through broken plays. Whit Tucker got behind the defence, and I happened to catch him for two touchdowns. But Saskatchewan controlled the game, controlled the ball. We just were drained emotionally and didn't have a whole lot going for us. It was just one of those things that happen in life, and you live with it.*

Some suggested that Ottawa lost because they got caught up in the festivities and didn't pay attention to the business at hand. "I don't think that's true," argued Ronnie Stewart. "Getting to the national final is what it's all about. We knew that. We just played a particularly good team that day. I think a factor was the death of our line coach Bill Smyth. Also we had come from behind in Hamilton to beat them and get to the Grey Cup. We had shot our bolt. The Grey Cup was kind of anticlimactic."

Hugh Campbell, who went on to coach the Edmonton Eskimos to five straight Grey Cup championships, summed up that wonderful year.

> *I remember most of it vividly; Eagle Keys telling us we may never get this opportunity again and we'd better take advantage of it. I remember Ed Buchanan catching a long pass on a pick play we had worked out to take advantage of Ottawa's man defence. And, of course, George Reed just romping through them.*
>
> *I remember the great satisfaction. We could hardly live with ourselves we were so proud to have beaten Ottawa because they were heavily favoured, and Saskatchewan had never won. I remember Reggie Whitehouse stealing the Cup and how we all went downtown to Trader Vics. My parents were there. It was a pretty proud night.*

Alan Ford felt the same way. "As a kid growing up in Regina, I watched the Riders. I never thought I'd be playing in a Grey Cup, let alone playing on the Roughriders."

He added ominously, "Since 1966 was my second year, and we had a fairly young team, I thought we were going to win this thing another five or six times."

It was not to be. Lancaster's Roughriders didn't win another Grey Cup while Jackson's Rough Riders didn't lose.

Grey Cup 1967

After a physical 1967 Western final against Calgary, Saskatchewan faced the ever-tough Tiger-Cats in the Grey Cup in Ottawa as part of Canada's centennial celebration.

The Roughriders had played four postseason games in a week and a half, all on frozen fields. Their bruises were deep. They were tired. Hamilton was on a roll, having finished first for the ninth time in 11 years. The Ti-Cats had not allowed a touchdown in the last six games of the regular season. Their opponents scored only 17 points in the last three games of the season, the Eastern final and the Grey Cup. Hamilton had one of the greatest defensive teams in CFL history. And they could score, too.

Things started to go wrong when the Roughriders arrived in Ottawa. "We had no facilities whatsoever," growled Eagle Keys. "The weather conditions were bad, but had we stayed in Regina where we could have had a cleared field to practice on, we would have been far better prepared. They put us on a practice field, but it was just like a skating rink. Hamilton, though, stayed home until the last moment."

On December 2, the big day arrived, freezing cold but dry. Hamilton opened the scoring with a touchdown. Saskatchewan replied with an Alan Ford 87-yard single—a Grey Cup record that still stands. It wasn't exactly a cherished Grey Cup memory for Ford. "No, it just means I had a good wind, I guess. I happened to hit it, it bounced and away it went."

The final score, Hamilton 24, Saskatchewan 1.

What most Rider fans remember about the game is a wide-open Ed Buchanan in the second quarter dropping a long bomb that would have scored a touchdown. A hero in 1966, Buchanan became a goat in 1967.

George Reed said, "I think there was a turning point in that game. Ed Buchanan was wide open. Lancaster laid the ball perfectly into his hands. It would have been about a 70-yard touchdown. He dropped the ball and that seemed to deflate us."

Hugh Campbell said, "In that game we were beaten so thoroughly that I didn't feel robbed. I suspect they had better players than us."

It was rumoured that Eagle Keys told Buchanan not to come back because he dropped that pass. "No, that's not true," Keys angrily replied. "I didn't say that. But Ed didn't like the cold weather. On a warm day, he would have caught it."

Ed Buchanan, who retired after that game, passed away in 1993 suffering from Lou Gehrig's disease.

Hamilton's first touchdown came when quarterback Joe Zuger capped off an 85-yard drive with a two-yard plunge for a touchdown. After Ford's single, Ralph Sazio remembered the play that broke the game wide open. "Joe Zuger hit Ted Watkins at the start of the second quarter. Saskatchewan was in a blitz, but Joe hit him quickly and he went 72 yards for a touchdown."

Tommy Joe Coffey converted both touchdowns and scored a single on a missed field goal. Zuger had three singles. Bill Ray Locklin picked up a Saskatchewan fumble and scooted 43 yards for the final score.

The win was the highlight of Zuger's career. "We had been ridiculed all year. They said we didn't have any offence, that we played boring football. So it was gratifying to score 24 points and win the Grey Cup.

"The weather was really brutal. We had to change shoes three different times. We started with broom-ball shoes, but we tore the soles off them. The field was so hard it was like playing in the street."

Although 24 points were scored on the Riders, the Saskatchewan defence was tough. Joe Zuger punted a record-tying 17 times for a second-best all-time total of 760 yards. Zuger always contributed significantly to his team's success. It would be natural to assume he was one of Steeltown's favourite sons, but that was not the case. "The fans got on my back quite a lot," Zuger admitted. "That bothered me personally, but the coaches believed in me and were behind me. That was the main thing. Those were the guys I had to answer to."

Still, the day belonged to the defence. "It was unbelievable," enthused coach Sazio. "We went the last four games of the regular season, the playoffs and the Grey Cup without giving up a touchdown. That was one of the best defences ever."

Grey Cup 1968

There was a new dog on the block in the Western Conference in 1968. GM Rogers Lehew had been quietly putting together a powerhouse in Calgary with the likes of defenders Wayne Harris, Joe Forzani, Larry Robinson, Dick Suderman, Jim Furlong, Frank Andruski, Jerry Keeling and John Helton. Lehew had a potent offence with quarterback Peter Liske and receivers Herm Harrison, Terry Evanshen, Gerry Shaw, Rudy Linterman and Ted Woods. The Stampeders were coached by the brilliant Jerry Williams.

Going into 1968, it had been 19 years since Calgary had played in a Grey Cup. They lost three of their last four games to finish second at 10–6, and 1968 hardly looked like the year the drought would end, especially since the Stampeders led the league in team losses while having the fewest yards rushing. But they peaked at the right time.

Calgary dispatched Edmonton in the semifinal 29–13 and then went into Regina and walloped the 12–3–1 Roughriders 32–0 and then swept them at McMahon Stadium in overtime 25–12, forcing nine turnovers. Calgary was off to Toronto to face the powerful Ottawa Rough Riders for the 1968 Grey Cup.

The Eastern champions finished in first place, two points ahead of the upstart Argos, and scored a league-high average of 30 points a game while surrendering 20. Linebacker Ken Lehmann won the Schenley for Outstanding Lineman while Whit Tucker was runner-up for the Canadian award. The Riders were led, of course, by Russ Jackson. General manager Red O'Quinn said of Jackson, "He could do it all. He was smart, he could run, he could throw deep. He was the greatest all-around quarterback."

Jackson's supporting cast included his old running mate Ron Stewart as well as Bo Scott, Whit Tucker, Vic Washington and Margene Atkins. They were strong on defence with Moe "the Toe" Racine, Ken Lehmann, Jerry Campbell, Marshall Shirk, Jay Roberts, Don Sutherin, Joe Poirier, Wayne Guardino, Roger Perdrix and Gene Gaines.

Grey Cup day, November 30, was damp and cloudy, with a temperature of 2°C.

The Stampeders out-passed the eastern Riders 258 yards to 185 and enjoyed a big edge in first downs, 24–13. But Ottawa had the edge that counted.

Liske propelled Calgary into a 14–4 lead during the first half by capping off a drive with a one-yard plunge for one touchdown and completing a 21-yarder to Terry Evanshen for the other. The defence came up big. Ottawa had five scoring chances in the first half and came away with four points on a single after Calgary recovered a blocked punt in their end zone and a Don Sutherin field goal.

Early in the third quarter, the Riders smothered punter Ron Stewart at midfield, taking over on downs. Russ Jackson engineered and scored on a touchdown drive to close the gap to four, the convert being wide. Soon after, Jackson pitched out to Vic Washington who dropped it. The ball bounced right back into Washington's hands and he scampered 80 yards for a touchdown.

Larry Robinson said, "They pitched him the ball, he grabbed it, then fumbled it, it hit the ground and bounced up back into his arms and I cut up too soon. I thought he was done, but he went around me. I got a hand on him, but I didn't get enough. He went down the sideline and scored."

Jackson closed out Ottawa scoring by combining with Margene Atkins on a 70-yard pass and run for a major.

In the fourth quarter, Dick Suderman recovered a Bo Scott fumble, setting up a Liske to Evanshen TD. Final score: Ottawa 24, Calgary 21.

Calgary was in no shape to play Ottawa. Their running back Dave Cranmer had broken a leg in the playoffs.

His replacement, Rudy Linterman, went out with torn knee ligaments in the first quarter, and Herm Harrison was hurt. If all that wasn't enough, the Calgary players came down with the flu when they arrived in Toronto. "Our trainer had a big bottle of cough syrup and just about every time we came off the field, we'd take a big swig of it," said Jerry Keeling. "We were lucky we stayed as close as we did in that game."

If it hadn't been for bad luck, Calgary wouldn't have had any luck at all.

"None at all," moaned Herm Harrison. "It was unbelievable. I broke five ribs in the first five minutes of the game. I still tried to play, but it just wasn't there. I lost 14 pounds before the game because of the flu. I just didn't have the strength." Harrison was the leading receiver in the league that year, 67 for 1306 yards. His inability to perform was a severe blow.

Getting to the Grey Cup "was a great feeling," said Rogers Lehew, "because we hadn't been there in 20 years. Everybody got excited, the whole team got excited. We played a helluva game. If it hadn't been for the play Washington made, we might have won it."

Russ Jackson said:

We got two big plays. The first one was where Vic Washington fumbled the ball. The Calgary defence sort of hesitated, and the ball bounced back to Vic who took it about 60 yards for a touchdown. The other play was to Margene Atkins, a touchdown pass that we had practiced the previous week but had not put on our list for the game. It was a semiroll to the right. Margene lined up on the right and went back against the grain. The Stampeders were playing a combination of zone-man defence. That defence was just beginning to come into the league then, and Calgary was very proficient at it. I felt we could take advantage of it, and it worked. The play went for about a 60- or 65-yard touchdown. It was probably a 45- or 50-yard pass in the air.

Grey Cup 1969

In 1969, Saskatchewan finished 13–3 in first place and swept the Stampeders in the Western final, setting up a rematch with Ottawa and one of the greatest performances in Grey Cup history, which was also Russ Jackson's swan song. It was also an opportunity for Ottawa to avenge their Grey Cup loss to Saskatchewan three years earlier.

The Rough Riders of Jackson and Ron Stewart were destiny's darlings. You didn't have to convince Eagle Keys. "There are some games you get the feeling you're not going to be allowed to win," he drawled. "That was one of them."

With police snipers stationed in the light turrets of Montréal's Autostad to protect against an FLQ terrorist threat, Jackson and Stewart put on a dazzling performance at the 1969 Grey Cup. But the game didn't start out that way.

Saskatchewan took a 9–0 lead on a 27-yard Lancaster to Ford touchdown pass, plus a safety touch conceded by Billy Van Burkleo. The Westerners added two singles in the third quarter, but that was it. The day belonged to Ottawa.

First of all, Jackson finished a long drive by completing a 12-yard pass to Jay Roberts for a touchdown. Soon after, Jackson tossed a short pass to Ronnie Stewart who ran 80 yards for the score, putting Ottawa into a 14–9 halftime lead.

The Red Riders' third touchdown came when Jackson eluded a fierce pass rush at the Saskatchewan's 12-yard line and found Jim Mankins alone in the end zone. Jackson admitted it was a broken play.

"Yep. We were rolling right, and McQuarters had me right in his grasp, and I happened to get lucky and get away from him. I came back across the grain, and Mankins was standing there just over the goal line."

Ottawa's last touchdown was similar. Cliff Shaw had Jackson in his grasp, but he somehow got the ball to Stewart who ran 32 yards for the score.

The final score was Ottawa 29, Saskatchewan 11.

The game was special for Ottawa because Jackson had announced he would retire at the end of the season. "It was a very emotional time for me personally and, I'm sure, for some of my teammates who'd played with me for a lot of years because I'd announced at the start of the season it was going to be my last year. After we got to the Grey Cup and I won the Schenley Award again, I knew the pressure was on everybody to make it a fairy-tale ending, which it turned out to be."

Saskatchewan's defensive end Bill Baker blamed the icy field for their defeat, believing it nullified their strength, the pass rush.

"Exactly," said Baker. "I thought it hurt us. I thought we had a better team than they did. It does neutralize a team because on ice, you're all the same. We had a heckuva defensive line, but we didn't do a very good job that day. We took it to them earlier in the season and really laid a beating on them. It was a completely different game in the Grey Cup."

Lancaster disagreed:

I don't really think the field conditions on that day would favour anybody. I mean, you're there all week practicing, and you sort of know what to expect. That was just one of those days where it went almost the way it was written—that Russ

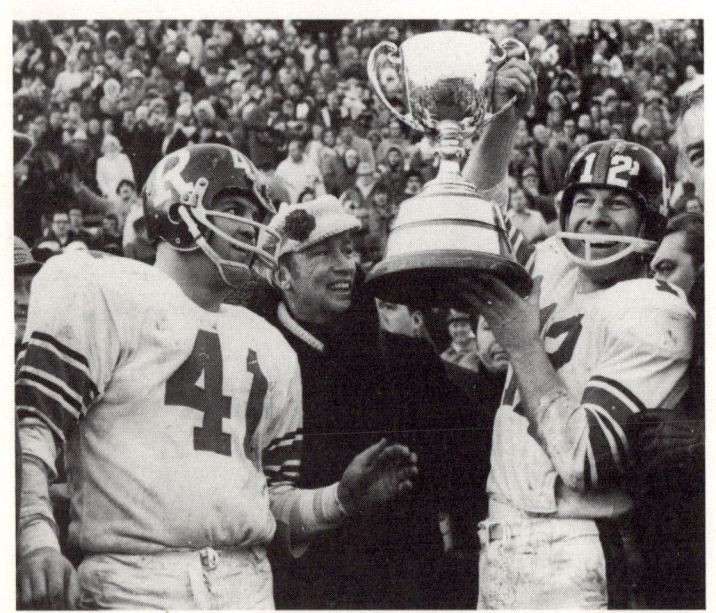

Ken Lehmann (left) and Russ Jackson (right) of Ottawa win the 1969 Grey Cup against Saskatchewan. The game was held in Montréal, and former Prime Minister Pierre Trudeau can be seen in the background.

was going to retire and he was going to win. Ronnie Stewart had a great game.

It was one of those days when it seemed like they were destined to win the game.

Hugh Campbell said, "In 1969, I felt like it was a movie where we were supposed to be the victims—or like a wrestling match where it was decided ahead of time the other guy was going to win. There was a big sensational thing over the fact Russ Jackson was retiring. It was his last game. It just seemed like everyone got on his bandwagon."

Responsibility for staging the Grey Cup rested with the commissioner's office, and, in 1969, Jake Gaudaur was presented with some special problems. "The game was in Montréal at the peak of the FLQ problem," Gaudaur said.

Leading up to that, people had been shot and killed in Montréal. There were threats that the FLQ was going to stage a march and walk toward the Grey Cup parade. In my mind's eye I could sort of see them running into the Saskatchewan band halfway down that parade going in the opposite direction. Day after day, I had to sit there wondering whether I should pull the game out of Montréal. There were a lot of conflicting opinions.

Finally the word came from Ottawa two weeks before the Grey Cup that a decision had been made. The Grey Cup was not going to be disrupted because the FLQ thought it would be counterproductive to their cause. So we took a gamble and went ahead and played the game in Montréal.

That game was played down in the Autostade. Around the stadium, built for Expo '67, there were a lot of light standards with little pods. There were both cameras and sharpshooters in those pods.

As a final condition of staging the game in Montréal, I went to meet with Mayor Drapeau and demanded his assurance that there would be adequate protection at the stadium site. He assured me there would be. So, as we always did at that time, I would get together with the police and work out security plans with them related to potential kinds of problems. We had to have those kinds of concerns, particularly with Trudeau at the game.

I said we had to have good crowd control down on the field. With three minutes to go, I'm looking down at the field, and all of a sudden I see all those police in riot gear coming out of the entrance. There were enough of them to ring the field shoulder to shoulder. I just about died. I guess they made the decision to overprotect.

There was always some special situation that arose concerning the Grey cup. I guarantee it never ran itself. It took an awful lot of planning.

After the 1969 Grey Cup, the trophy was stolen. Gaudaur took action.

"What I did along the way was take the original Grey Cup and put it safely in the Hall of Fame where nobody could touch it and had a replica produced. I did that the year after it was stolen and recovered by the Ottawa police early in 1970. At that time, I decided that we shouldn't lose the symbol of what we were supposed to be all about and decided to protect it in that way.

"Traditionally what happened back then, the team that won the Grey Cup took it back to their place and used it for promotions or whatever they wanted. There was high potential for it being stolen and lost forever."

Soon after Russ Jackson retired, coach Frank Clair did the same, and an era came to a close, ending Ottawa's golden era. Ron Lancaster played on.

The 1960s were years of futility for the Alouettes, brought about by the disastrous Etcheverry-Patterson trade at the beginning of the decade. Averaging only four wins per year, the Larks didn't win a single playoff game after 1962.

Grey Cup 1970

In 1970, the Alouettes' new owner, Sam Berger, hired Red O'Quinn as general manager and Sam Etcheverry as head coach. The team finished third but got by Toronto and Hamilton to advance to the Grey Cup against third-place Calgary who had pulled off a stunning upset over 14–2 Saskatchewan when Larry Robinson kicked a last-play field goal into a gale-force wind to end the coldest football game ever played in Regina. It was the first time that two third-place clubs played in the big game.

Every coach tells his players to be on the their best behaviour at all times in public. Etcheverry had to deal with every coach's worst nightmare when starting receiver Bob McCarthy and star running back Dennis Duncan, who had led the Alouettes in scoring three times and rushing twice, failed to heed that advice. Just before the semifinal, Etcheverry was forced to cut them both.

Red O'Quinn explained what happened. "Duncan and McCarthy were in a night club before the game and got into a brawl. It was reported to *The Gazette*, everybody got hold of it and so Sam had no choice."

McCarthy was a former Stampeder, but he hadn't been a problem. "No," said Calgary quarterback Jerry Keeling, "he was just one of those far-out guys that did his own thing. Getting into a fight in a bar wouldn't have surprised me at all."

An outside linebacker on the team was Mark Kosmos who went on to play in three more Grey Cups with two different teams. He supported Etcheverry's decision. "Dennis Duncan and Bob McCarthy were tremendous contributors to our team. I remember being shocked by it all, but we had so much respect for Sam that whatever he did was okay with us."

Minus two important contributors to the team, the Alouettes prepared to play the 1970 Grey Cup in a sea of mud, par for the course in Toronto.

The field had been resodded the week earlier, Kosmos recalled. "The turf was ripping up in almost two-foot squares. After a play, you'd reach down, grab the thing and spread it out, almost like you were making your bed. They had laid it in big squares like that, thinking the weight would keep it down, but it didn't work."

Calgary great John Helton disputed the notion that the field was the same for both teams.

"My feet would slip out from under me. I think I could have beaten Goliath on a fast track, but if the field was muddy or slippery, I was done. My greatest playing weight was 247 pounds. By November, it was 238. Without speed and strength, I wouldn't have been able to play. All the linemen I played against were bigger than me. On a bad field, I was nullified."

The Stampeders took advantage of the first break of the game when they converted a fumbled punt into a Hugh McKinnis touchdown. Soon after, a long Montréal march stalled deep in Calgary territory. The Als gambled on third-and-one. Moses Denson was tackled below the waist by Terry Wilson. The quick-thinking halfback then tossed the ball to Ted Alfin in the end zone.

The teams traded field goals before Alouette Tom Pullen scored on a seven-yard running play after being set up by an Al Phaneuf interception, his second of the day.

In the fourth quarter, Sonny Wade passed to Gary Lefebvre for a touchdown. The final score was 23–10 in favour of Montréal.

Two nights before the game, Calgary's Wayne Harris won his third Schenley Award for Most Outstanding Lineman. Runner-up Ti-Cat Angelo Mosca said, "I find nothing to be ashamed of in being second to a guy who is not only the greatest lineman in Canada but the greatest football player, too."

Grey Cup 1971

Although the Alouettes had won their second Grey Cup, the marriage made in heaven between owner Sam Berger and Montréal greats Sam Etcheverry and Red O'Quinn didn't last long. Both left in 1972. Asked why he had left the GM's job in Ottawa to take over the Alouettes, O'Quinn replied, "Stupidity, I guess. Ego more than anything. The Alouettes had been going through all that mess and turmoil over there, and I wanted to straighten it out because I'd had some great years in Montréal.

"We got along fine the first year, and it was Utopia. We won the Grey Cup. Unfortunately, we had no place to go but down. Sam Berger stayed out of the operation the first year because he had lost an eye and was quite ill. But when he got well, he started getting into everything. He interfered so much that we just couldn't live together. I left in July of 1972."

Having never won a Grey Cup as a player, it would be reasonable to assume Sam Etcheverry regarded winning the championship as a coach the crowning achievement of a distinguished career.

Not so, said Etcheverry. "I enjoyed playing in the Grey Cup more than winning it as a coach. My coaching experience with the Alouettes wasn't a good one even though we won the Grey Cup. We didn't have a good season. We were just fortunate to put four good games together and win it all. But it was an unhappy experience for me. I regret ever having coached the Alouettes."

Toronto had appeared in the Grey Cup only three times in the modern era. Russ Jackson, the latest big-name saviour, had just been fired as head coach and was licking his wounds at the Florida retreat of the man who swung the axe, owner Bill Hodgson.

Until Ralph Sazio moved down the Queen E from hated Hamilton in 1982 to restore Toronto fortunes, the Argos led the league in spending, were number one in self-proclaimed superstars, first in attendance and last in the Eastern Conference 18 times. Seldom in the history of sports have so many spent so much to achieve so little.

Even a blind squirrel finds an occasional nut, and in 1967 Argo GM Lew Hayman hired Leo Cahill away from the Toronto Rifles of the Continental Football League. The new coach got the team into the playoffs his first year. In 1968, the Argos finished second with a 9–5 record, two points behind the powerful Rough Riders. It was Toronto's first winning record in seven years.

Toronto rolled over Hamilton 33–21 in the semifinal and then edged Ottawa 13–11 in the first game of the final at CNE. The Argos came back to earth with a thud in the nation's capital when the Riders won 36–14.

In 1969, Toronto again finished second, two points behind Ottawa. They eliminated Hamilton and beat Ottawa in the first game of the final, 22–14. Up by eight, Cahill was so convinced the good ship Argonaut was about to come in that he proclaimed, "Only an act of God can stop us from winning the game." They lost 32–3.

Toronto finished second in 1970 but were upset by Montréal in the semifinal, 16–7. New owner John Bassett demanded that changes be made, starting with the quarterbacks.

Because Bassett didn't think Tom Wilkinson looked like a quarterback, he was sent to BC. Bassett didn't like his other quarterback either, so Don Jonas and receiver Jim Thorpe were dealt to the Bombers. Both quarterbacks went on to win Schenley awards.

That left Cahill without a quarterback. A gifted recruiter, he signed veteran Greg Barton away from the Detroit Lions and got Notre Dame All-American Joe Theismann to come north. After three years in Toronto, Theismann became an NFL star with the Washington Redskins and, upon retirement after a devastating knee injury, a television football commentator.

Cahill also signed U.S. college football's outstanding defensive lineman Jim Stillwagon.

Although pundits predicted Greg Barton would lead the Argos, the rookie stepped up instead. Theismann led the Big Four in passing and was named to the Eastern All-Star team. The Argos beat Hamilton in the Eastern final and headed to Vancouver for their first Grey Cup encounter since 1952. Their opponent was the Calgary Stampeders. The Argos were favoured to win.

For the first time, Calgary would play a Grey Cup in the West, in Vancouver. Again they faced poor playing conditions.

"It rained all week," said Jerry Keeling. "That was Tartan-Turf, the first one in Canada. It didn't drain at all. Water came up every time you took a step. It was that way the whole game."

Defence dominated the 1971 Grey Cup, not surprising since the Stampeders only yielded an average of 13.6 points per game, Toronto 17.7.

The offensive star of the game for Calgary was Rudy Linterman, who set up both Calgary touchdowns with his running and receiving. In the first quarter, after a 40-yard Linterman reception, Keeling hit Herm Harrison in the end zone for a 13-yard touchdown. Harrison described the play.

> *The wide receiver and slot ran deep, creating an alley. I would come right down between them in that alley, and then I would cut across the middle because they were clearing out all those guys. Because Dick Thornton was cheating on the speed side, Keeling said, "Herm, it's there." He said he would hit me just before I got to Dick, and that's exactly what happened. As soon as I caught it, Dick bumped me.*

Said Keeling, "Herm didn't have much trouble getting in for the touchdown. Of course, it was also the type of game where because it was so wet, defensive backs had a lot harder time changing direction than receivers did." After 7:17 of play, it was Calgary 7, Toronto 0.

Early in the second quarter, Toronto drove down to the Calgary four-yard line where John Helton, Fred James, Dick Suderman and Craig Koinzan forced them to kick an Ivan MacMillan field goal. Seven minutes later, recalled Keeling, "I threw a pass out in the flat to Rudy Linterman. He was splashing around. Someone came in to tackle him and dove to cut his legs out from under him. He went up and over him and ran down to the six-yard line."

Jesse Mims scored on the next play. At the half, Calgary led 14–3.

Special teams accounted for the Argo touchdown, which came in the third quarter when Jim Silye fumbled Zenon Andrusyshyn's punt. Joe Vijuk picked up the ball and lateralled to lineman Roger Scales, who ran 36 yards for the only major of his career.

Near the end of the third quarter, Calgary conceded a single. They led 14–11 after three quarters.

With the game almost over, Keeling, deep in his own end, threw his third interception of the game, picked off by Dick Thornton.

Scrimmaging from the Calgary 14, Bill Symons swept right and lost three yards. John Helton described what happened next.

"[Leon] McQuay was running to the left, and when he was getting ready to turn up field, he slipped, his elbow hit the ground, the ball popped out, Reggie Holmes recovered it and snuffed out their opportunity."

Argo end Mike Eben said, "Poor Leon didn't fumble the ball. That ball was gang-tackled. I had a good view of the play, and I saw how it unfolded. He just didn't let the ball drop out of his hands. It was Larry Robinson's helmet on the ball that popped it free. It was a very strong, aggressive play on their part."

The always modest Robinson described the play. "I was the one who actually hit him. I was forcing the sweep; we both slipped at the same time and bumped together. His elbow hit the ground, and the ball popped out."

But Toronto wasn't done. Calgary couldn't pick up a first down and had to punt, giving the Argos a last opportunity to move into field-goal range. But Harry Abofs mishandled the ball and kicked it out of bounds, thinking that the last team to touch it had possession. Not so. In that situation, the kicking team took over. The Stamps ran out the clock. The term "Argo Bounce" took on new meaning.

Calgary had won their first Grey Cup in 23 years, 14–11.

Leon McQuay's fumble was uncharacteristic for the rookie who had had the kind of year in 1971 that players only dream about. He led the Eastern Conference in rushing. His average per carry of 7.1 yards and per kickoff return of 26.7 were among the best in CFL history. He fumbled only once during the regular season.

Leo Cahill disputed the referee's call:

I don't think it was a fumble by the rules then. The rule then was that the ground couldn't make you fumble. We were on the right hash mark, and [McQuay] ran to the left. I had sent in the word to get into the middle of the field so we could kick in an easy chip shot for a field goal in case the play didn't work.

So he ran to the left. The off-tackle play opened up. When he planted his outside foot to make the cut, it just gave away. He fell on his elbow, and when he hit the ground, the ball came out. They recovered it. That was the end of the story. Leon slipped, and I fell.

The myth persists that McQuay's fumble cost Toronto the Grey Cup.

Not so, said the great Wayne Harris. "He definitely wasn't going to get back to the line of scrimmage. Everybody still refers to it as Leon McQuay gave it to us. It wasn't him. They had only crossed the 55-yard line three times the whole day. We had a super defensive unit. They may have kicked a field goal to tie it, but they definitely weren't going to score a touchdown on the run.

"We dropped a punt that led to the one touchdown they got. So they only kicked a field goal and a single against us. We held them in check all day."

The Calgary defence efforts were recognized. Harris was named the Grey Cup MVP and Dick Suderman the Outstanding Canadian.

Harris believed that Grey Cup experience was a factor in Calgary's win: "It probably had a lot to do with it," said Harris. "A whole bunch of us were getting very long in the tooth; certainly there wasn't going to be another chance to play in many more, if any. In my case, that was my 11th year; Keeling and Robinson the same. Some of our defensive backs had been around 10 years or so. We were really an old, veteran football team."

Veteran Herm Harrison said, "I thought that team could have beaten an NFL team. The defence was just awesome. Everybody was playing as a unit, was dedicated to the game. Nobody put themselves forward as a standout. The team effort was so strong. We always won as a team."

Grey Cup 1972

Familiar faces were back in 1972. The Saskatchewan Roughriders finished third at 8–8, four points behind Winnipeg and Edmonton. After edging the Eskimos 8–6, the Green and White headed for Manitoba and the Western final, a sudden death affair for the first time since 1949.

Leading 21–0 at the end of the first half, the Bombers were making plans to go to Hamilton for the Grey Cup. But in the second half, Ron Lancaster engineered one of his patented comebacks, pulling his Roughriders into a 24–24 tie going into the final minute of the game.

On the last play of the fourth quarter, the Riders' Jack Abendshan was wide on his field-goal attempt. Paul Williams punted out of the end zone; Lancaster punted it back. Williams punted it out again, and Lancaster caught it, but Winnipeg was called for no yards. Abendshan had another chance. He kicked the Riders into their fourth Grey Cup appearance in seven years.

Hamilton was back after a five-year absence. Their head coach was former Stampeder leader Jerry Williams, who had recently been fired by the Philadelphia Eagles. The Cats tied with Ottawa for first place, each with a record of 11–3. Hamilton squeaked by the Rough Riders 30–27, in the two-game total-point final.

The Ti-Cats had a rookie quarterback in Chuck Ealey and an 18-year-old place-kicker named Ian Sunter. They faced a Saskatchewan squad loaded with Grey Cup veterans.

The 1972 Grey Cup was special to Hamilton because it was the first time since 1944 they had hosted the event.

Angelo Mosca of the Hamilton Tiger-Cats holding up the Grey Cup in 1972 at Ivor Wynn Stadium in Hamilton

This was the fifth meeting between the teams, the fourth in Steeltown. The home team had not won the Grey Cup since 1952 when Toronto turned the trick against Edmonton.

In the first quarter, Al Brenner picked off a Lancaster pass, and Ealey directed his team 52 yards for the opening touchdown, a 16-yard pass to Dave Fleming in the end zone. The Riders argued vehemently that Fleming, after leaping up for the ball, had come down out of bounds. The film confirmed that.

"Isn't that too bad?" sneered Angelo Mosca.

Saskatchewan responded with a 75-yard drive, capped off with an eight-yard TD pass to Ohio State rookie Tom

Campana. The Ti-Cats argued that defensive back Gerry Sternberg had been the victim of an illegal Bob Pearce pick.

"Isn't that too bad!" said Wayne Shaw.

The teams exchanged field goals after which the game settled into a tight defensive struggle until the dying moments of the fourth quarter. Deadlocked at 10, Chuck Ealey went to work.

With 1:51 left in regulation time, Hamilton scrimmaged on their own 15-yard line. Although he had done nothing throughout the game, second-year homebrew and all-Canadian tight end Tony Gabriel caught three consecutive passes of 27, 12 and 15 yards, bringing the ball to the Rider 41. Ealey ran for two yards and threw to Garney Henley who made a circus catch at the 27. Ian Sunter trotted onto the field. "Keep your head down, kid," Henley advised. Sunter did, kicking it right down the middle. Final score: Rookies 13, Grizzled Veterans 10.

The loss was the result of more than the Riders running out of luck. In the first place, they didn't help their cause on special teams. Although Sunter was named player of the game, Bob Krouse blocked a Saskatchewan punt, partially blocked another and fell on the ball when John Williams blocked a third. And coach Dave Skrein made at least two coaching errors that cost his team their second Grey Cup.

George Reed described his day.

I thought the game was going along quite well; I thought we should have won the game. Probably that's the second most bitter defeat because I thought we were controlling the ball, controlling the tempo of the game and I thought the referees gave them a touchdown. Fleming was clearly out of bounds, and everybody sees that now, so he got a touchdown he shouldn't have got.

We had a turning point in that game. We punted the football when we shouldn't have. We were on about our 35-yard line. We had a third-and-two. We went for it and made it with ease. We got close to mid-field, and we had the same situation, a third-and-one or two, and the coach elected to punt. We could always get one or two yards when we wanted to get them. If we had gone for it, they wouldn't have had a chance to come back and win the game.

Skrein's second major mistake was listening to assistant coach John Payne. Linebacker Wayne Shaw explained:

We had a middle linebacker by the name of Steve Svitak who was a big tough American kid, but he was a rookie. He was good against the run, completely lost on the pass.

When we were in a zone defence, he'd drop back 10 to 12 yards in the middle of the zone. He had that problem all year. I used to tell him, "Don't drop so deep."

All day long, I'm playing on that big Canadian tight end Tony Gabriel. He never caught a ball on me until the fourth quarter.

When it was late in the game and Hamilton needed some action, they took Garney Henley who was a great defensive back and put him in at flanker, and I'm worried.

Late in the game, Gabriel had not caught one pass. I can handle him. I'm hitting him off the line all day, and I'm with him. My job was to play on him, hit him right off the line and cover him to the curl zone, 10 or 12 yards deep.

Now what happened, I hit Gabriel. I stopped in the curl zone, I'm with him. I see Ealey looking inside at Garney Henley. He had lined up outside and came into the hook zone.

I look, no sign of Svitak. I made a step inside. Ealey threw to my guy. I made a mistake trying to cover up for Svitak. We stopped them, they don't score. I go on the bench. The offence goes out, doesn't do anything. Skrein sends in a rookie Bill Manchuk.

I was hitting him off the line. Manchuk was faster than I was, but he couldn't cover him [Gabriel].

The opposition saw it the same way as Shaw. Ti-Cat linebacker Mark Kosmos observed, "I played against Gabriel when I was in Montréal. I found Tony very easy to keep on the line of scrimmage. I don't think he ever experienced people that would get him up in front and not let him off the line. But Tony was the kind of guy whenever he was on the field he was dangerous. If somebody gave him a break like they did in '72 and '76 and gave him some room, he was going to kill you."

The win capped a spectacular first year for Chuck Ealey. He made the Eastern All-Star team and won the

Schenley Rookie Award. Unfortunately, his blaze of glory was short-lived. Less than two years later, Ralph Sazio dealt him to Winnipeg. "He got dinged a couple of times and we traded him," the GM explained.

Over the next three years, Saskatchewan lost the Western final to Edmonton (see Chapter Nine for Grey Cups 1973–75).

Grey Cup 1976

The Roughriders got back to the Grey Cup in 1976 against Ottawa whose tight end was none other than Tony Gabriel. The Westerners were without the immortal George Reed, who had retired before the season began.

On November 25, 1976, Ron Lancaster won his second Schenley Outstanding Player Award. Tony Gabriel won for Outstanding Canadian.

Grey Cup day in Toronto in 1976 was windy and cold. As in the Roughriders' last Cup appearance in 1972, it was the veteran King of the Quarterbacks versus a downy-cheeked youngster, this time Tom Clements from the Fighting Irish of Notre Dame. Saskatchewan was favoured over Ottawa by seven. As in 1972, the villain was Tony Gabriel. And once again, coach John Payne made critical errors.

The darkest day in the history of Saskatchewan sports was about to begin.

Saskatchewan's first drive began on their 40-yard line. Steve Molnar ran 20 yards and fumbled. Wonderful Monds picked it up and ran 60 yards to the end zone, but the play was ruled dead. On the next play, Molly McGee fumbled, Ottawa recovering at their 45. After Gerry Organ missed a 57-yard field goal, the Roughriders scrimmaged at their seven. On second down, Lancaster went back into the end zone to pass, scrambled to elude linebacker Mark Kosmos and slipped and fell at the one. Footing on the slick field was a problem all day for Saskatchewan. Ottawa didn't seem to have that problem.

Bob Macoritti kicked from 14 yards deep in his end zone. The Green defence came up big, forcing Ottawa to settle for a 31-yard field goal. Ottawa 3, Saskatchewan 0.

The Roughriders scrimmaged at the 35. After two incomplete passes, Macoritti got away a 40-yard punt into the wind. The stiff breeze held the ball up for a second or two. Rookie Bill Hatanaka fielded the ball on the run. Saskatchewan's Ted Provost lunged desperately at him. Hatanaka brushed Provost aside and out-raced Lou Clare and Macoritti to the end zone. In 68 seconds, Ottawa had scored twice to jump into a 10–0 lead.

Ottawa's head coach George Brancato didn't consider the return a broken play. "It's a good special teams play," he said. "There has to be some good blocking and certainly some good running by the returner. You work on those things every week, and you just hope that one day you'll break one."

The second quarter belonged to Saskatchewan. Starting out at their 48, Lancaster alternated hits and misses. To McGee for 23, Leif Pettersen for 14 and 12. First down at the Ottawa 13. Incomplete, nine yards to Rhett Dawson, third and a foot at the four.

For 13 years, whenever the Roughriders needed a yard, George Reed was Mr. Automatic. It was second nature to

Lancaster to call the fullback's number in this situation. Not this time. Fullback Steve Molnar piled into the line and didn't gain an inch.

The Green defence came up big again, forcing Ottawa to punt. Although Ottawa took advantage of good field position to put three points on the board, a golden opportunity had been lost. Saskatchewan had to rely on Ron Lancaster's arm—and he had a magnificent day—as did his primary receivers Leif Pettersen and Bob Richardson.

However, the Green and White's inability to pick up short yardage on the ground would be their undoing.

Saskatchewan's next possession was set up by Steve Mazurak's 24-yard punt return. From the 45, Molnar picked up eight yards, McGee one. Faced with another crucial third down, Lancaster kept it, and Ottawa was offside. It was a 16-yard toss to Mazurak at the 15. Lancaster then threw left to Mazurak across the middle. Mazurak got a great block from Rhett Dawson to make it to the end zone. Tie ball game.

Three plays later, Ted Provost intercepted Clements at the 51, returning it 26 yards to the Ottawa 25. Lancaster promptly hit Bob Richardson at the 10. The big tight end shook off Ron Woodward and thundered into the end zone. Saskatchewan 17, Ottawa 10 at the half.

Lancaster completed 15 of 21 passes for 170 yards and two touchdowns. Clements was having a miserable afternoon with only 25 yards through the air. The football universe was unfolding as it should.

Saskatchewan opened the second half with a 51-yard Bob Macoritti field goal. Gerry Organ replied on their next possession with a 40-yarder into the wind.

With about a minute left in the third quarter, Ottawa was third-and-10 at their own 37. Organ went back to punt, but to everyone's surprise, he ran for 52 yards.

Ottawa couldn't cash in. With a first down at the Saskatchewan 21, Clements was picked off by Cleveland Vann. The quarter ended with the Green and White holding a seven-point lead. But the Eastern champions had outplayed the Westerners in the third quarter and had the wind for the final 15 minutes.

Ottawa got a break early in the final quarter when, punting from the enemy 52, Gary Brandt snapped the ball high. Macoritti jumped up and pulled it down. The punt dribbled away. Ottawa took over on their 54, only two yards beyond the Saskatchewan line of scrimmage.

Neither offence could do much, but the Roughriders were being punted into poor field position. Halfway through the fourth quarter, Ottawa capitalized on field position and narrowed the score to 20–16 with a 32-yard field goal.

From his 35, Lancaster and Leif Pettersen moved the ball to the 55-yard line. On second-and-one, Lancaster again eschewed the quarterback sneak and gave it to Molnar, who slipped and fell a good yard short. Macoritti punted, Ottawa started out at their 26.

Tom Clements had only two good drives in the entire game. They came exactly at the right time. Behind almost perfect protection, he threw to Jeff Avery for 13 yards. After an incompletion, he hit Art Green for 16, who took the hand-off to the Saskatchewan 51.

On the next play, Tony Gabriel got off the line, cut across the middle, cradled Clement's picture-perfect pass and ran 41 yards to the Roughrider 10. The young quarterback, cool as a cucumber, had the best secondary in the CFL back on its heels. As Yogi Berra would say, it was déjà vu all over again.

Or was it? Perhaps lightning wouldn't strike twice. Art Green picked up two yards. On second down, Clements carried down to the one where he fumbled, but the ball was ruled dead. On third-and-goal, Saskatchewan's defence held firm. Saskatchewan took over on their one-yard line with 1:32 left to play.

On first down, Tom Campana sliced off a tackle for five yards. Lancaster called the same play again. Campana got a yard. Macoritti punted. Ottawa took over at the Saskatchewan 35.

Art Green picked up a yard on first down. With 40 seconds left, Tony Gabriel got off the line, cut across the middle and caught one for 10. With 20 seconds left, Gabriel faked inside and ran to the end zone where he got behind the secondary and broke a million Saskatchewan hearts. His touchdown gave the Ottawa Rough Riders their ninth and final Grey Cup victory by a score of 23–20. In comparison to the depression that settled over the land of the Roughriders, Mudville would have seemed positively euphoric.

Tom Clements had 151 yards passing in the second half, 104 of them on his last two possessions.

Ottawa linebacker Mark Kosmos was more than surprised at Saskatchewan's conservative strategy.

> *I was shocked. I'm calling the defensive plays. I remember us getting in the huddle and I said "GAP defence." That's almost like a goal-line stand defence. I'm basically saying we're going to stop the run because that's all they were going to do. If Ronnie would have thrown the ball, the guy would still be running. None of our guys were playing the pass. We knew they were going to run. They had to know that we were going to play the run.*

Coach George Brancato said, "What I thought would happen was that they'd give up two points and kick off and get us out of field position because there was less than a minute left in the game. They surprised me when they punted the ball, and we took over in good field position at their 35."

Playing conservatively was Saskatchewan's first mistake. Not surrendering a safety was the second error.

John Payne's third mistake was his strategy against Tony Gabriel. Everyone in the ballpark knew Clements would go to Gabriel, but they couldn't stop it from happening. Remember 1972 when Wayne Shaw kept Gabriel in check by hitting him on the line of scrimmage? This was the same John Payne who was the Rider defensive coach four years earlier and made the decision to pull Shaw and get somebody with more speed on the big tight end. Didn't work then, didn't work now.

"If the situation had been reversed and I had been playing against that team," said Mark Kosmos, "Gabriel would never have left the line of scrimmage. In those days, you could hit people coming off the line.

"Tony came out on that play, nobody touches him at the line and he gets this beautiful pass from Tommy. That was it. Everybody knew the ball was going to Tony. Tony was running free as a bird."

Gabriel described the dramatic moment:

I'd been hit hard on the previous play by Cleveland Vann, and I was dazed and seeing stars. I got back into the huddle, and Tom Dimitroff had sent in Gary Kuzyk, the wide receiver, with a play from the bench. Time was counting down, and Tom Clements shouted, "No!" and called the play that won the Grey Cup.

It was a Fake 324, fullback through the four hole and a tight end slash. Ironically, the set they were in defensively, [linebacker] *Roger Goree was off the line of scrimmage, and they had a defensive end lined up over me. That allowed me to escape the line. Ray Odums followed our wide receiver and left my area empty.*

When the ball was coming, my heart was pounding and my eyes were open wide. If I had dropped that pass, I may as well have retired right then.

Because Gabriel was seen running away from him, Ted Provost has been wearing the goat horns ever since, unfairly according to George Brancato.

"It was the corner, the outside guy, Ray Odums," said Brancato. "He jumped on the underneath guy. It was a three-deep defence, and the corner didn't get back. Tony broke for the corner. Provost was actually in a good position, taking the middle away. But he had no help on the outside. You usually blame the guy closest to the ball. It just so happened that the guy closest to the ball was not responsible. He was just chasing."

Of the four Grey Cups that Lancaster lost, 1976 was the hardest one for him to take:

> *In 1972 during that last series, you could see it going by you. In '76, we thought we were good enough to beat anybody. We weren't overconfident, but we did have confidence, whereas in '67 and '69, you could see at the start of the game we were going to get dominated.*
>
> [The year] *1976 was the beginning of the end of an era. I think people sensed that. A lot of us had played a long time together, and the team was starting to disband. People probably felt like I did. That was the year. If we were going to win it, that had to be the year to do it.*

chapter nine

Dynasty—The Edmonton Eskimos, 1973–75 and 1977–82

In the 10 seasons between 1973 and 1982, the Edmonton Eskimos went to the Grey Cup nine times and came away with six wins, including five straight, from 1978 to 1982, a feat likely never to be equalled. That time was a stark contrast to the 1960s when they missed the playoffs five times and failed to win a playoff game after 1960.

But the period wasn't entirely for naught, in that two personnel moves were made that laid the foundation of the greatest dynasty in Canadian football history. The first, in 1966, saw Norm Kimball named general manager. The second, in 1970, came when Ray Jauch was named head coach.

In Jauch's rookie season, the Eskimos finished second, and he won the Coach of the Year Award. He wasn't satisfied and was particularly upset with the attitude of some of his players before the team's semifinal loss to Calgary. "Although we were in the playoffs, the guys all had their cars packed and in the parking lot, ready to go home. I thought that was a bunch of garbage. I wanted them to have to walk down the street the next day. It's a matter of attitude, of playing harder, of having to face the fans rather than getting out of town."

After making wholesale changes, the team finished last in 1971 with a record of 6–10. The next time the Eskimos missed postseason play was in 2006!

Jauch built his team with men of character. "What I look for in an athlete is honesty," he insisted. "Find the best players with the right attitude—self-motivators. Those people take care of themselves."

Key was the quarterback. The Eskimos signed Tom Wilkinson, a man loaded with character, in 1972. To say he was unprepossessing would be an understatement. He would have easily stumped the panel on *What's My Line?*

The great middle linebacker Dan Kepley recalled his first encounter with the man who led the Esks to the promised land. "I got into Edmonton October 1975. Wilkinson came walking up to me. He was a little chunky. He had that double dip of Skoal and a Styrofoam cup, and he was spittin' and chokin'. He said, 'Nice to meet you. I'm the quarterback.'

"I said, 'Yeah, sure, you're my quarterback.' I thought he was the equipment manager."

Kepley soon learned that looks can be deceiving. "He wasn't pretty, but he was effective. I still hold Wilkie as probably the best all-around athlete I have ever seen in my life. The best. He was drafted by Major League Baseball. He can shoot the eyes out of a basketball. He is the most intelligent athlete I have ever met."

During his 15-year CFL career, Wilkinson completed 1613 of 2662 passes for 22,579 yards and 154 touchdowns. His percentage completion rate of 60.6 is fifth best in league history.

Wilkinson was the CFL All-Star quarterback in 1974, '78 and '79. He won the Schenley Most Outstanding Player Award in 1974. When the Eskimos instituted the Wall of Honour at Commonwealth Stadium in 1982, his was the first name on it. He entered the Canadian Football Hall of Fame in his first year of eligibility, in 1987.

The Wyoming graduate began his pro career in 1966 with the Toronto Rifles of the Continental Football League. When Rifles' coach Leo Cahill went to the Argos the following year, he took Tom Wilkinson with him. In 1971, Cahill signed Joe Theismann and shipped "Wilkie" to the Lions. He was cut by the Lions in favour of Don Morehead after spending the season riding the pine.

"Wilkinson called me," explained Ray Jauch. "We had [Bruce] Lemmerman at the time, but I didn't really have a backup. Tom said he was driving to Greybull, Wyoming, and wanted to know if I was looking for a backup quarterback. I said sure, come on by. So he did. He still lives in Edmonton. He never did get to Greybull."

Hugh Campbell coached Wilkinson from 1977 to 1981 and said, "Wilkinson was our leader. He was a competitor at the highest level. He was the single best leader I've ever been around as far as team play goes."

One of Wilkinson's favourite targets was receiver George McGowan. In 1971 Jauch brought him in as a defensive back but soon realized he had the potential to be a receiver. McGowan had a good year in 1971, improved in 1972 and won the Schenley Award in 1973.

McGowan credited Wilkinson with his transformation from average receiver to superstar. "Wilkinson—he turned it around for the Eskimos and me also. I was a late bloomer. We had that happen in Edmonton in all kinds of positions. Look at the people from BC: Tom, Larry Highbaugh, Ron Estay, Bob Howse, Wayne Matherne. Sometimes the conditions, the surroundings, the city you're in, change a ballplayer."

Ray Jauch deserves credit, too. When other teams thought players were over the hill or lacking in talent, his insightful judgement of personnel turned losers into champions. But he did make the occasional mistake.

Dave Cutler's magnificent kicking career was almost nipped prematurely in the bud.

> *In 1969, my rookie year, I was lucky they paid me two cents to play. Then in 1970, I was very lucky in training camp because my holder had once held for George Blanda, so I started to get better. But I missed a convert in Vancouver, and soon after, I had a field goal blocked. Jauch then told Peter Kempf to get ready to kick, but Kempf didn't have his shoe on, so I was sent out again to kick from the 43. I sunk it, and I was back on track. That kick turned my career around.*

When Jauch was reminded that he almost cut one of the greatest kickers in CFL history, he laughed. "We always weren't so smart, were we? Thank God Kempf couldn't find his shoe."

Working the other side of the kicks was Edmonton's premier return man, Larry Highbaugh, who had a career average of 35 yards per carry, still the best mark in CFL history. In 1974, Highbaugh averaged an incredible 43.3 yards per return.

What a scenario! Highbaugh would run back the kick-off to his own 50-yard line. Wilkinson would complete a couple of seven-yarders, and Cutler would kick a field goal. Opponents quickly found themselves on the wrong end of the scoreboard.

With a mixture of rejects and rookies, the Eskimos entered their greatest era. Thirteen of them would land in the Hall of Fame.

In 1972, the Eskimos reversed a 6–10, fifth-place finish from the season before, finishing 10–6 and tied for first with Winnipeg. Edmonton lost the semifinal 8–6 to Saskatchewan.

Grey Cup 1973

The tie-breaking formula favoured Edmonton when they tied Saskatchewan for top spot in 1973. The Eskimos beat the Roughriders in a thrilling final of 25–23 to return to the Grey Cup for the first time in 13 years. Edmonton's opponent was Ottawa.

After Russ Jackson's swan song in 1969, coach Frank Clair retired, replaced by his assistant, Jack ("Jocko") Gotta. Faced with a massive rebuilding job, Jocko's Rough Riders were 4–10 in 1970, 6–8 in 1971 and 11–3 in 1972. Gotta won his first Coach of the Year Award for his efforts. He expected to pick up where he left off in 1973, but Ottawa lost their first four games. "I was hung in effigy in both official languages," he said. Instead, they won 11 of their next 12 games, including the Eastern final and the Grey Cup.

The only offensive category the Riders led in 1973 was scoring, helped by kicker Gerry Organ's 123 points. Although Hugh Oldham, Rhome Nixon, Jim Evenson, Jim Foley, Art Green and Jerry Keeling were solid performers, clearly Ottawa's strength was defence, called the Capital Punishment Gang. This was reflected in the All-Canadian team. No Riders made it on offence, four made it on defence, including tackle Rudy Sims, linebacker Jerry Campbell and defensive backs Dick Adams and Al Marcelin. Gerry Organ won the Most Outstanding Canadian Award.

The 1973 Grey Cup hinged on the health of the quarterbacks. Edmonton's Bruce Lemmerman hurt his elbow in the playoffs, and Tom Wilkinson was nursing a variety of injuries. Ottawa's Jerry Keeling had a knee injury, so backup Rick Cassata had to go all the way.

Early in the opening quarter, running backs Calvin Harrell and Roy Bell romped through the Ottawa defence, Bell scoring the first TD. Cassata countered with a 38-yard pass to Rhome Nixon to tie. Dave Cutler kicked the Esks into a three-point lead.

Giving their opponent's quarterback a rough ride was part of the Capital Punishment Gang's strategy. Wayne Smith was penalized for roughing the quarterback on Edmonton's first possession of the game. Near the end of the first quarter, Wilkinson rolled to his right at the Ottawa 12-yard line and was trying to get out of bounds. Jerry Campbell hit him in the face with a forearm, driving him to the turf, and Smith piled on and smashed Wilkinson in the ribs. Dick Adams also hit him. Ottawa was penalized for roughing, a small price to pay for getting Wilkinson out of the game with broken ribs. The injured Lemmerman entered the fray.

Said Jack Gotta, "Let's get to the quarterbacks and really pound them. That was the point we really tried to get through to the players."

The only scoring in the second quarter came when Eskimo punter Gary Lefebvre fumbled the ball in the end zone conceding a safety, and Gerry Organ added a 46-yard field goal. Ottawa led 12–10 at the half.

In the third quarter, Jim Evenson rumbled 18 yards for a major, and Organ added three points. Lefebvre scored an 85-yard punt single, the second longest in Grey Cup history. In the last minute, Wilkinson, in relief of Lemmerman who ripped open his elbow again, returned in the fourth quarter and connected with Lefebvre for a major. The final score: Ottawa 22, Edmonton 18.

Rick Cassata had the finest game of his career, and Charlie Brandon was named Grey Cup MVP, the only time an offensive lineman has won the award. Still, injuries seemed to be the key to the game's outcome.

Eskimo tight end Tyrone Walls dropped several passes because of a broken hand. Ray Jauch had no doubt about the difference in that game.

We used both our quarterbacks quite a bit. We had both of them hurt going in, so we had a problem right there. You're going into the biggest game of the year, and you've got both your quarterbacks hurt. Wilkie could play, but we knew if he took one hit, it was all over. I knew if they got Wilkie out of there, we were in trouble. Then Wayne Smith got him on the sideline.

Bruce went into play just on sheer guts. He shouldn't have been playing. Then he got hit, and Wilkie had to go back in. I think that if we had had a couple of healthy quarterbacks, we would have had a good shot at them. Their offence wasn't that great.

Grey Cup 1974

During the rest of the decade, Edmonton faced Montréal in the Grey Cup every year except 1976. Their first Grey Cup match-up took place in Vancouver, on November 24, 1974.

The rainfall was so heavy that tractors with huge roller brushes had to be used to push water off the artificial turf at Empire Stadium. Although most of the fans were under the roof, the players were soaked to the skin minutes after taking to the field. Still, the game was played with great intensity and speed.

Although the Eskimos appeared healthy, Wilkinson had an injured shoulder. That year he won the Schenley Outstanding Player Award and was the All-Canadian quarterback.

While strong offensively, Edmonton wasn't formidable on the other side of the ball. The front four was solid, but the linebacking and secondary were suspect. They bent

From left to right, Junior Ah You, Marv Levy and Peter Dalla Riva with the Grey Cup in 1974. Montréal won against Edmonton 20–7.

but didn't break. Bending was all Alouette kicker Don Sweet would need.

Sweet tried eight field goals, making four and a single. He converted Montréal's only touchdown scored on Larry Sherrer's second-quarter five-yard run. Earlier, Edmonton had moved into a 7–0 lead on Wilkinson's eight-yard pass to Calvin Harrell. Montréal shut them out the rest of the way to win 20–7.

Once again the Eskimos lost their quarterback because of a late hit. With the ball on the Alouette 23, Glen Weir nailed Wilkinson and Junior Ah You piled on. Montréal was assessed 15 yards, bringing the ball to the eight. The Eskimos scored on the next play, but Wilkie was done for the day, replaced by Lemmerman.

"We were in pretty good shape going into the Grey Cup," recalled Ray Jauch, "and then Wilkinson got hurt on the first series we went in and scored on. Well, you could say, 'You're all right. You've still got Lemmerman,' but Wilkinson had just won the Outstanding Player Award and established himself as our leader, our number one quarterback, and then we lost him. From a morale standpoint, that had as much effect on us as anything.

"Our offensive line had a hard time with their defensive line. That was one of the reasons we lost. But in both Grey Cups we played well until our quarterbacks got hurt."

A star for the Easterners that day was Johnny Rodgers. Twice Larry Highbaugh was called for holding because he couldn't handle Rodgers' dashes through the secondary.

Rodgers joined the Als in 1973. A Heisman Trophy winner from Nebraska, he was everybody's All-American. He rushed, caught passes and was spectacular on returns. Rodgers spurned an offer from the NFL San Diego Chargers in favour of the wider field in Canada. He won the Schenley Rookie of the Year Award.

Rodgers stirred up controversy by making a statement that made him sound like a blowhard when that was not his intent. When asked if he would be a superstar in the CFL, he replied that if that came to pass, he wanted to be an ordinary superstar who didn't lose the common touch. All the reporter passed on was the term "ordinary superstar."

In his four-year CFL career, Johnny Rodgers made All-Canadian three times—twice as a receiver and once as a running back. In 1974, he led the league with 1024 yards on 60 receptions. He picked up 2054 all-purpose yards and was runner up to Wilkinson in '74 and Calgary's Willie Burden in 1975 for the Outstanding Player Award.

The 1974 Grey Cup was the first for Montréaler Wally Buono. "I look back on 1974 in Vancouver with a lot of fond memories. It rained every day that week, but it didn't really affect us at all because we were really pumped for the game. We came out and played a tough game."

Back in Edmonton, Jauch retooled his team for the 1975 season, adding Canadian players who would be part of Edmonton's success for years to come. Homebrew rookies from the previous year included defensive lineman Dave Fennell, receiver John Konohowski, halfback Stu Lang and linebacker Dale Potter. In 1975, offensive lineman Bill Stevenson, linebacker Tom Town and DB Pete Lavorato joined the team.

Grey Cup 1975

For the third straight year, the Eskimos finished first and defeated Saskatchewan in the Western final. Montréal finished second to Ottawa but still advanced to the Grey Cup, held in Calgary for the first time.

When the game was awarded to Calgary, the major concern was the weather. The organizing committee produced charts proving the weather could be quite balmy on November 23. It wasn't.

The first four days of the 1975 Grey Cup were relatively warm. The weather turned cold on Friday and colder

Saturday. On game day, all "metal chimpanzees" were judiciously moved indoors, and the temperature at game time was −10°C, with the wind chill −30°C, the coldest Grey Cup in history. Despite the weather, McMahon Stadium was full 30 minutes before the kickoff. Fun-loving fans eager to watch the pre-game show got more than they bargained for. As the bands were playing, a female streaker took to the field and did a dance that lasted several minutes. For a few seconds, everyone thought she was part of the show.

The playing conditions turned the game into a defensive struggle. It was only the third Grey Cup in which no touchdowns were scored (the others were in 1933 and '37). It was the first Grey Cup since 1945 that all points were scored by Canadians, and it was the first Cup in which the points were scored by just one player on each side. The final score was Dave Cutler 9, Don Sweet 8.

Sweet kicked Montréal into the lead with a 30-yarder in the first quarter, matched by Cutler from 40 yards. Near the end of the half, Sweet set a Grey Cup record with a 47-yarder and added a single. The Als led 7–3 at the half.

In the second half, Cutler struck twice, a 25-yard field goal and then one from 52 yards out, breaking the record Sweet set a quarter earlier. Edmonton was ahead 9–7 going into the final 15 minutes, but Montréal had the wind.

In the dying minutes of the fourth quarter, Sonny Wade replaced Jimmy Jones at quarterback and marched his team downfield. Larry Smith picked up 26 yards on a screen pass, and Joe Petty made a razzle-dazzle play for a 46-yard gain. Two running plays later, it was third-and-seven at the

Eskimo 12. With just under a minute left, the Alouettes lined up to try a field goal.

Wayne Conrad snapped the ball back to Jimmy Jones, who dropped it. Already moving forward, Sweet kicked the ball on the ground, sending it into the end zone where the Eskimos conceded a single point.

But 45 seconds remained. It was imperative that Edmonton retain possession by picking up a first down. Wilkinson took off from his 35 on an option play and got the job done.

According to Wilkinson, the wind was a bigger problem than the cold. "When you were playing, you didn't notice the cold all that much, but the wind you did notice, especially from my perspective as a quarterback. The wind could hold the ball up very easily."

Southerner Dan Kepley did notice the cold. That Grey Cup was his first. "I had no idea what a Grey Cup was. But I knew I had to win that game just to pay for the down-filled jackets and clothes I had to buy my dad and his best friend when they came up for the game.

"I knew Canadians were a little crazy when I saw that woman streaking. Tom Wilkinson came out to the centre of the field with the other captains for the coin toss and said to Junior Ah You, 'Wasn't that your wife?' That really started things off well. Junior didn't have much of a sense of humour."

Said Wally Buono, "We felt we had really outplayed them. We had ample opportunities to put the game away. We had the game very much under control, but then Johnny

Rodgers fumbled a punt. Another time going into score, Rodgers fumbled the ball again.

"And then everyone can remember the last-second field goal we missed. It was really caused by Jimmy Jones not being able to put the ball down, not Don Sweet missing it. It wasn't a very good hold because his hands were cold." He sighed. "It wasn't our day."

Both Edmonton and Montréal slipped to third the following year.

Hugh Campbell

At the end of the 1976 season (see Chapter Eight: The Riders), Edmonton coach Ray Jauch startled the football world by deciding to leave coaching for the front office. "They told me they were going to hire a director of football operations. They said I could do one or the other. I decided to get into the administrative end, which was a mistake. I soon realized I wasn't ready to quit coaching."

The man chosen to succeed Jauch was Hugh Campbell, former outstanding receiver with Saskatchewan. Campbell had been head coach at Whitworth College in Spokane, Washington, taking over a program in 1970 that was nearly extinct and building teams that won two-thirds of their games. He was selected Coach of the Year in the Pacific Northwest Conference three times. Still, coaching young collegians is one thing, looking after grizzled old pros another. When he was informed that no one had ever successfully made the head-coaching jump from small college to pro, Campbell replied, "Gee, I didn't know that. Maybe I shouldn't have taken this job."

Campbell knew what was expected of him in Edmonton. "When I was hired, Ray and Norm Kimball told me that one of the reasons they had selected me was that because I wasn't here as an assistant coach, I would have a more open mind about new people and change.

"Ray told me the team needed a lot of changes, and that was one reason he hired me instead of Vic Rapp [Esk assistant]. Vic wouldn't make the changes that had to be made. He had favourite players. The year before the team had finished third. Ray felt there were some players who were aging, and it was hard to make those changes when you've had those players for years."

At age 36, Campbell was the youngest head coach in the CFL. He immediately began the task of hiring assistants, favouring older men with a wealth of experience. "That was one of the things Jack Gotta told me," Campbell confided. "By doing that, you're not afraid of someone stabbing you in the back for your job. You get people around you who are experts at their positions."

The exception, and Campbell's boldest move, was hiring Don Matthews as assistant defensive coordinator.

"Don and I had a relationship that went back to Spokane when I was at Whitworth, and he was coaching at Ferris High School."

Matthews had no coaching experience beyond the high school level except for a graduate assistantship at Idaho. Some people thought Campbell had taken leave of his senses.

"When I hired Don Matthews," said Campbell, "the headline in the Edmonton paper was 'Campbell Hires High

School Coach.' They said it was a big negative that we had a high school coach. What about all the guys that have coached pro ball that are looking for jobs right now, they asked? But I knew Don was special."

Hugh Campbell's other picks were veterans Joe Faragalli and, in 1978, Cal Murphy.

Campbell discussed his coaching philosophy. "Involve yourself with the most talented and best people you can. I believe in getting the right people and having them be thinkers and contributors."

With the full support of Kimball and Jauch, Campbell changed direction. Slowly but surely, Campbell fashioned a dynasty. "Too many teams put their Canadians at the receiver positions, and because they were always worried about protecting the quarterback, they used two or three imports on the offensive line.

"I think it was about the third season that we finally went to an all-Canadian line. The thing I think I brought to the Eskimos was playing an all-Canadian offensive line.

"We got [fullback] Neil Lumsden for Bruce Lemmerman when I guaranteed Hamilton they would make the Grey Cup if they had Bruce as their quarterback. I loved and respected Bruce as a player, but we had Wilkinson and Warren Moon, so I felt we could give up one of our really good quarterbacks for an outstanding Canadian like Neil."

Grey Cup 1977

In 1977, the Eskimos finished in a three-way tie for first with the Lions and Blue Bombers. Edmonton got the bye.

Lui Passaglia kicked the Lions past the Bombers in the semifinal, but the Eskimos crushed them 38–1 to return to the Grey Cup, this time at Montréal's Olympic Stadium against the Alouettes. On paper, the teams were evenly matched. It was reasonable to expect a close game.

Events, however, conspired against the Eskimos. The weather in Montréal was reasonably pleasant the first half of the week. On Thursday night, a blizzard hit the city, dumping tremendous amounts of snow on Olympic Stadium. At that time, the Big O wasn't closed in, so the field was exposed. The stadium workers put salt on the snow to melt it. When the temperature plunged the next day, the field turned into a sheet of ice. Despite the billion dollars spent on the Olympic Stadium, it had no tarpaulin.

Even though a transit strike was going on, a record crowd of 68,205 watched what should have been an excellent football game. Instead, they were treated to a sorry spectacle resulting from the incompetence of stadium officials. The score was 41–6. For the sake of the crowd, it was a good thing Montréal had the 41.

The shellacking absorbed by Hugh Campbell's Eskimos was the third worst in league history. What surprised the crowd was how the Alouettes handled the slippery field with ease while the Eskimos floundered. Als quarterback Sonny Wade unleashed an aerial attack, completing 22 of 40 passes for 340 yards and three touchdowns. Don Sweet set two records, one by kicking six field goals and another for total points, 23.

During Grey Cup week, Alouette coach Marv Levy had cloistered his team away, thinking only about football.

Rumour had it they were staying in a monastery. "It was pretty close to being a monastery," recalled Larry Smith.

If the Eastern champions were essentially inaccessible, the Eskimos were highly visible everywhere, including the lobby bar at the Chateau Champlain, as loose and carefree as a bunch of kids when school's out.

It was only natural to examine a number of factors to explain the Eskimos' lopsided loss. It couldn't have been the field conditions or the −9°C temperature because the conditions were the same for both teams.

What had made the difference, it turned out, was that the Alouettes had put heavy-duty staples on their shoes in order to get a grip on the ice. They worked perfectly, giving the home team a significant edge. According to Buono, the late Tony Proudfoot thought of it. "The big thing for us was seeing what shoes would be adequate. Tony, very ingenious, always thinking, felt we needed something steel-tipped to cut through the crust of the ice. He came up with the staples idea.

"All we did was get two staples and cross them. You put them on the outer part of the toe where you get the grip. I think it was a psychological edge more than anything."

Dan Kepley wasn't buying it. "We were set up. The ice and snow came, and all of a sudden, there just happened to be staple guns all around the place. I mean, if Custer had known the Indians were on the other side, he wouldn't have walked over there."

Wally Buono had no doubt why Montréal won:

We didn't win because of staples; we won because we were a better football team. We had beaten the Eskimos [25–20] in Edmonton that year. We had a closely knit group of guys who really played hard. That's why we won.

We had a great defence. We never allowed more than 20 points a game. We had excellent special teams. There were very few turnovers.

The guys had a great sense of pride, a great willingness to pay the price to win. They had a great sense of confidence in one another that no matter what, they were going to win.

Back in Edmonton, Hugh Campbell took the defeat in stride. "After winning the West, I felt that we had done as well as we could possibly do," he confessed. "However, that game served as our motivation for five straight Grey Cups."

Grey Cup 1978

From the moment the 1978 training camp began, the Eskimos desperately wanted a return Grey Cup match with the Alouettes. They knew about the staples and felt they'd been had.

In addition to a deep, talented receiving corps, running back Jim Germany was coming off a 1004-yard season. Tom Wilkinson and Bruce Lemmerman were joined by a Rose Bowl hero named Warren Moon.

The defence was the best in the West with Dave Fennell, David Boone, Ron Estay and York Hentschel on the line, with Dan Kepley, Tom Towns and Dale Potter behind it and a superb secondary with Larry Highbaugh, Joe Hollimon, Ed Jones, Greg Butler and Pete Lavorato.

In spite of their talent, 1978 wasn't a cakewalk because the Stampeders, who had finished last the previous year, were revitalized by Jack Gotta and challenged for top spot, finishing one point behind Edmonton. The Eskimos beat Calgary 36–13 in the final and moved on to the rematch with Montréal in Toronto.

"Our team was very well motivated," said Campbell. "Montréal was an excellent football team with a bunch of old pros who had been there, and we had a mixture of very young and very old players. Not only were we hungry, we were pretty talented."

Dan Kepley described the atmosphere that Grey Cup afternoon. "There was really a tremendous amount of revenge involved. It was one of the most physical games I can remember. There was so much hitting going on, and it was constant. It was a really tough, defensive struggle that we won 20–13."

Jim Germany and Dave Cutler staked Edmonton to a 10–0 lead in the first quarter. Cutler added seven more points compared to three by Don Sweet. Going into the fourth quarter trailing 17–3, Montréal closed the gap when Joe Barnes ran 10 yards for a touchdown, and Sweet kicked a field goal. The rally fell short when Cutler wrapped things up with a final three-pointer during the last minute of play. For the first time in 14 years, a Western team had won a Grey Cup on eastern soil.

Grey Cup 1979

The following year, the Eskimos and Alouettes met again in Montréal, their fifth Grey Cup meeting in six years and their last. Each had won the Grey Cup twice.

1979 Grey Cup winners Tom Wilkinson (left) and Dan Kepley (right) of the Edmonton Eskimos. Former Prime Minister Joe Clarke is in the background.

Joining Edmonton in 1979 was a red-headed rookie from Washington State, Brian Kelly. Over a nine-year career, Kelly caught 573 passes for 11,169 yards, placing him 10th all-time in CFL history. His 97 touchdown passes placed him all-time behind Milt Stegall and Allan Pitts and seven ahead of Geroy Simon going into 2012. Kelly averaged 1241 yards a season, second only to Calgary's Pitts. Kelly is Edmonton's all-time leading receiver.

Montréal breezed through the East, finishing first with a record of 11–4–1. Running back David Green led the league in rushing with 1679 yards, winning the Schenley Most

Outstanding Player Award for his efforts. Defensively they were led by Dickie Harris and Junior Ah You.

Despite two explosive offences, the 1979 Grey Cup was again a tough, defensive struggle. The Alouettes won all the awards, but Edmonton took home the Grey Cup, winning 17–9. Montréal couldn't get the ball into the end zone, settling for three Sweet field goals.

The Eskimos relied on two big plays for victory. In the first quarter, Tom Wilkinson hooked up with the CFL's leading receiver Waddell Smith on a 43-yard pass and run for a touchdown. Smith was so wide open that he could have crawled into the end zone.

In the third quarter, after Sweet had kicked the Als into a 9–7 lead, Hugh Campbell replaced Wilkinson with Warren Moon, who threw a touchdown strike to Tom Scott. Cutler closed out the scoring with a 38-yard field goal.

Grey Cup 1980

The Eskimos began the decade of the 1980s by becoming the first team in CFL history to score over 500 points. Dave Cutler led the league in scoring, Jim Germany picked up 1019 yards rushing, Tom Scott caught 73 passes for 1245 yards and Warren Moon was second in passing. Edmonton youngster Hank Ilesic had the best punting average, and Larry Highbaugh was first in punt returns. Nine Eskimos made the All-Canadian team and a dozen were Western Conference All-Stars. The club finished at 13–3 in first place.

Edmonton defeated Ray Jauch's Blue Bombers 34–24 in the Western final. The Esks went on to Toronto to face the

Tiger-Cats in one of the few clear Grey Cup mismatches. They won their third straight Cup 48–10.

By this time, Warren Moon had displaced Tom Wilkinson as the starting quarterback. During the season, Moon completed 181 passes for 3127 yards and 25 touchdowns, at the time an Eskimo record. Wilkie wasn't exactly riding the pine, hitting the target 83 times for 1060 yards. During the 1980 Grey Cup game, Moon completed 21 of 33 passes for 398 yards and three touchdowns. The Eskimos netted 606 yards to Hamilton's 201. Tom Scott caught three touchdown passes, a record that still stands. Bernie Ruoff had three field goals and a single for the losers. Moon was the Grey Cup MVP, while Dale Potter was named the best defensive player and outstanding Canadian.

Grey Cup 1981

The 1981 Eskimos finished first at 14–1–1 but just squeaked by BC in the Western final 22–16. Making their fifth straight appearance in the national classic, Edmonton's opponent was Ottawa.

Ottawa went 5–11, 13 points behind Hamilton in second place. After beating the Als in the semifinal, the Riders upset the Ti-Cats late in the fourth quarter when quarterback J.C. Watts hooked up with Pat Stoqua for a 102-yard pass-and-run touchdown.

The Rough Riders prepared to meet the greatest CFL team of all time, in Montréal. What should have been a hopeless situation turned out to be one of the most glorious days in the history of the Ottawa franchise.

How does a head coach instill confidence in a team facing a hopeless situation?

Rider assistant coach Bob O'Billovich said:

It's easy to get players motivated for those kind of games. When you're the hopeless underdog, I think that's easier than when you're heavily favoured because nobody expects you to win. Psychologically, I think that works to your advantage. The other guys start reading about how much better they are, and sometimes they aren't ready to play the way they should be.

By playoff time, we were a lot better than our record indicated. We knocked off Hamilton in Hamilton when they had the second best record in the league.

One of Ottawa's stars was defensive end Greg Marshall, an Eastern all-star four times and All-Canadian twice. He won the Schenley for Outstanding Defensive Player in 1983. Marshall described the team's frame of mind during Grey Cup week. "We actually were pretty confident about our chances. We knew we could play with them. We just looked at it like we didn't have anything to lose, nobody expected us to win, so we were just going to go out and play hard and see what happened. If we could get something going early, we thought we'd have a chance."

That's exactly what happened.

Warren Moon, a member of both the CFL and NFL Halls of Fame, celebrated his 25th birthday four days before the 1981 Grey Cup. His winning percentage was .790.

Though obviously a consistent performer, Moon came out flat against Ottawa.

In the first quarter, Gerry Organ made field goals of 34 and 37 yards to give Ottawa a 6–0 lead. A minute and a half later, capitalizing on a turnover, Jim Reid finished off a drive with a one-yard touchdown. In the second quarter, Sam Platt ran 14 yards for a major, giving the Eastern upstarts a 20–0 lead. All the mighty Eskimos could produce was a single on a missed field goal.

Just before the end of the half, Campbell pulled Moon and sent in the forgotten Wilkinson. With a seven-yard pass here and a Jim Germany run there, Wilkie strung together a few first downs and kicked the sputtering offence into life, giving the Esks some semblance of optimism when they headed for the dressing room down 20–1.

In the dressing room, head man George Brancato told the players to "Just keep doing what you're doing." Brancato said, "I think more or less they did. We came out and got a pass interception right away and took the ball into field-goal range and got a field goal right at the start of the third quarter. And then that was it. Edmonton woke up."

What did Campbell do at halftime to shake his team out of the doldrums? "The big adjustment was mental," he recalled. "Wilkie had already adjusted us going into the second half. Wilkie had gone into the game because Warren Moon wasn't doing anything, nor was the entire team. Wilkie went in and moved the football.

"At halftime, we discussed in a businesslike way what we had to do for a shorter time than normal and in an emotional way for a longer time than normal. We ended halftime saying we had to win the third quarter. [They outscored Ottawa 14–0.] Most teams believe they have to win the fourth quarter, but I've always thought that if you win the third, the fourth will take care of itself."

Early in the second half, Dan Kepley and Dave Fennell made crushing tackles and stopped the Riders cold deep in their own end. Soon after, the great Eskimo offence made a dent in Ottawa's stalwart defence. First, Jim Germany ran for a touchdown, and after holding Ottawa on the subsequent possession, Warren Moon drove his team to the goal line again, where he went over on a quarterback sneak. At the end of the third quarter, Ottawa led 20–15.

Gerry Organ upped the Riders' lead to eight with a 28-yard field goal halfway through the final quarter. Shortly after, Moon scored again, and with the two-point conversion pass to Marco Cyncar, the Eskimos tied the game.

Near the end of the game, J.C. Watts threw to Tony Gabriel at the 55, but Gabriel was called for offensive interference. With the penalty, Ottawa was hemmed in deep and had to punt.

Starting around midfield, Moon quickly marched his charges to the Rider 20. Dave Cutler kicked the winning field goal with three seconds left on the clock. The final score: Edmonton 26, Ottawa 23. The Eskimos became the first team to win four straight Grey Cups.

Greg Marshall thought mistakes turned the game in favour of Edmonton. "To me, the key to the game was we had a turnover deep in our territory where they got the ball.

They kicked a field goal to make it 20–4. Shortly after that we fumbled the ball on about our own 10-yard line. They recovered and were able to take it in on a third-down play for a touchdown. That got them seven points real quick and got them back in striking distance."

A key mistake was made by an official. Watts had completed a pass to Tony Gabriel at the 55, but it was called double interference. The ball went back into the Riders' own end where Watts was sacked. Ottawa punted, and Edmonton got the ball in good field position and moved in for the kill.

Gabriel recalled what happened. "I was coming back to the ball, and Gary Hayes was draped all over me. I made the catch, but the official called double interference. That official never worked another playoff game. I came out after that play. I had been wearing a brace, and I was hurt and sore. It was a disappointing way to end my career, not only because of the penalty but because we had a 20–1 lead and let it slip away."

Marshall was incensed at the call. "Probably the worst call in the history of the CFL. That call was utterly ridiculous. In retrospect, it really did cost us an opportunity to win the ball game. To this day, every time I see it, I can't believe it was called that way."

But Marshall praised the opposition:

Warren Moon played an excellent second half and made some great plays. I remember in particular when they went for the two points to tie it up. I thought he made a great play.

That was just one of several big plays he made in the second half. Wilkie came in near the end of the first half and maybe calmed things down a bit. But he only put one point on the board. Warren Moon was definitely the catalyst in the second half.

Coming so close to pulling off the biggest upset in Canadian sports history was something the Ottawa Rough Riders could feel good about. "I suppose," said George Brancato, "but a loss is a loss. It's hard to take, especially a Grey Cup loss. It hurts to lose a game like that."

Grey Cup 1982

For three complete seasons, the Eskimos lost a grand total of six games. At the halfway mark of the 1982 campaign, Edmonton faced Calgary in the Labour Day Classic at McMahon Stadium. The Stamps won 32–20, leaving the Grey Cup champions in last place with a record of 3–5.

The injury bug had struck the Eskimos. Brian Kelly and Marco Cyncar missed parts of the season, as did the unappreciated running back Jim Germany. It was no coincidence the team returned to their winning ways when Germany returned.

The Eskimo comeback began minutes after their Battle of Alberta loss in Calgary. Hugh Campbell addressed the troops:

I said to the team that I hadn't given up, but that we had lost all our margin for error. We had to virtually win every game just to make the playoffs.

I said we were capable of doing that, and any players who didn't think we could, I would guarantee them their contracts. All they had to do was step forward and say they wanted out. I promised them they would still get paid, but I needed them out of the way because we were going to the Grey Cup.

The players did a lot of talking among themselves, and as a group we all agreed to play the best football possible and let the chips fall where they may. We then won 10 sudden-death games in a row, including the Grey Cup in Toronto against the hometown team. The odds against doing that are phenomenal.

One of the few rookies on the 1982 team was Laurier graduate and centre Rod Connop, who went on to win the Outstanding Offensive Lineman Award in 1989 and was an all-star seven times. "I remember that speech well," he said. "It was something. Instead of letting the media in after the game, he closed the door and spent the next 20 minutes explaining things the way he saw them. When people talk about great turning points in seasons, they always mention Hugh Campbell's speech."

Connop then added a qualification. "It just so happened that Jim Germany and Brian Kelly came back in the lineup. People never understood how good Germany was because he did everything so easily, so smoothly. He wasn't flashy, so he didn't stand out. Anyway, after Labour Day, the team basically got healthy for the first time that year."

Almost nothing went wrong the rest of the way. Saskatchewan collapsed, Calgary's defence fell apart and British

Columbia lost both their quarterbacks. Edmonton ended the season tied for first with Winnipeg and got the bye into the final, which they won 24–21.

The man of the hour in 1982 was Warren Moon, who threw for 5000 yards, the first quarterback in CFL history to achieve that mark. He completed 333 passes, 36 for touchdowns.

It was cold, wet and windy for the last Grey Cup game played at the CNE in Toronto on November 28, 1982.

For Hugh Campbell, it was his last Grey Cup as a CFL coach. Soon after, he left to coach the Los Angeles Express of the United States Football League (USFL) and then the NFL Houston Oilers. As beloved as any coach could ever have been, the players desperately wanted Campbell's CFL coaching career to end on a winning note.

Edmonton opened the scoring against the Argos with a Dave Cutler 38-yard field goal. Minutes later, Condredge Holloway hit Emmanuel Tolbert on a hitch pattern. He turned up field and ran 84 yards for a touchdown, the first offensive Grey Cup major Toronto had scored in 30 years. Cutler added another field goal, but Toronto took the lead again when Terry Greer scored on a 10-yard pass from Holloway.

Before the half ended, Cutler struck again, and Brian Kelly picked up a major to give the Eskimos a 20–14 lead. Neil Lumsden added a major, and Cutler a fourth field goal, giving him a record-setting Grey Cup career total of 18. All Toronto could muster in the second half was a safety touch. Final score: Edmonton 32, Toronto 16.

Toronto boss Bob O'Billovich explained the loss. "They were a better football team, but we played them pretty even the first half. The weather did come into play in the second half. They had a much better offensive line, and they could run the ball with Germany and Lumsden better than we could. That, along with Warren Moon's ability to run, when the weather got bad, made them tougher."

Defensive lineman great Dave Fennell commented on winning a fifth straight Grey Cup. "The challenge after a team matures becomes quite different," he explained. "It's sort of like having sex five times a night. The first time is always the most exciting. You're not as enthusiastic the fifth time as the first, but it's still great." Fennell won the Grey Cup awards for top defender and Canadian.

Warren Moon, the Grey Cup Most Valuable Player, commented on the win:

> *I think winning the Grey Cup in 1982 was the most satisfying because at Labour Day, everyone had written us off. People were calling for Coach Campbell to be fired. The finger was being pointed at a number of players for not performing properly.*
>
> *We went though a little bit of soul-searching. Then we won 10 straight games. That was a team accomplishment. I think I'm prouder of that than anything. It is the ability of a team to overcome adversity that is really the mark of a champion. It's easy to be a front-runner. What really counts is your ability to pick yourself up when you're down.*

Hugh Campbell offered another perspective. "A lot of people don't realize how hard it is to beat a team in a Grey Cup in their home stadium. Before we won in 1978, no Western team since 1964 had won a Grey Cup on eastern soil, let alone in the other guy's home stadium. We won five in a row on eastern soil, and two of them in the other guy's home stadium. It is rare for a team to do that."

chapter ten

Feline Frenzy, 1983–88

Between representing the Big Four in the 1971 and 1982 Grey Cups, the Toronto Argonauts missed postseason play eight times. Despite the coaching services of luminaries like Eagle Keys, Jackie Parker and Cal Murphy, the BC Lions only made the playoffs eight times between 1964 and 1982. Two of the greatest general managers in CFL history turned these perennial losers into champions: Ralph Sazio in Toronto and Bob Ackles in BC.

Sazio was brought to Hamilton as an assistant coach and player in 1950 by Carl Voyles, who had been his coach at the College of William and Mary. Thirteen years later, Sazio became head coach of the Ti-Cats, making the playoffs every year and winning three of four Grey Cups. He was the general manager or president from 1968 until six games into the 1981 season (when he joined the Argos), missing the playoffs only twice by a grand total of three points.

He quickly decided a coaching change would be made.

"Willie Wood [Argo coach and former Green Bay Packer great] had the great name, and he was a nice guy, but not the kind of guy who could handle that team," said Sazio.

To replace Wood, Sazio hired Ottawa assistant Bob O'Billovich.

"You've got to have a guy who has a background in the Canadian game. Bob's ideas, Bob's value of Canadian players, things like that made us hit it off together," said Sazio. "I felt I could work with him, and he was willing to work with me, which was important. He thought much like I did. We made a lot of changes, we cleaned house."

In 1982, O'Billovich's rookie year, he took the Argos from worst to first and was on the verge of winning it all, only to lose to the Edmonton Eskimos 32–16 in the Grey Cup. Toronto breezed through the 1983 regular season with a record of 12–4, which was a surprise considering their offensive coordinator Darrell "Mouse" Davis quit during training camp, quarterback Condredge Holloway injured his hand twice, running back Cedric Minter missed two games and superb blocking back Bob Bronk sustained a season-ending injury in August.

No other team in the Eastern Division had ever won 12 games before. Toronto's consecutive top-place finishes were the first for the team since 1937–38 and the first back-to-back Grey Cup appearances since the Teddy Morris teams of 1945–47. O'Billovich—the easily underestimated and overlooked boy from Butte, Montana—had done a tremendous job.

Toronto's best season ever was almost ruined by third-place Hamilton (5–10–1), who advanced to the Eastern final with a narrow 33–31 win over Ottawa. The Argos, trailing the Ti-Cats by 10 points going into the fourth quarter, pulled it out with only 27 seconds left when Cedric Minter scored the winning touchdown. The final score was 41–36.

Grey Cup 1983

Toronto's opponent in the 1983 Grey Cup was the Lions, playing at home in their brand-new dome, BC Place. The Leos were the best in the West in points for and against, percentage completion and sacks. Defensively, they surrendered the fewest points and yards in the league. BC finished first at 11–5 and dispatched Winnipeg in the Western final.

The Lions were led by former Eskimo defensive coordinator Don Matthews, his first year of an illustrious career as a head coach. The Lions' offensive stars were guard John Blain, quarterback Roy Dewalt, running back John Henry White and receiver Mervyn Fernandez. Kicker Lui Passaglia led the league in scoring with 191 points. Defensively, Larry Crawford had a CFL high 12 interceptions. Crawford, lineman Mack Moore and DB Kerry Parker were All-Canadians.

Lion GM and former water boy Bob Ackles explained why he hired Don Matthews. "Don knows how to win. Some people don't particularly like him, but Don knows how to win football games. He knows talent, he knows coaches, he knows how to hire coaches and let them work. Don took a decent football team and put it into the Grey Cup his first year."

Both teams were hungry. Toronto hadn't won the Grey Cup since 1952. BC was making their first appearance since 1964. The Argos had won both regular-season match-ups.

Come Grey Cup day, the Argos found themselves down 17–7 at the half. Merv Fernandez and John Henry White tallied majors for the Lions, and Passaglia added the converts and a field goal. Fernandez had 130 yards receiving through the first 30 minutes.

Argos slotback Jan Carinci took a pass from Condredge Holloway and worked his way 14 yards to the end zone. Kicker Hank Ilesic had missed three field goals but was not concerned. O'Billovich was not amused. "I finally said to Ilesic after he missed the third one, 'Hank, you've got to start making some of those; we're going to need those points.' He said, 'Don't worry, coach, I'll make it when it counts.' Sure enough, late in the fourth quarter, he made a 44-yarder that was the key kick. If he had made the ones he should have made, the game never would have been that close."

O'Billovich changed quarterbacks for the second half. Joe Barnes was one of those rare players who was comfortable sharing the starter's role. In Saskatchewan, he was part of the J.J. Barnagel quarterbacking tandem along with John Hufnagel. Previously, Barnes had shared the duties with Sonny Wade in Montréal. Condredge Holloway and Barnes were a good fit in Toronto.

O'Billovich explained why he made the quarterback change:

> *They had done a great job of defending us in the first half. They were doing some overloads with their defence, and they were keying the flow of our fullback. They were just well prepared for our offence and the stuff that Holloway did really well.*

In the second half, we went to more conventional stuff, more misdirectional stuff, bootlegs, sprint-outs that Joe Barnes was good at. We ran the ball a little more. Those adjustments made our offence get into gear in the second half. Joe came in and got us going.

All season we went with a two-quarterback system. Whenever we felt we had to make a change, we'd do it. Both our quarterbacks were comfortable with that. It just worked out that in that particular game, Barnes got the call and delivered the goods.

In the second half, Ilesic closed the gap to five points with a field goal and two singles. With four minutes remaining in regulation time, Toronto was second-and-six at their 53. Barnes threw to Paul Pearson over the middle. When Pearson was tackled, the ball flew out of his hands. Emanuel Tolbert picked it off without missing a beat. Three passes later, Barnes hit Cedric Minter for a three-yard touchdown.

The Argos failed their two-point conversion attempt, but the defence held the enemy at bay. The final score was Toronto 18, BC 17. The 31-year drought was over.

Joe Barnes won the Player of the Game Award, but in reality, either the defence or Hank Ilesic deserved the credit for the Argo's 11th Grey Cup—the defence shut the Lions out in the second half.

"We had the best defence statistically in the league," said O'Billovich. "Eighteen points for one team, 17 for the other, doesn't say a whole lot for either offence. Both defences were paramount. They both controlled the game.

"The key thing that contributed to our defence being as good as it was, was the punting of Ilesic in the second half. That helped give our defence really good field position all second half and kept them in their end."

Two big plays hurt BC in the second half. When running back Ray Crouse was heading for pay dirt, Carl Brazely ripped the ball out of his arms. Late in the fourth quarter, Roy Dewalt found receiver Jacques Chapdelaine wide open in enemy territory, but the rookie dropped it.

The 1983 Grey Cup was one of heartbreak and tragedy for Don Matthews.

> *I don't remember a lot of that game. My children got in a very bad car accident the day before the game, and I spent the entire night before the game at the hospital. Two of them broke their backs.*
>
> *In fact, I told my coaches at the start of the game, "I can't help you; my mind's not even here. All I can tell you is just try to stay aggressive."*
>
> *I was there, but I didn't have any input into the game. I was completely ineffective as a football coach.*
>
> *My children were in the hospital for over two weeks. When they finally got out, they had to wear a back brace for over six months. They both healed perfectly and went on to play high school and college football, which was great.*

At the time, the doctors couldn't tell us if they were ever going to walk again. It was a major traumatic time in my life, so I remember bits and pieces, but I really wasn't into that game.

Losing at home was particularly hard on Vancouver-native Lui Passaglia.

That was the hardest Grey Cup to swallow because we waited so long to be in it. We had a great defence, offence and coaching staff. The team was well run, but we just couldn't get the job done. And to play in front of 60,000 fans the first year in BC Place. I recall after the game a lot of tears from professional athletes. A lot of the guys were there for seven or eight years. To take that long to get a taste of it and then to blow it away by a point! When it comes to championships and anything in life, whatever you are doing, when you get that one shot at it, you've got to take it and grasp it.

Grey Cup 1984

Neither BC nor Toronto made it back to the big game the following year. Hamilton, under the direction of coach Al Bruno, emerged as the power in the East and represented that division in the Grey Cup three years in a row. In the West, former Eskimo assistant Cal Murphy had got the Blue Bombers flying again. In 1984, Winnipeg and Hamilton met for the 11th time in the first Grey Cup game ever played in Edmonton.

In 1983, two-time Schenley-winning quarterback Dieter Brock, citing the personal happiness of his family, had gone on strike to force the Bombers to release him from his $1 million contract so he could finish his career in the U.S. General Manager Paul Robson refused to void the contract and instead traded Brock to Hamilton for Tom Clements.

Safety Paul Bennett won Outstanding Canadian in 1993 as a Bomber. He was traded to Toronto, who cut him, and then he was picked up and released by Edmonton and went on to star with Hamilton.

So, Brock was upset on offence, and Bennett was in a funk on defence. That left special teams. Kicker Bernie Ruoff had been earlier convicted of marijuana possession while a Bomber. He was cut and picked up by Hamilton, who now had three stars all thirsting for revenge.

In 1984, Winnipeg didn't miss a beat with Tom Clements at the helm, scoring 61 touchdowns, 21 more than the year before. They led the league in points, touchdowns and total offence. Willard Reaves picked up 1733 yards rushing, winning the Schenley Most Outstanding Player Award. Centre John Bonk won for offensive lineman. Clements, Bonk, Reaves, receiver Joe Poplawski and offensive linemen Chris Walby and Nick Bastaja made All-Canadian.

Winnipeg's biggest improvement was on defence. They reduced their points allowed from 402 to 309. They were ferocious at forcing turnovers. There were three keys to the Bombers' rejuvenated defence. Scott Flagel, a Winnipeg native, developed into such a promising safety that Cal Murphy was able to trade Paul Bennett to Toronto for standout defensive back Donovan Rose. Murphy then traded defensive back Ken Ciancone to Montréal for linebacker Delbert Fowler. About the same time, Saskatchewan cut Frank Robinson, who joined

Fowler, Aaron Brown and Tyrone Jones as a fearsome foursome of linebackers.

While Winnipeg was 11–4–1 in the West, Hamilton tied for second in the East at 6–9–1. The Ti-Cats won the semifinal 17–13 over Montréal and edged Toronto 14–13 in overtime to advance to the 72nd Grey Cup.

On a cold Sunday afternoon in Edmonton, it looked like the Ti-Cats were peaking at the right time, jumping to a 17–3 lead. By the end of the game, 44 more points were scored; unfortunately for Hamilton, they were all by Winnipeg. But in the first quarter, the Ti-Cats looked like world-beaters. Dieter Brock marched his team smartly downfield to the enemy 15-yard line. He dropped back to pass, found no one open and scampered up the middle for a touchdown. Later in the quarter, Brock hit Rocky DiPietro in the end zone for a seven-yard score. Trevor Kennard and Bernie Ruoff traded field goals.

Then fate intervened. The Bombers' Tom Clements was having trouble moving the ball. Early in the second quarter, he lost a contact lens and had to leave the field, replaced by John Hufnagel. Hufnagel explained what happened:

> *At that point I had been in the league for quite a while and understood the defences. That helped my playing because once I got on the field, I knew 100 percent what I wanted to do.*
>
> *Basically we had put in a play, just an easy play, where we would release the back in the flat. In our preparation, it looked like the back would be open, and he was. I just ran it a couple of times,*

> *dumping the ball. I think what it showed was that if you're patient and make some decisions, you'll start moving the football. Once Tom got back on the field, whether I helped him or not, I don't know, we moved the ball awfully well.*

Cal Murphy recognized Hufnagel's contribution. "Huf started to do the things we thought could go. Then Tom got another [contact] lens, and I was betwixt and between as to whether I'd send him back in. I thought, 'Heck, he's the guy, and so that's where we're going.'"

Before losing his contact lens, Clements had managed only one first down. Hufnagel was in for three plays. The ball was on the Hamilton 54. He took them to the 18 and retired to the sideline. A couple of plays later, Willard Reaves ran it into the end zone.

Good defence continued the revival. "I still remember the big hit Tyrone Jones made on Dieter Brock," Murphy said. "Stan Mikawos picked up the ball and ran for his only career touchdown. You look at the interception that David Shaw made. It was plays like that I really believe turned the game around."

For Winnipeg-native and defensive lineman Stan Mikawos, it was a dream come true.

> *I saw Tyrone Jones from the corner of my eye come in on a blitz and hit Brock, causing him to fumble. As I was rushing Dieter, the ball bounced, I scooped it up and ran 22 yards for a touchdown. That was a key point in the game because we were down to Hamilton, and that touchdown*

gave us a spark of new life, and we went on to win the game.

After the Shaw interception, Clements and Poplawski combined for a 12-yard touchdown. Kennard added two more field goals. The score at halftime was 30–17. Winnipeg's 27 second-quarter points is a record that still stands.

Kennard kicked a 16-yard field goal in the third quarter. Reaves plunged over from three yards out in the fourth, and Hufnagel threw a four-yard touchdown pass to Jeff Boyd. The final score was 47–17. Winnipeg had won their first Grey Cup in 22 years.

Hamilton's coach Al Bruno bemoaned his fate. "We were going pretty well. Dieter was hot, hitting passes. We ran the ball fairly well. We had too many turnovers, and that just kills you. I mean, a lineman picked up a fumble and went for a touchdown. It wasn't a good day for us. They had a good ball club, but it wasn't really our day to play."

Grey Cup 1985

BC finished first in the West for the third year in a row in 1985 with a record of 13–3. The race was tighter down east with Hamilton and Montréal tying for first at 8–8. The Als eliminated Ottawa 30–20 before bowing to Hamilton 50–26. The Lions crushed an injury-riddled Bomber squad 42–22 to advance to the Grey Cup in Montréal.

The dynamic duo of quarterback Roy Dewalt and receiver Mervyn Fernandez led the Leos. Dewalt played in constant pain. He had broken his ankle in 1984, but that didn't bother him as much as turf toe.

"I got injured in 1982. My big toe is sore to this day. I reinjured it during the 1983 Grey Cup. I have had pain with each and every step for the last four or five years. Now it is arthritic."

When Dewalt first came into the league, he was a scrambler. The turf toe put an end to that but made him a better passer, the main beneficiary of which was Mervyn Fernandez, who won the Schenley Most Outstanding Player Award in 1985, catching 95 passes for 1727 yards and 15 touchdowns. Fernandez got hurt in the division final and couldn't play in the Grey Cup.

The Lions jumped into the lead in the 1985 Grey Cup on their second possession when Dewalt hit Ned Armour streaking down the sidelines. Ti-Cat Less Browne and the receiver arrived at the same time, but Armour wrestled the ball away and headed to the end zone. Lui Passaglia kicked the convert and added two field goals.

Early in the second quarter, Grover Covington recovered a Lion fumble on the BC 49. Soon after, Ken Hobart connected with Ron Ingram for a 36-yard major. Near the end of the quarter, Hobart engineered a drive culminating in a Johnny Shepherd one-yard plunge for a touchdown. Hamilton 14, BC 13.

Then came the climactic moment. Just as a broken kicking play was instrumental in BC's first Grey Cup victory in 1964, a kicking play turned the 1985 Grey Cup in the Lions' favour.

Near the end of the first half, the Lions were forced to punt. After taking the snap and starting to move forward, Lui

Passaglia saw Mitchell Price coming at him. He pulled the ball down and took off, picking up a first down at BC's 51. On the next play, Dewalt hit Armour for his second touchdown. Passaglia described the pivotal play:

> *They were leading 14–13. They kicked off to us but stopped us right away and had some momentum going. We were ready to punt from around our 40-yard line.*
>
> *When I was ready to drop the ball, I could see yellow and black jerseys, in fact, two of them, coming up the middle. If I had kicked it, they would have blocked it, and who knows what would have happened.*
>
> *I think somebody just missed by about an inch of tripping me up. I just happened to go outside and get the first down, and we scored on the very next play. I got another field goal just before the half.*

Less Browne recalled the play vividly:

> *I'm always the guy who goes for the block. I'm not a big man so they don't put me on somebody to block.*
>
> *I remember going in, and I thought, "Oh, man, I'm going to get this, I'm going to get this." And then, all of a sudden, damn. He just took off with it, right past Mitch Price who had his fingertips on him. That's when they say it's a game of inches. He was just an inch off. He had his fingers right on his jersey. I kept thinking, "Grab him Mitch, just grab him." He couldn't, and they*

ended up getting that first down, which kept their drive alive.

The Westerners went into the dressing room leading 23–14.

The Lions maintained their momentum in the second half. Jim Sandusky scored a touchdown, and Passaglia added two field goals and a single. Hamilton rounded out their scoring with a Steve Stapler TD and a Paul Osbaldiston field goal in the fourth quarter.

BC had won their second Grey Cup 37–24. It was Don Matthews' first Grey Cup win as a head coach.

"We scored early on a long bomb that Armour stole right out of Less Browne's hands," recalled Passaglia. "That gave us confidence knowing we could go deep. Mervyn had been our deep guy all year, but Ned caught two bombs that day and a couple of long balls in the Western final."

Coach Al Bruno pointed the finger at Less Browne.

"Less Browne got beaten twice on long touchdown passes. On the first one, Less tried to pick it off. He had fairly good coverage, but I don't think he realized how quick that kid Armour was."

Less Browne presented the case for the defence:

I was step for step with Ned, and when he caught it, I caught it. My mistake was going for the interception.

The second touchdown wasn't on me at all. We were in a three-deep zone, Ned Armour runs a post, which means when he leaves my area to

> *catch the ball in the middle of the field, there ought to be somebody there.*
>
> *I took the blame for that in the locker room when they asked me about it, and I remember the guy [Paul Bennett] I took the blame for came up to me afterwards and said, "I just want to thank you because most guys would probably sit there and point the finger and say whose man it really was." And I didn't.*

Bruno released Less Browne at the first opportunity.

The Grey Cup had extra meaning for BC Sports Hall of Fame centre Al Wilson:

> *I was scared stiff going into that game because I knew that was my last one. Even though I didn't retire until the next year, I knew that was probably my last one.*
>
> *All we had to do was play our game and we could win. But was I overconfident? No. Going in, did I think I was going to win? No. We had to go out there and do something, play the game. Hamilton was tough. They played hard the whole game.*
>
> *It wasn't until there were 30 seconds left and we had a 13-point lead that I would kiss my wife who was leaning over the railing in the stands.*

For Al Bruno, Hamilton's loss had been another disappointment. But every cat has his day, and for Bruno, that day came on November 30, 1986, at BC Place.

Grey Cup 1986

After winning his fifth straight Grey Cup in 1982, Edmonton Eskimos coach Hugh Campbell left for the United States Football League (USFL) Los Angeles Express but returned to Edmonton in 1986 as GM. The Eskimos' then-GM Norm Kimball hired Pete Kettela to replace Campbell but soon realized he made a mistake, firing Kettela halfway through the '83 season. The great Jackie Parker took Kettela's place.

If hiring Kettela was a mistake, replacing him with Parker was a stroke of genius, typical of Kimball's wonderful insights about people. "Jack probably did one of the best coaching jobs that anybody ever did for us," Kimball said, "at a time when it would have been very easy for us to go the other way."

As Parker explained, his job wasn't easy. "The guys that were great players for Edmonton over the years are still very good friends of mine, but I had to tell them they couldn't play anymore, which is hard to do. Some realize on their own their careers are finished, but most don't. So they have to be told. It was very difficult."

Making wholesale changes, Parker had three third-place finishes and then came out on top in 1986. Crucial to success was the quarterback, and the Eskimo scouting system produced another great one, Matt Dunigan.

Dunigan quickly established himself in the CFL. As a backup to Warren Moon in 1983, he completed 14 of 26 passes for 239 yards. In 1984, he was fourth in the league in passing and also fourth in rushing. The following season,

Dunigan was fifth in passing, fourth in rushing and made All-Canadian.

In 1986, the Eskimos were 13–4–1. They defeated Calgary 27–18 in the semifinal (four western teams were in the playoffs) and crushed the Lions 41–5 in the final, setting the stage for what turned out to be a thoroughly wretched Grey Cup appearance. Edmonton's opponents, the Hamilton Ti-Cats, had to survive an incredible two-game total-points Eastern final. They lost the first game at home 31–17. They fell behind 10 more points in the second game at Toronto before coming back to win the game 42–15 and the round 59–56.

Despite being overwhelming favourites in the Grey Cup, the Eskimos were humiliated 39–15 by the Ti-Cats. Usually when a team wins by a big margin, they do so with a powerful offence. But it was the Hamilton defence that savaged the Eskimos that day in one of the most ferocious displays ever witnessed in a Grey Cup. Edmonton's total offence at the end of the half was minus one yard! Grover Covington, Mike Walker and Mitchell Price ripped the Edmonton offensive line apart and did all manner of unspeakable things to Matt Dunigan.

Things started to go wrong the moment the Western champions left the dressing room. When the players were introduced, they were greeted by thunderous boos from the largely BC crowd, still smarting over the defeat of their beloved Lions the week before.

On Edmonton's first play, Grover Covington laid an enormous hit on Dunigan, knocking the ball loose for Mitchell Price. On the next play, Hamilton quarterback Mike Kerrigan connected with Steve Stapler for a touchdown.

1986 Grey Cup celebration with then Tiger-Cats president Harold Ballard and Ben Zambiasi (number 31)

Rod Connop explained what happened. "Hector Pothier got suspended for a drug conviction, and Leo Blanchard [eight-year veteran and All-Canadian that year at guard] switched from the right side over to Hector's left tackle spot and just never adjusted."

Minutes later, Mark Streeter blocked a punt, and Jim Rockford recovered for another Ti-Cat major. Two Edmonton mistakes, two Hamilton touchdowns.

Less than four minutes later, after a Kerrigan to Stapler pass covered 43 yards, Paul Osbaldiston kicked the Ti-Cats into a 17-point lead. Osbaldiston tied Don Sweet's Grey Cup record of six field goals. He also added three converts.

The score was 29–0 at the half and 36–0 by the 13-minute mark of the third quarter, when Damon Allen replaced the concussed Dunigan and finally got the Eskimos on the scoreboard with six-yard run for a touchdown.

Edmonton rounded out their scoring when Allen threw to Brian Kelly in the end zone and added a two-point convert. In the dying moments of the travesty, Osbaldiston rubbed salt in the wound with a final field goal. The Eskimos allowed 10 sacks and gave up 10 turnovers, a still-standing Grey Cup record.

Jackie Parker explained the defeat. "We had to change our offensive line around. That really killed us because Hamilton was a really good defensive team."

General Manager Hugh Campbell said, "We knew we were really the underdog. We knew we had a problem on the offensive line. We had covered it up for two weeks on an icy field. The key for us was to make some plays early and put off for as long as possible Hamilton finding out how superior they were to us. But they found out real quickly."

"It was like a track meet to see who would get to me first," Dunigan recalled. "I was sacked 10 times and had to have my knee and elbow operated on after the game. They got good pressure on me."

Al Bruno discounted Edmonton's offensive-line problem as a determining factor in the outcome. "I was aware they had lost an offensive guard, but we would have kicked the hell out of them anyway."

Grey Cup 1987

The 75th anniversary of the Grey Cup came in 1987 and was contested by Edmonton and Toronto. Both teams had appeared in the national classic more often than their division rivals. Both teams were steeped in Grey Cup tradition.

Before the 1986 season, Eskimo GM Norm Kimball retired, replaced by Hugh Campbell, back from the NFL. Kimball came out of retirement soon after to assume ownership and control of the struggling Montréal franchise. It didn't work.

In 1987, the Alouettes folded, replaced in the Eastern Division by the Winnipeg Blue Bombers. The Argos and Bombers battled to the regular-season wire with Winnipeg finishing first in the East with a record of 12–6, one point ahead of the Argonauts (11–5–1).

After polishing off the Ti-Cats 29–13, the Argos went to Winnipeg Stadium for the Eastern final. The Bombers had lost a grand total of three home games in four years, yet they were no match for the Argos, losing 19–3.

For the Eskimos, the 1987 season began on an ominous note when head coach Jackie Parker had to relinquish his position because of ulcers.

"Jackie Parker was a great coach," said Rod Connop. "I was so disappointed when he had to retire. When we won the Grey Cup that year [in 1987], Jackie didn't get enough credit. He put that team together."

Joe Faragalli had been at the helm of the Alouettes when they folded. GM Hugh Campbell wanted someone familiar with the Eskimo tradition, the community and the team's will to win, so he hired Faragalli as coach.

Under Faragalli, the 1987 Eskimos scored a league record of 617 points. Because of injuries, the team had to replace most of the secondary, and for much of the season, they had the worst pass defence in the league. But come playoff time, the new players had adjusted, and the Eskimos were tough. The Eskimos knocked off Calgary and BC to advance to the Grey Cup, once again played in Vancouver.

The first quarter of the 1987 Grey Cup was one of missed opportunities for the Argonauts. Kicker Lance Chomyc was wide on a field-goal attempt. Eskimo Henry "Gizmo" Williams returned it to his 22. Minutes later, Toronto lined up for another three-pointer. Again Chomyc missed the mark, and again Williams caught the ball, this time five yards behind his own goal line. He exploded out of the end zone and down the sideline to midfield. Williams then changed direction, crossed the field and raced down the other sideline to the end zone. His 115-yard touchdown run is still the longest return in Grey Cup history. Edmonton led 7–0.

Williams explained the play:

Most of the time, if there's less than five yards or they miss it to the far right or left, I bring it out. If they miss it deep, I usually down the ball. That time Chomyc missed it farther to the left, but I had enough time because the ball got down there pretty quickly. The first guy I had to get around was an offensive lineman, and once I got around him, there was a clear sideline. I could run it up there.

Was Gizmo faster than a speeding bullet? It seems a fair description according to lineman Dan Ferrone:

> *He slipped by me so fast I didn't even see it. We didn't think he was going to run it out. I think everybody just casually started walking away thinking he was going to give up the one point. Once he got started, he kept going.*
>
> *I remember him starting to go to the right side of the field—his right, my left—and I tried to pick an angle of pursuit. I should have intercepted him within 10 yards, and I missed him by 20. He just ran by and went pretty much untouched. I think it was partly a case of us forgetting who was back there catching the ball.*

No blocks were thrown on the runback because, according to Esk Danny Bass, "You don't want to take a chance on making a block because when you do, sometimes you'll clip a guy."

The Argos got on the scoreboard before the quarter ended when Chomyc finally split the uprights from 34 yards out. Rookie Eskimo kicker Jerry Kauric replied two minutes into the second stanza, giving his team a 10–3 lead.

Toronto struck back with a vengeance when quarterback Gilbert Renfroe hit rookie Gill Fenerty on a sensational 61-yard pass and run for a touchdown. Fenerty's TD tied the game at 10. A few minutes later, he scored again, set up by a Darnell Clash interception. Shortly after, Glen Kulka knocked the ball loose from Matt Dunigan, and Doug Landry picked it up and went 54 yards for a touchdown. Dunigan was done.

"It was a concussion," Dunigan recalled. "Kulka put a forearm across my chest and slammed me to the ground. When Glen hit me, there was no way that I could go out there and do the things I was required to do as a leader and a quarterback. Unlike getting your bell rung, you can't play through a concussion." He was replaced by Damon Allen.

With the first half nearly over, the Argos were firmly in command, leading 24–10 with Mr. Momentum wearing double blue. Unfortunately for the Argonauts, Lady Luck was dressed in green and gold.

Just before the half ended, rookie Argo Stanley Blair blocked a Hank Ilesic punt. Three plays later, Allen capped a 40-yard drive with a six-yard pass to Marco Cyncar in the end zone, halving the Argo lead.

Early in the third quarter, Edmonton cut the Argo lead to four on a Kauric field goal.

Turn-about being fair play, Argo quarterback Gilbert Renfroe was driven from the game with an injury. Both starting quarterbacks were out, the only time that has happened in Grey Cup history. Renfroe's replacement was Danny Barrett.

The only scoring later in the third quarter came on a 50-yard Lance Chomyc field goal and a Kauric single. This set up a wild and woolly final 15 minutes that saw the lead change five times.

First, Brian Kelly caught a touchdown pass, setting a still-standing mark for career Grey Cup TD receptions at five. Toronto regained the lead with a field goal. Damon Allen responded by leading the Eskimos 80 yards for a touchdown, which he scored on a 17-yard run. Barrett brought the

Feline Frenzy, 1983–88

James Zachary (left) and Dan Kearns of the Edmonton Eskimos in 1987 with the Grey Cup

Boatmen back to the enemy 25, from where he scampered to pay dirt. The two-point convert failed. The Argos led by a single point with 2:47 remaining in regulation time.

Tom Richards returned the Argo kickoff 16 yards to the Esks 21. Allen threw to Stephen Jones for 21 yards, and Milson Jones picked up 23 more on two plays, bringing the Esks to the Toronto 43. An incomplete pass and a three-yard run set the stage for Jerry Kauric to be the hero. He banged it through from 49 yards out with 23 seconds left on the clock. The Eskimos had won their 10th Grey Cup 38–36.

Before Matt Dunigan was knocked out of the game, he had been ineffective. The injury to the Edmonton quarterback was a break for the Eskimos. On the other hand, Gilbert

Renfroe was playing very well when he went down. Danny Barrett struggled the rest of the way.

So the injury to Renfroe hurt Toronto, and the injury to Dunigan helped Edmonton?

"Exactly," Argo coach Obie replied, "mainly because Damon was running the ball when they needed some key downs, and he hit some key screen passes to Milson Jones.

"Gilbert Renfroe was having a heckuva game for us, and then he got hurt early in the third quarter. Actually, our own guy fell on his knee. We then had a drop-off. When Danny Barrett came in, he didn't play all that badly, but Gilbert had such a hot hand, we were really clicking with him in there."

Grey Cup 1988

Going into 1988, both Matt Dunigan and Damon Allen were unsigned. Both wanted to start for Edmonton, and Dunigan wanted more money. BC needed a quarterback. Lion GM Joe Galat and Hugh Campbell pulled off a blockbuster trade.

BC sent receiver Jim Sandusky to the Eskimos for Dunigan. At the end of the season, the Lions would protect two players plus Dunigan. Edmonton could then choose anyone they wanted from the Lions roster. The Lions would then protect two more players and Edmonton would select again. The Esks chose linebackers Greg Stumon and Jeff Braswell, DB Andre Francis and running back Reggie Taylor. Part of the deal was BC's 1989 first-round draft choice, who turned out to be Leroy Blugh, an Eskimo stalwart for the next 11 years.

Edmonton got all the players, but BC got a trip to the 1988 Grey Cup. The Lions finished third, two points behind Edmonton and Saskatchewan. BC clobbered the Riders 42–18 and then upset the Eskimos 37–19. The Lions were coached by Larry Donovan, who had taken over in October 1987 when Joe Galat fired Don Matthews even though BC was just two points out of second place.

It was West versus West, with the Winnipeg Blue Bombers representing the Eastern Division.

Murphy's Law was in effect that year. The Bombers lost five All-Canadians, including quarterback Tom Clements and Willard Reaves. Murphy (Cal, that is) signed veteran Roy Dewalt only to find he had nothing left. Backup Tom Mueke got hurt just before the playoffs, leaving the team in the hands of quarterback Sean Salisbury.

Although the Bombers finished in second place, 10 points behind the Argos, they eliminated Hamilton 35–28 and then the Argos 27–11. Led by sophomore coach Mike Riley, the Blue Bombers were the underdogs.

The 1988 Grey Cup was played in Ottawa. Despite the usual fears, the weatherman was in a good mood that week, and the Bytowners staged a tremendous festival. The big day dawned sunny, warm and one of the windiest days in Grey Cup history. Although the team from windy Winnipeg handled the breeze better than BC, coaching mistakes proved to be the difference in the ball game.

The Bombers opened the game with a Bob Cameron single, set up by a 40-yard Sean Salisbury pass to James Murphy. Then, starting on his 35, BC's Matt Dunigan drove the distance in five plays, capped off by a Tony Cherry 14-yard run for the touchdown. Near the end of the opening quarter, Salisbury and James Murphy teamed up for a beautiful, dipsy-doodle 71-yard pass and run that brought the ball to the Lion six. Two incomplete passes later, Trevor Kennard kicked a 13-yard field goal.

Early in the second frame, Kennard tied the game with a 43-yarder. Dunigan came back, running the ball to the Bombers 36. After a 10-yard pick-up, Benny Thompson blitzed. Dunigan read it perfectly and hit David Williams in the end zone. Winnipeg tied it up, once again Salisbury to Murphy, 65 yards. Lui Passaglia responded with a single, sending the Lions to the dressing room with a 15–14 lead. So far, the wind hadn't been a factor.

BC's Anthony Drawhorn opened the second half with a long kickoff return. After a pass to Jan Carinci and a run by Scott Lecky, plus some facemask and roughing calls, BC was at the Bomber 10. Again, the defence held, and the Lions had to settle for a field goal.

Winnipeg couldn't move the ball, but Bob Cameron punted the Lions in deep. Two plays later, it was third-and-one on the BC 18. The Lions had the wind, enabling them to send the Bombers reeling toward their goal line. Instead, BC coach Larry Donovan called for a quarterback sneak.

The Big Blue stopped the Lions cold. "They were third down in their end of the field," said Winnipeg's Stan Mikawos. "That was the biggest turning point right there. If they had kicked it and maybe held us down in our end, it would have been a different game. But we stopped them, and at that point, momentum swung our way."

Matt Dunigan distanced himself from Donovan. "I don't think anybody in our huddle would have called that play."

Lion offensive coordinator Adam Rita agreed.

It was on the 18-yard line on the right hash with the wind behind us, third down and one-and-a-half. The head coach asked me what I wanted to do. I said, "Punt it."

Our defence was playing well. Winnipeg was minus 14 yards rushing and only had one first down. So all we had to do, really, was play field position and we would have had our chances. But, you know, it was his first year as a head coach in the CFL.

Still, the defence rose to the occasion, holding Winnipeg to a 21-yard field goal. Not much harm done. The Leos still led 18–17.

The next Lion drive stalled on the enemy 36. Willie Fears broke through and blocked the 43-yard field goal attempt. Shortly afterwards, missed opportunities continued when Rod Hill picked off Dunigan and returned it to the 26. All the Bombers could muster was a game-tying single when Kennard missed a 33-yard field goal.

The teams exchanged singles to close out the third quarter 19–19.

Both defences were magnificent throughout the final 15 minutes. With only 2:55 left in the game, Winnipeg was finally able to use the wind to their advantage.

Kennard kicked a 30-yard field goal set up by a short Passaglia punt and a no-yards penalty.

With Winnipeg ahead by three, the Lions started out at their 35. Tony Cherry swept around the end on an electrifying 52-yard run, bringing the ball to the Bomber 23. After an offside, Cherry ran to the 10, picked up a first down and then pushed through to the seven. The Lions, going into the wind, had gone 68 yards on the ground in three plays and were squarely in front of the goal posts. Passaglia waited to tie the game.

On the second down, Dunigan went back to pass. Although a receiver was wide open in the corner of the end zone, Dunigan was looking straight ahead. He released the ball. Linebacker Delbert Fowler deflected it up in the air. Defensive lineman Michael Gray made the interception. A few seconds later, the Bombers conceded a safety touch, and Winnipeg went on to win the Grey Cup by a score of 22–21.

Winnipeg had been the first team to win the Grey Cup for the West way back in 1935, and now they had just become the first Western team to win the Grey Cup for the East.

Dunigan explained his throw:

I had called a play called "54 Yankee." I had Jan Carinci coming over the middle. He was open, but the ball got tipped at the line of scrimmage and went about 30 feet up in the air. Michael Gray, of all people, caught it about six yards downfield. What he was doing six yards downfield was news to me, but he came up with the key interception.

If you look at the film, you'll see David Williams worked the defensive back so bad he made him fall down and was open in the corner of the end zone. But my read took me to Jan Carinci.

BC's Adam Rita made no apologies for the call.

What happened was Jan Carinci had come off the field at a time-out and said he could get open on the guy because he was playing so far outside. He could run a 54 Yankee across the field. And he was open, except we had blocked Delbert Fowler fairly well. He came up off the ground. Matt didn't see him because you see a lane and throw the ball. Fowler got up and tipped it, the ball was up in the air, and Michael Gray caught it. It was the right call, except Michael Gray makes a big play. Stuff happens.

The thing that disappointed me was that basically we got beat because we didn't make the right decision in the third quarter. The right decision was to punt. I had never heard of anybody going for it at a time when you have the wind at your back and it is just before the fourth quarter. That one baffled me.

Recalled Winnipeg GM Cal Murphy, "Salisbury completed two passes in the second half, but [Bob] Cameron just popped the ball the whole second half. Bob's kicking into the wind was the deciding factor in that football game."

Cameron recalled that great day in a distinguished career.

I was fortunate enough to win the Outstanding Canadian Award. That was an in credible win for our team because no one gave us much of a chance to win. Everything we needed to happen, did happen.

We needed a big wind. A windy day gave us the advantage because we had a good running game. We had a tough defence. Our offence usually just scored enough points to win. We had excellent special teams, and our coverage was phenomenal. Our net was around 40 yards a punt, which is really unheard of.

chapter eleven

The Greatest Grey Cup Ever, 1989

The Old Testament tells the story of how Joseph told the pharaoh the meaning of his dream, saying, in part: "Seven years of great abundance…will be followed by seven years of famine…when all the abundance in the land…will be forgotten" (Genesis 41:29–30).

Joseph was a piker—try 11 years of feast and famine. Children in Saskatchewan grew into adults wondering why their football team could never win. Little heads began to wonder, contrary to the bedtime stories they were told, whether Ron Lancaster, George Reed and the Big Bird from Turkey Neck Bend, Eagle Keys, ever existed.

The Roughriders in the Grey Cup? Finding the Holy Grail would have been easier.

First, the feast. From the 1966 season through to 1976, the Roughriders won more games than any team in the country—117 out of 176 for a winning percentage of .665.

They appeared in five Grey Cups, winning one. They garnered 48 All-Canadian selections, three Schenleys and one Coach of the Year Award. They appeared in the Western final 11 straight years. There are 11 Roughriders in the CFL Hall of Fame from that era.

Then a curse settled upon the land.

After one of the most incredible periods of success in Canadian football history, the Riders authored a new, likely never-to-be-broken record for futility, missing the playoffs 11 years in row. The Great Depression lasted only 10 years.

They went through seven head coaches and four general managers. Aggravating the situation was the fact that the worst economic downturn since the Dirty Thirties meant the good people of the Wheat Province had little money for football tickets. After the 1986 season, the team executive cleaned house, bringing in former Rider great and Interprovincial Pipe and Steel Company executive Bill Baker as general manager. He stayed only two years before becoming the fifth commissioner of the CFL.

Baker faced a gargantuan task. The team had sold only 12,756 season tickets for 1987 and was virtually bankrupt. Tired of losing, the faithful stayed away in droves. The first thing Baker did was convince the players to accept $700,000 in salary cuts. Then he hired Winnipeg offensive line coach John Gregory as head coach, who had never been a head coach at the professional level.

In 1987, the Riders won five games. They scored the fewest points, with all their quarterbacks combining for just

12 touchdowns. The defensive stats were almost as bad, but they were on the field most of the time.

Then, in 1988, the Riders finished tied for first place with Edmonton, each with marks of 11–7. The playoff drought was over. But they lost the semifinal 42–18 to the Lions in Regina.

Not since the days of Ron Lancaster had the Riders been as strong at quarterback. Sharing the duties were Kent Austin and Tom Burgess. A quarterback controversy is a given in Regina, and 1989 was no exception. Although Burgess had been getting more playing time, a lot of people thought Austin should be the starter. Coach Gregory disagreed. "Each has special things they do. I like Austin, I like Tommy. Both have areas to improve on. Whichever one makes the biggest improvement will be the quarterback."

Austin started the season against Calgary, played miserably and was replaced by Burgess, who brought the team back from a 14-point deficit with less than two minutes left to win 32–29.

Through the first third of the season, Burgess threw 19 touchdown passes. The Riders started off 4–1 but then lost four straight. On September 16, trailing Toronto 24–9 at the end of the third quarter, Gregory pulled Burgess and gave Austin another chance. Saskatchewan won 29–24. The following Sunday, Austin got his first start since opening day, leading the Green to a 48–35 win over Edmonton. He started the rest of his career in Saskatchewan.

The Roughriders closed out the regular season by losing in Edmonton 49–17. A quick exit from the playoffs seemed guaranteed.

But no. Beginning the most magical period in Saskatchewan Roughrider history, they went into Calgary and knocked off the Stampeders 33–26. The key play came on a second-and-long at the Stampeder 46. Austin ran a draw with little-used Canadian fullback Brian Walling. He ran the ball in for the winning touchdown.

Surely that would be it. Edmonton had just finished a record-setting season, 16–2. They had defeated the Roughriders twice during the regular season. The Esks were well rested and ready. But the Roughriders upset the mighty Eskimos 32–21.

So it was off to Toronto to play Hamilton for the Grey Cup christening of SkyDome. The Riders were the underdogs. The only team Saskatchewan couldn't beat during the season had been Hamilton. A dozen Ti-Cats from the 1986 Grey Cup win over Edmonton were still on the team in 1989. Coach Al Bruno said his Ti-Cats preferred to play Edmonton. Given the outcome, maybe Bruno knew something nobody else did.

Hamilton had beat Saskatchewan 34–17 on a stormy July night in Regina. On August 18 in Hamilton, they had won 46–40 with a blocked kick playing an important role. The losing quarterback in both cases was Tom Burgess.

Saskatchewan led the league in passing yardage and touchdown passes. The Ti-Cats were second in passing yardage and completions. Neither team had a good pass defence. Everything pointed to a shoot-out of epic proportions.

The Roughriders had a superb offensive line with Mike Anderson at centre (his father Paul played for the Riders in the 1950s), Bob Poley and Roger Aldag were the guards, and Vic Stevenson and Ken Moore the tackles. They faced Grover Covington, Mike Walker, Ronnie Glanton and Tim Lorenz. The Ti-Cat linebackers were Frank Robinson, Darrell Corbin and Pete Giftopoulos.

The Rider wide receivers were Don Narcisse and Mark Guy, and at slotback were Jeff Fairholm and Ray Elgaard. Tim McCray and Milson Jones were the backs, and Kent Austin was the quarterback. John Gregory explained why he chose Austin:

> I knew we were going to play Tommy Burgess against a blitzing team and Kent against a zone team. Hamilton was a zone team. They were in all kinds of different zones and coverages.
>
> A lot of people questioned me. In fact, they even had a pick-the-quarterback contest and everybody called in, which I was very upset about. My thought was with the guys on the field. They were a zone team, and I really felt Kent would give us the best chance to win. He played a great football game.

Austin would be attacking a Hamilton secondary comprised of Will Lewis, Stephen Jordan, Jim Rockford, Sonny Gordon and Lance Shields. They had a long afternoon.

Defensively, Saskatchewan's front four were Bobby Jurasin, Chuck Klingbeil, Gary Lewis and Vince Goldsmith. They faced centre Dale Sanderson, guards Jason Riley and

Darrell Harle and tackles Miles Gorrell and Mike Dirks. The Rider linebackers were Eddie Lowe, Dave Albright and Dan Rasovitch. The secondary of Steve Wiggins, Larry Hogue, Glen Suitor, Richie Hall and Harry Skipper would defend against wide-outs Wally Zatylny and Tony Champion, slot-backs Rocky DiPietro and Richard Estell, running backs Derrick McAdoo and Jed Tommy and quarterback Mike Kerrigan, the hero of Grey Cup '86.

Terry Baker and Dave Ridgway would do Saskatchewan's kicking, while it was Paul Osbaldiston for Hamilton.

On Hamilton's second possession on Grey Cup day, they moved from their 54 to the 35 and kicked a 42-yard field goal. Four plays later, Austin's pass was deflected into the arms of Frank Robinson. The Cats kicked their second three-pointer to lead 6–0. Saskatchewan replied with a single.

Hamilton scrimmaged at the 35. Offside Saskatchewan moved the ball to the 40. McAdoo picked up the first down. Kerrigan hit Winfield for 15 and 19. At the Rider 28, Kerrigan threw to Estell for 15. Then it was into the end zone for Tony Champion. Hamilton led 13–1 at the end of the quarter. Kent Austin wasn't worried.

"No. I just felt we had a good offence; we certainly had enough weapons to put points on the board. Offensive football in the Canadian league is very much a matter of tempo. The sporadic start didn't allow us to get into a groove. Once we put a couple of first downs together, we ended up having an unbelievable second quarter."

The fun began on Saskatchewan's second possession. Starting at their 48, Austin hit Jeff Fairholm for 22 yards.

Testing the secondary, Austin missed on a long bomb to the end zone but then connected with Ray Elgaard for 16. After an incompletion at the 24, it was a strike to Don Narcisse to the five. Elgaard then caught one for a touchdown. Hamilton 13, Saskatchewan 8.

After taking the Rider kickoff to their 53, Kerrigan picked up a first down to Estell. He completed a pass to DiPietro at the 30 and then to McAdoo for the touchdown. Hamilton 20, Saskatchewan 8.

The Riders were not to be outdone. With first down at their 35, Austin dropped back to pass and found Jeff Fairholm streaking down the left side. At the moment Fairholm caught the ball, a flag came down, but the second-year slotback broke through the interference and ran 75 yards for the touchdown. Hamilton 20, Saskatchewan 15. That was the signature play of the 1989 Grey Cup.

Fairholm was a study in concentration. "On that catch I made for the touchdown, I didn't even know I had been interfered with. I didn't even know the guy was on my back. I just caught the ball, ran for a touchdown, looked back and saw the flag and thought, 'Oh, my God, somebody held.' I had no idea that the guy was all over my back until I saw the film the next day."

"We caught them in a man-to-man situation," explained Austin.

> The safety was really cheating with my eyes. We picked that up in the first quarter. We just sent Jeff on a streak route, and I looked the safety back to the field, and Jeff got behind his man.

Really, the only chance he had was to kind of pull Jeff down. He got an interference call on it, but Jeff still pulled away from him and caught the ball and went 75 yards. The ball came over his outside shoulder, and he kind of looked back. It was a tough catch.

Hamilton was not impressed. With two strikes of 9 and 15 yards to Tony Champion, five runs for 37 yards by McAdoo and an 11-yard completion to DiPietro, Kerrigan marched his team 71 yards for a touchdown. Hamilton 27, Saskatchewan 15.

So what, said Saskatchewan. Three passes to James Ellingson, plus strikes to Narcisse and Elgaard brought the Riders to the five, where Austin found Narcisse alone in the end zone. At halftime, it was Hamilton 27, Saskatchewan 22.

Saskatchewan had launched an all-out aerial attack in the second quarter. Austin was 11-for-16 and had three touchdowns in the second quarter. He went exclusively to the air "because we got down, and Hamilton kept scoring. We didn't run the ball one time in the second quarter. We couldn't afford to. We had to keep scoring to keep pace with those guys and stay in the game. We got on a roll with the passing game in the second quarter, and we didn't get away from it."

In the third quarter, the teams traded field goals on their first possessions. At the 10-minute mark, Terry Baker pinned Hamilton at their three-yard line with a thunderous punt. Three plays later, Osbaldiston conceded a safety touch.

The Greatest Grey Cup Ever, 1989

After the ensuing kickoff, Saskatchewan scrimmaged at their 33. After a two-yard gain by Tim McCray, Austin hooked up with Narcisse on a 47-yarder to the Hamilton 28. The Cats took an interference call on the next play, and McCray crashed over from the one.

At the end of the third, the Roughriders had their first lead of the game, 34–30. Just over a minute later, Dave Ridgway kicked a 25-yard field goal for Saskatchewan. Starting at the 35, Kerrigan fired a pass upfield but was picked off by Glen Suitor at the Ti-Cat 51. Austin drove the Riders toward the Hamilton goal line where an interception was thrown by Ray Elgaard.

"We ran a reverse pass," said coach Gregory. "It was a run-pass option. He should have run. The thing that was too bad is we probably could have gotten a field goal out of it."

Added Austin, "That was right after we got an interception by Suitor. We were up by seven and in scoring range, so that was a big turnaround for Hamilton because had we gone in to score, we may have pulled away from them."

The teams twice exchanged punts. At the 8:39 mark, Osbaldiston kicked a 47-yard field goal to close the gap to four. Ten plays later, Ridgway replied with a 20-yarder of his own, making the score 40–33 Saskatchewan with 1:58 left in regulation time. Austin thought that drive was critical. "It helped us maintain the atmosphere and the tempo. It helped show Hamilton that they were going to have to keep scoring to stay with us."

Can do, said Kerrigan. Starting at the 35, he threw to Lee Knight for 18 and DiPietro for 9. McAdoo ran for six. After an incompletion, Saskatchewan was called for interference at

The Saskatchewan Roughriders celebrating with the Grey Cup

their 11. McAdoo for two, an incomplete pass. With third-and-eight, Kerrigan threw to the right side of the end zone. Tony Champion made a dazzling over-the-shoulder catch while falling backwards to the turf. The convert was good. With 44 seconds left, it was tied 40–40.

Saskatchewan ran the kickoff back to the 36. There was no thought of playing conservatively, hoping to win in overtime. For once, in the last minute of a Grey Cup, the Riders attacked.

"When Kent went out there," recalled Gregory, "we said use the clock wisely—which he always did—they're probably going to play zone, so read the coverage and hit the spots. That's exactly what he did."

Said Kent Austin:

On the first play of that drive, I went to Narcisse on a stop-and-go and overthrew everybody, but that was really more to send a signal to Hamilton that they weren't going to squat on a route. There were three more passes. Elgaard caught one, Guy, two.

I didn't feel like they could stop us. That was plenty of time to get into scoring range for the best kicker I ever played with. I knew if we got it close, Dave would make it. We actually drove it down there into pretty decent range for him. It was a pretty easy kick for him. [He laughed.] *Although in that type of pressure situation, no kick is easy.*

But Ray Elgaard made a big second-down catch on the sidelines that kept the drive alive, and then Mark Guy came through with a big catch. On the first one over the middle, he took a good hit from the safety and held on to the ball.

With the ball on the Hamilton 26, Austin went down on one knee to stop the clock. The teams exchanged timeouts. Then at 14:58 of the fourth quarter, before 54,088 anxious fans, the greatest moment in the history of Saskatchewan sports took place—the kick.

The snap was back. Suitor put the ball down as Ridgway moved toward it. For a split second, the great domed stadium was silent. Then, as the ball flew toward the goal posts, the roar grew louder. When the ball split the uprights, all

Saskatchewan fans were immediately on cloud nine. *Wow! We did it! We won!*

But two seconds remained on the clock. Ridgway kicked off. Steve Jackson punted it back down the field to Glen Suitor, who ran it out of bounds. The greatest Grey Cup of them all was over. Final score: Saskatchewan 43, Hamilton 40.

Dave Ridgway talked about the kick:

There's no doubt there was a tremendous amount of pressure. I was totally oblivious to the meaning of what that kick was until after the fact, and then I sat down and said, "Holy Cow! That was a big kick!" It was an afterthought.

When we got out there, there were two timeouts, and I asked my holder Glen Suitor to talk to me about something other than football. He got me laughing, and before I knew it, it was time to attempt the kick. I get a strange kick out of doing it. I like walking on the field in that situation, and I expect to make it.

Still, I would rather that game hadn't come down to a field goal because that's an awful lot of pressure on one person's shoulders to come back to the province here. It was the deciding factor. I just don't see living in this province if I had missed in that situation.

Kent Austin was sensational, completing 26 of 41 throws for 474 yards and three touchdowns, winning him the Grey Cup MVP Award.

Mike Kerrigan wasn't exactly a shabby Tabby, completing 23 of 35 passes for 303 yards and three touchdowns.

Saskatchewan always livens up a Grey Cup. The record SkyDome crowd rocked and rolled for an hour before game time and until well after the last Roughrider left the field. At one hotel, the caped crusader—known as the Torch or the Flame—with gunpowder on his helmet strode through the lobby with his minions in tow. At another inn, a wandering band of musicians spotted Ron Lancaster and George Reed and played a rousing chorus of "On Roughriders."

Coach John Gregory reminisced:

The thing I always appreciated about the players in Saskatchewan, they played hard. A lot of times I think we played over our heads. It was really a good group of people.

The fan support was great. After we won the Grey Cup, that was fun. I was really proud for the Saskatchewan people who supported that team so strongly. It was interesting how it affected everybody from the farmers to the meat cutters to the presidents of banks.

Indeed. After 10 years of depression, low wheat prices, rural depopulation, crop failures and losing football teams, winning the Grey Cup was just what a beleaguered people needed to enter the last decade of the century with confidence. The Roughriders' 23-year Grey Cup drought was over.

chapter twelve

Yankee Doodle Dandy, 1990–97

The decade of the 1990s was dominated by American expansion and the rise of the Calgary Stampeders and their star quarterback Doug Flutie. Interspersed in there was a three-ring circus for the 1991 Grey Cup in Toronto and a heroic defence of our nation's honour in Vancouver.

Neither Hamilton nor Saskatchewan made it back to the Grey Cup in 1990. Wally Buono, in his first year as a head coach, brought the Calgary Stampeders home first with a record of 11–6–1. Edmonton was second at 10–8. After avenging their 1989 playoff loss by beating Saskatchewan 43–27, Tracy Ham's crew from Edmonton thumped the upstarts from the south 43–23 in the Western final.

In 1989, the Blue Bombers had slipped to 7–11, causing coach Cal Murphy to retool. There were eight new faces on defence, seven on offence, including three receivers, the entire backfield and one lineman. The most important change for

Winnipeg was Tom Burgess coming over from Saskatchewan to quarterback, replacing Sean Salisbury who left for the NFL.

Winnipeg finished atop their division with a record of 12–6. They overcame a stubborn Toronto team to advance to the 1990 Grey Cup at BC Place, where they handed the favoured Eskimos their worst drubbing in Grey Cup history.

Grey Cup 1990

The star of the Grey Cup in 1990 was Blue Bomber linebacker Greg Battle.

On their opening drive, Tracy Ham marched the Eskimos to the Winnipeg 20-yard line. Then Battle intercepted Ham in the end zone and returned it to the Edmonton 43. Moments later, Trevor Kennard kicked a 13-yard field goal.

Recalled Battle:

> *I could see Tracy Ham, but I know he couldn't see me because generally you don't have a deep player coming from where I was coming from. The coaching staff came up with that scheme where we brought down the safety. If the quarterback is reading properly, when the safety disappears, you throw into the middle. But I showed up. If Ham had had a clear throwing lane, he probably wouldn't have thrown it because he would have seen me.*

Winnipeg added to their lead when, after recovering a fumble, Burgess drove down to the 11. From there, he found Lee Hull in the end zone. Winnipeg 10, Edmonton 0.

Esks kicker Ray Macoritti made it 10–4 at the half on a single and a field goal.

In the third quarter, deep in Edmonton's own end, Ham went back to pass to Michael Soles. Again, Battle picked it off and this time ran 32 yards for a touchdown. The Bombers scored 28 points in the third quarter—still a Grey Cup record—and added 12 in the fourth. Edmonton's only TD came when Larry Willis took a 20-yard pass from Ham. Final score: Winnipeg 50, Edmonton 11.

It was Greg Battle's finest hour in his finest season. He won the CFL's Most Outstanding Defensive Player Award that year and was named Outstanding Defensive Player in the Grey Cup.

"In my football career, nothing will ever top that Grey Cup week," Battle exulted. "Not only the awards but having my granddad and my wife there to share everything with me. Everything was perfect. Playing the game was almost secondary."

Grey Cup 1991: Three-ring Circus

In 1989, the Toronto Argonauts fell to 7–11, and coach Bob O'Billovich was fired. His replacement was Don Matthews, who brought the team to second place and on the verge of a long run of success. He had acquired Matt Dunigan from the Lions, and Ralph Sazio had signed running back Michael "Pinball" Clemons.

Clemons was so good that he became the CFL's all-time combined yardage leader with 25,385 yards, a mark he still holds. No player is even within striking distance.

The five-foot-six 170-pound phenom was named the 1990 CFL Outstanding Player.

There was bad news for Toronto, though. Because of a disagreement with GM Mike McCarthy, Don Matthews resigned, replaced by Adam Rita.

The Canadian football world was delighted when it was announced in February 1991 that Bruce McNall, Wayne Gretzky and John Candy had bought the team. Newspaper coverage of the Argos moved from the lingerie ads to the front page overnight.

The new owners possessed star power, deep pockets and a deft marketing touch. Movie star John Candy toured all the CFL training camps to promote the league and accompanied the Argos on most of their road trips. His sideline presence sold thousands of tickets in every stadium in the league.

Understanding Toronto's hunger for big-league status, the ownership triumvirate signed the NFL's projected top draft pick, Notre Dame star Raghib "Rocket" Ismail, to a contract estimated between $18 million and $26 million.

The audacious signing of the Fighting Irish star sent a message to Torontonians that the man who brought the greatest hockey player in the world to Los Angeles was dead serious about his ownership of the Argos and that the people of Toronto could regard their team as major league.

When the Argos opened their 1991 rookie training camp, a large tent was erected for a press conference with Gretzky, Candy, McNall and Ismail. The setting was appropriate to kick off a year-long three-ring circus.

Over 41,000 fans turned up at SkyDome on July 18 to see a glittering array of Hollywood personalities and the "launching" of the Rocket. Ismail didn't disappoint, with 213 yards overall as Toronto won their home opener over Hamilton 41–18. The Argos didn't taste defeat under the Dome until over a year later.

The 1991 edition of the Argos finished first with a record of 13–5, despite the fact that quarterback Matt Dunigan went down early in the first quarter of the home opener and missed 10 games. He returned to lead his team to a 34–25 win over the Lions on August 27. On September 15 in Calgary, Dunigan was injured again, breaking his collarbone in several places. Michael Clemons missed seven games.

But the Rocket Man picked up 3049 all-purpose yards, third highest total in CFL history, including 1300 yards on 64 receptions. He made All-Canadian but lost the Outstanding Rookie Award to BC's Jon Volpe, who picked up 1077 fewer yards. Maybe the voters punished Ismail for his indifference to the press.

Dunigan returned for the last game of the regular season. During the course of a 42–3 romp over the Blue Bombers in the Conference final, he reinjured his collar bone. During Grey Cup week in Winnipeg, his arm in a sling, it looked for certain that he would be watching the 79th Grey Cup from the sidelines.

Not so. The day before the game, the rumour mill had Dunigan working out in a hotel ballroom.

"Oh, yes," he confirmed. "I had my shoulder shot up to see if I could throw a football. They wanted to see if I could do what they said they were going to do the next day. They shot it up with the medication and gave me a few minutes, and I was throwing the rock to Mike McCarthy. We were trying to get it right. I said, 'Hey, this is pretty good.' That's what happened."

Dunigan described the night before a Grey Cup game.

You have trouble sleeping before any game, but particularly the Grey Cup. You never get over that. That's part of it. The anxiety, the adrenalin, the anticipation, the getting ready for the contact and the physical abuse, the mental warfare, being prepared.

It is constant trials, physical and mental struggles of everybody. It comes down to one game. How do you sleep the night before something like that? You know you've got to bring it off and make it work, not only yourself but 36 guys alongside you as well as everyone in the organization with millions of people watching you. It's crazy. Hell, I mean nobody's going to sleep right.

November 24, 1991, was the first time the Grey Cup had been played in Winnipeg. When the Bombers were awarded the game, purveyors of doom and gloom made dire predictions about the weather. Unfortunately, they were correct.

It was the coldest Grey Cup ever played. The temperature at game time was −19°C, and with the windchill factored in, it was about −30°C. Despite the conditions, the week was a huge success, with Winnipeggers taking to heart the exhortation of their mayor to personally make all visitors feel welcome. They had a wonderful time.

The game itself would be a Rocket-propelled 747 against the Little Engine That Could, the Hollywood All-Stars versus the No-name Nobodies. Toronto versus Calgary. The oddsmakers gave the Argos the edge.

The Stampeders hadn't appeared in a Grey Cup since their 1971 win over Toronto. It would be Calgary's outstanding six-pack receiving corps of Allan Pitts, Carl Bland, Shawn Beals, Pee Wee Smith, Dave Sapunjis and Derrick Crawford against a strong Toronto secondary featuring Reggie Pleasant, Carl Brazely, Dave Bovell, Don Wilson and Ed Berry.

The Argos had great speed offensively with Dave Williams and Rocket Ismail the wide-outs and Paul Masotti and D.K. Smith in the slots. Both teams liked to throw to their running back, Keyvan Jenkins for the Stampeders and Pinball Clemons for the Argos.

The Stamps were led by Danny Barrett, unspectacular but steady. His passing totals were average except for one remarkable statistic—he had thrown only five interceptions all year.

One of the oldest clichés of sports is, "The team that makes the fewest mistakes will win." Throughout the season, Calgary was the team that made the least mistakes with 18 fewer turnovers than Toronto. Come game time, however, all of that meant nothing.

Toronto had the first possession at their own 37. Dunigan threw two incompletions; Hank Ilesic punted.

On Calgary's very first play at their 44, Danny Barrett was picked off by Ed Berry who returned the ball 51 yards for a touchdown. "I can't remember the last time I threw an interception for a touchdown," moaned the disconsolate Stampeder quarterback. Just over a minute into the game, it was Toronto 7, Calgary 0.

Stampeder receiver Dave Sapunjis explained what happened. "Danny was a little nervous and threw a bad ball, and the receiver didn't do anything to knock it down."

Return man Pee Wee Smith also had the jitters, fumbling the ensuing kickoff at the 30-yard line. Kevin Smellie was held to no gain, and Dunigan overthrew his receiver. Lance Chomyc's field-goal attempt went wide for a single.

Two plays later, Barrett was sacked by Brian Warren.

Sapunjis described the mood at the Calgary bench. "You are quickly humbled. It is obviously discouraging when you go out in a big game and you don't start off well. So we had to kind of gather our thoughts, calm each other down and go out and start doing what we had to do—start to play a little better."

The Stamps started at their 33. On first down, Barrett threw to Sapunjis for 11 yards, Calgary's first gain of the ball game. Nine plays later, Barrett plunged over from the one. The play had been set up by an end-zone interference call on Carl Brazely.

In the second quarter, the teams traded field goals, making the score at the half, Toronto 11, Calgary 10.

The Rocket opened the third quarter with a blazing 43-yard kickoff return, giving the Argos the ball at the enemy 35. Completions to D.K. Smith and David Williams brought the ball to the 22, but Dunigan went incomplete and then was hit by Will Johnson.

"I hit Dunigan a couple of times. That one time I hit him, he coughed the ball into the air, and Tim Cofield caught it and got a few yards before an offensive lineman grabbed him."

The Stamps drove to the Argo 35, where Mark McLoughlin scored a single on a 42-yard field-goal attempt to tie the game. Four minutes later, McLoughlin connected from 27 yards to put Calgary into the lead for the first and last time, 14–11.

The name of the game in football is field position. For most of the game, Toronto had it. Their advantage in field position was attributable to the marvellous performance of the Rocket as well as the abysmal performance of Calgary punter Jerry Kauric, the worst in modern Grey Cup history. Kauric's average was 28 yards, his net punting average 19 yards. Of all the injuries the Stampeders suffered during the season, perhaps the most damaging in the final analysis was the one to punter Brent Matich in October. Matich ranked third with a 42.7 average. Hank Ilesic was first at 44.4. Late in the third quarter, Kauric kicked from his 38-yard line. Toronto scrimmaged from the Calgary 48 without benefit of a return. On the next play, Dunigan threw to Smith for a touchdown.

On the opening play of the fourth quarter, Barrett was intercepted a second time by Reggie Pleasant at the Stampeder 40-yard line. He returned it to the 12. Again the defence came up big and forced the Argos to settle for a field goal. Toronto 22, Calgary 14.

On the next possession, Kauric got away a good punt, pinning the Argos at their six-yard line. After going incomplete, Dunigan ran for eight, and Ilesic got off probably the worst punt of his postseason career, 16 yards. Starting at the 31, Barrett hit Sapunjis for 18 yards. He then isolated Allan Pitts on Carl Brazely and threw to him for a touchdown. The Stampeders trailed by one, but Mr. Momentum seemed to be on their side.

Not for long. In 58 seconds, it was over.

Mark McLoughlin kicked off to Rocket Ismail, who streaked 87 yards to the end zone. Toronto was ahead by eight points with 10:26 remaining, hardly an insurmountable lead. But then Keyvan Jenkins allowed the kickoff to bounce off his foot, and Keith Castello recovered his second fumble of the game at the 36. Two plays later, Dunigan hit Paul Masotti in the end zone for a touchdown. At the 5:19 mark of the final frame, the scoreboard read Toronto 36, Calgary 21.

The Stampeders had a chance to get back in the game when they marched from their 31 to the Argo two-yard line. Instead of running, Calgary chose to throw. The first was incomplete, Barrett was sacked for a nine-yard loss on the second, and the third-down gamble failed.

"I looked the wrong way, and by the time I saw my receiver, it was too late," Barrett lamented. "That series hurt us more than anything else. When I got sacked, that probably cost us the ball game."

All-Canadian defensive end Will Johnson questioned the strategy. "With two yards to go, I'd have run a sweep or a quarterback sneak or quick-hitting dive play."

The Argos won their 12th Grey Cup 36–21.

"We lost because of special teams," argued Sapunjis.

Rocket's touchdown sort of put us away. When you get beaten so badly on special teams, it starts to drain you on both sides of the ball. Your offence and defence are ready to go out, and then they return the ball for 70 yards. You start off poorly, you do some things fairly well. As the game goes on, you start to get your confidence back, and all of a sudden a guy like Rocket returns it all the way. Our emotions just drop, and we lose our energy.

The cold was a factor in the game.

"It was minus 19 that day," said Dunigan. "Regardless of whether you are hurt or not, those are difficult conditions to play in. The ball is certainly a lot harder. There's no give. It's like throwing or catching a brick. There's no feel for it. It's a difficult situation to play in.

"But what makes the CFL so grand, so unique, are the conditions football is played in year in and year out. It gives it a lot of colour."

Grey Cup 1992: Doug Flutie

In Wally Buono's first year as head coach in 1990, Calgary lost to Edmonton in the final. In 1991, the Stampeders beat the Eskimos in the playoffs but lost the Grey Cup. Looking ahead to 1992, Buono wanted his team to turn it up a notch and take that final step.

The key to taking the final step was Doug Flutie.

After playing in the United States Football League (USFL) with Donald Trump's New Jersey Generals and backing up with the NFL Chicago Bears and New England Patriots, former Heisman Trophy winner Flutie headed to BC, signing a contract with Murray Pezim, the flamboyant owner of the Lions. When Pezim couldn't afford to keep Flutie, fellow snake-oil salesman Larry Ryckman, the owner of the Stampeders at that time, signed Flutie to a personal services contract worth over $1 million.

Ryckman then traded Danny Barrett to BC for Rocco Romano, the rights to Jamie Crysdale and $250,000 in stocks. Ryckman claimed the stocks were delivered late and were worth only $30,000. Pezim said that's the way it goes; a deal's a deal—sometimes the value of stocks goes down. Ryckman wasn't satisfied and threatened to boycott Calgary's game at BC on July 23. Pezim called Ryckman a chicken and had 10,000 rubber "Chicken Ryckmans" made for distribution to the Lion faithful. Calgary won the game 37–19.

Doug Flutie was the dominant player of the decade, winning the CFL's Most Outstanding Player Award six of the seven years he played in Canada, with the exception of 1995 when he missed a third of the season because of injuries.

He was an All-Canadian quarterback six times. He led the league in passing five times. He ranks sixth all-time in passing and still holds the records for most touchdown passes in a season (48) set in 1994, and yards in a season (6619) set with BC in 1991. He rushed for 4660 yards during his Canadian career. Flutie appeared in four Grey Cups, winning three. He holds the record for highest percentage completion (78.9) in the 1997 Grey Cup, and is second in five other categories. When TSN picked their Top 50 CFLers of all time in 2006, Flutie was voted number one.

The Stampeders started the 1992 season with four wins in a row. Flutie, hailed as the conquering hero, was typically modest. "I've been on a roll," he allowed, "and the media and fans think it is all the quarterback, and it's not. You're dependent on the people in front of you. If you don't have time to throw the ball, you can't get it done. If you don't have guys working to get open and catching the ball, you still don't get it done. There is too much emphasis on the quarterback. It takes 12 men to win."

Flutie and receiver Allan Pitts were made for each other. Pitts recalled in 1994:

> We were watching film the other day, and a situation came up where I was running a route, and me and Doug just clicked on that particular play. Normally I would have kept on going to the outside, but I stayed inside, and he was with me all the way, and we were able to connect. I had a sixth sense where to go, and it worked out because the quarterback was on the same page with me.
>
> What Doug brings is the creativity which opens up other opportunities. With the type of mobility he has, we are able to do more things offensively.

The two players formed a mutual admiration society. "[Pitts] was a big, physical presence," said Flutie. "Great movements. Great body position. Ran great routes. All the tools. I've never seen a player dominate a game the way Al could. When we were rolling, we'd walk the ball down the field. Second-and-10, second-and-15, third-and-a-bunch, the idea was 'Get Al the ball.' I trusted him to make the play."

After their fast start, Calgary split the next eight before finishing with seven straight wins and a final mark of 13–5, good for first place. The Eskimos scraped by Saskatchewan in the semifinal and headed for Calgary and a third consecutive Western final.

As usual, it was a thriller, a marvellous duel between two great quarterbacks. With 1:30 left, the visitors were leading 22–16. Flutie then marched his Stampeders to the three-yard line via strikes to Sapunjis and Pitts. With precious seconds ticking away, Flutie audibled to tackle Ken Moore and slipped, minus a shoe, into the end zone behind him. Shoeless Doug Flutie had found a way to win. The final score was 23–22. After the game, the former All-American said the comeback was his greatest moment in football, even greater than the play that made him famous, the "Hail Mary" touchdown pass that beat Miami 47–45 when Flutie played for Boston College.

The year earlier, Calgary couldn't beat Toronto in Winnipeg. Maybe they could beat Winnipeg in Toronto. At least the weather wasn't a problem for the 1992 Grey Cup.

All the attention was on the offence. Allan Pitts led the league for the second straight season, catching 103 for 1591 yards and 13 touchdowns, the first Stampeder receiver since Herm Harrison to have three consecutive 1000-yard seasons. Dave Sapunjis caught 72 passes for 1317 yards, and Carl Bland picked up 1052 yards on 72 receptions. Derrick Crawford and Pee Wee Smith were both effective.

Flutie wasn't the only newcomer to the 1992 Stampeders. Rocco Romano came back to Calgary from BC as part of the Danny Barrett deal and soon blossomed into an All-Star. The anchor of the line was 10-year veteran Ken Moore. He proved invaluable in mentoring Calgary's first-round draft pick, Bruce Covernton, the rookie at left tackle. The six-foot-five, 294-pound newcomer learned his lessons so well that he won the league's top honour in that category.

It takes coaching courage to replace most of your offensive line when you have a team that made it to the Grey Cup. Often overlooked with this array of offensive power was the fact that Calgary's defence led the league in most categories.

The Stampeders faced a Blue Bomber team that had overcome significant adversity. They lost their coach and general manager when Cal Murphy entered the hospital at the University of Western Ontario in London for a heart transplant and wasn't fit to run the team any longer. Urban Bowman took over the reins at age 55, his first head coaching opportunity. QB Matt Dunigan started 13 games, with Sammy Garza and Danny McManus handling the rest. Dunigan was at the helm when Winnipeg crushed Hamilton 59–11 in the Eastern final.

After Toronto won the Cup in 1991, Argo GM Mike McCarthy would only renew Matt Dunigan's contract on a per-game basis because of his injury history. In 1990, Dunigan only played eight games, the same in 1991. Dunigan refused McCarthy's offer and signed with Winnipeg. He made it through the entire 1992 season, as well as the first 16 games in 1993.

The Bomber's main weapon was rookie running back Michael Richardson who gained 1123 yards. Calgary's weakness was defending against the run, but Winnipeg's was stopping the pass. If Calgary could jump into an early 10-point lead, they would force Winnipeg out of the running game and render the Bomber defence less effective by making it play cautiously.

That is exactly what happened. Calgary scored on four of their first five possessions, making Matt Dunigan put the ball in the air. Richardson picked up only 21 yards in the first half, 27 overall. Winnipeg ran only once in the second half.

The Stampeders took an early lead when Mark McLoughlin kicked a 37-yard field goal. Four minutes later, he picked up a single on a missed field-goal try. Four minutes after that, Flutie finished a touchdown drive with a 35-yard pass to Dave Sapunjis. McLoughlin kicked two 17-yard field goals in the second quarter to give Calgary a 17–0 lead at the half.

The third quarter was scoreless, a tribute to outstanding defence by both teams. At 2:36 of the fourth, Flutie completed a 15-yard pass to Pitts for a touchdown. "It was called a 144X-Smash," Pitts explained. "I'm the receiver, and that's a corner route by me. They were in man coverage that play. I just beat the guy, and Doug did a real good job of putting the ball in a very good spot."

With 6:37 left in the game, Winnipeg finally got on the scoreboard when Troy Westwood kicked a 46-yard field goal. Four minutes later, Gerald Alphin scored the Bombers' only touchdown. Final score: Calgary 24, Winnipeg 10. The Stampeders had won their third Grey Cup.

Flutie was Most Outstanding Player of the game. He completed 15 of his first 20 passes and 17 of 25 by the half. He finished the game with 33 out of 49 for 480 yards and two touchdown passes, the second best performance in Grey Cup history. Dave Sapunjis was again the Canadian player of the game with seven receptions for 85 yards and a touchdown. Honourable mention should have gone to Derrick Crawford, who caught six passes for 162 yards. It was his finest hour in a Stampeder uniform.

The 24–10 score flattered Winnipeg. "We moved the ball a whole lot, yes," agreed Pitts, "but we didn't finish off drives like we should have."

A healing Cal Murphy took it all in stride. When it was suggested that Calgary dominated on both sides of the ball, he laughed. "You're being kind. We were never in it. It was Flutie, Flutie and more Flutie."

Flutie was spectacular; Dunigan was not.

"Dunigan didn't have a good day," said Sapunjis. "You know what? They did not have good coaching that game. They were playing linebackers on guys like me, and we're going to beat them every time."

Bomber Greg Battle agreed. "Their scheme was such that we were put in bad situations. Several times I had to go and cover Derrick Crawford. That's definitely a mismatch. Now, if Flutie was running the ball up the middle, that would be my forte, and I'd have the advantage. They were running a package that caught us off guard, and we didn't make any adjustments."

Dunigan did not question Urban Bowman's game plan. "We had opportunities early, but we were just missing. You hear often that football is a game of inches. In that game, I believe it was. We were maybe an inch away offensively from making it happen. A receiver would stumble or let up. We did not make the plays. Calgary did, so you take your hat off to them and move on."

That Grey Cup was the apex of Doug Flutie's Calgary career. He wouldn't win another wearing red and white.

Grey Cup 1993

Uppermost in coach Wally Buono's mind preparing for the 1993 season was the fact that the Grey Cup would be played in Calgary.

The Stampeders came out of the starting gate like Secretariat, winning 10 in a row. Their winning streak ended at Commonwealth Stadium in Edmonton on September 10, with a 29–16 loss to the Eskies. Allan Pitts, running back Keyvan Jenkins and cornerback Junior Thurman sustained season-ending injuries that game.

The Stamps responded to adversity by winning their next four straight and five of the remaining seven to finish first with a mark of 15–3. Calgary was undefeated at home. They didn't lose a regular-season game at McMahon Stadium until August 18, 1995.

The top four Western teams made the playoffs in 1993. Calgary beat BC 17–9, while Edmonton destroyed Saskatchewan 51–13. The Alberta rivals prepared to meet in the final for the fourth year in a row.

The few days leading up the game were bitterly cold and blizzard-like. Long-time observers couldn't remember more daunting weather for a Western final. The artificial turf was sorely tested.

The Stamps started in dramatic fashion with Pee Wee Smith returning a punt 64 yards for a touchdown three minutes into the opening quarter. Mark McLoughlin added a field goal to give Calgary a 10–0 lead after one quarter of play. In the second frame, Edmonton scored on a 73-yard pass from Damon Allen to Jim Sandusky plus a single. McLoughlin replied with another field goal. Calgary led 13–8 at the half.

Halftime was extended to allow the stadium crew to clear the snow off the field. That seemed to be all Edmonton needed. Damon Allen completed TD passes to Sandusky, Eddie Brown and Jay Christensen while holding Calgary to a safety, winning 29–15. Flutie left the game in the fourth quarter complaining about cold hands. Losing the right to defend their title in their stadium to their arch-enemy was a bitter pill to swallow for Calgary. The Eskimos took great delight in occupying the Stampeders' dressing room for the Grey Cup.

Because of dissension and discipline problems, Hugh Campbell had fired Joe Faragalli after the 1990 season. He then turned to his old Saskatchewan battery mate Ron Lancaster to clean up the team's act and restore Edmonton's reputation as a class organization.

Lancaster finished first in 1991 and second in '92. In preparation for the 1993 season, Campbell and Lancaster had done a massive overhaul, making the biggest trade in CFL history by swapping a total of 16 players with Toronto.

Edmonton got QB Rickey Foggie; receivers Darrell K. Smith, Eddie Brown and J.P. Izquierdo; DBs Don Wilson and Ed Berry; linebacker Bruce Dickson and defensive lineman Len Johnson. Toronto received QB Tracy Ham; receiver Craig Ellis and Ken Winery; DBs Enis Jackson and Travis Oliver; LB John Davis, RB Chris Johnstone and defensive lineman Cam Brousseau. The deal was done on January 28, 1993.

The next month, Edmonton traded LB DeWayne Odum, QB Dechane Cameron and a draft choice to Hamilton for QB Damon Allen.

All did not go well, largely because anytime Foggie or Allen faltered, Lancaster gave them the hook. On September 26, 1993, Edmonton was clobbered at home 52–14 by Winnipeg to drop them into fourth place with a record of 7–6. A frustrated Allen went to Lancaster and asked for the ball to be put in his hands. The coach agreed.

"After we lost to Winnipeg," said Lancaster, "we said the heck with it, Damon, you're going to start and finish and play this season down the line, and you're going to take us as far as we can go. And that's what we did."

Allen took Edmonton to the Grey Cup, where their opponent was Winnipeg.

On August 13, 1993, Matt Dunigan had run in three touchdowns and threw for three others as the Bombers routed the Eskimos 53–11. On September 26 in Edmonton, just before the end of the regular season, the Bombers trounced the home team again.

With two games left on the 1993 schedule, Dunigan blew his Achilles tendon. Winnipeg finished first at 14–4, 16 points ahead of second-place Hamilton. But without Dunigan, the Blue Bombers just squeaked by the Ti-Cats 20–19 in the Eastern final.

The absence of Dunigan didn't affect Lancaster's approach to the Grey Cup game. "But the players, let's face it, knew he wasn't playing. They knew he had tremendous success against us. From their standpoint, just knowing he wasn't going to be there gave them a psychological lift. A coach can't say 'Because Matt's not playing, that's going to help us.' If you start thinking that way, you're likely to get your rear end kicked."

It seemed that Murphy's Law was bedevilling Winnipeg's coach Cal Murphy because whatever could go wrong, did. Near the halfway mark of the opening quarter of the Grey Cup game, centre Nick Benjamin snapped the ball over punter Bob Cameron's head. The veteran should have run to the end zone and conceded a safety touch. Instead, he tried to kick the ball, it was blocked and Edmonton recovered it on the four-yard line. Lucius Floyd scored on the next play.

Blaise Bryant fumbled the ensuing kickoff. Damon Allen hit Jim Sandusky in the end zone. On Winnipeg's next possession, Garza was intercepted by Dan Murphy. Sean Fleming then connected on the first of a record-tying six field goals. In five minutes, Edmonton had scored 17 points.

In the second quarter, Edmonton upped their lead to 21–0 on the basis of a single by Fleming and a three-pointer from 26 yards out. Winnipeg got on the scoreboard with a Michael Richardson two-yard plunge. The teams exchanged field goals, making the score 24–10 for Edmonton at half time. It was mistakes that did the Bombers in. Edmonton converted seven Winnipeg turnovers into 23 points.

The Bombers closed the gap in the third quarter when Garza finished off a drive with a quarterback sneak for a touchdown. Winnipeg was down 24–17 heading home.

At 4:19 of the fourth quarter, Troy Westwood narrowed the gap to four with a 32-yard field goal. The Bombers might still have pulled it out had David Williams not dropped a pass in the end zone, or had Sammy Garza not dropped the ball on his 35.

Westwood tallied another field goal, and Fleming kicked three. Final score: Eskimos 33, Winnipeg 23.

Rod Connop of Edmonton analyzed the game.

What was important was the first quarter when they had three turnovers, and we scored two touchdowns and a field goal.

Also, if I could pick one thing, it would be the last drive that Damon put together for a field goal. We were up seven points. We got the ball with about three minutes left. We put together about a 9- or 10-play drive, keeping the ball inbounds almost the entire time. When we stalled on their 12-yard line and kicked a field goal, we were up 10 points with just a few seconds left in the game.

Cal Murphy agreed. "We made one mistake on one play on that drive. Damon broke outside, scrambled and hit Soles. We came off the thing for some unknown reason. It was such a big play for them. It really was. Up until then, they were in the doo-doo."

Murphy believed that, without the first-quarter errors, the Bombers played Edmonton straight up. "I know we did," he averred, chuckling ruefully. "I mean, I like Blaise Bryant, but he was a one-man wrecking crew.

"How often do you see David Williams drop a pass in the end zone? That's a touchdown. If we get that, it's a different ball game. And Sammy Garza just dropped the ball. He started to run, and the ball slipped out. It was just one of those things where you try to do too much at once."

Grey Cup 1994: American Expansion

The collapse of the Montréal Alouettes in 1987 sent the CFL into a tailspin. Fan interest and revenues sank with each passing season. In 1992, the league hired former Alouette Larry Smith as commissioner. His goals were to bring the CFL back to Montréal, which he did with spectacular success, and he also broadened the league's financial base through expansion.

"Shortly after becoming commissioner," Smith said on May 10, 1994, "I made a formal approach to the league governors about expansion south. After looking at the financial situation, I felt we had to get into bigger markets where we had more revenue opportunities."

In 1993, the Sacramento Gold Miners joined the CFL, fielding a lineup comprised entirely of Americans. The Gold Miners finished last with a mark of 6–12, largely because their coaches and players had practically no CFL experience. But what would happen if a coach came along who understood the nuances of the Canadian game and recruited Americans who had been All-Stars in the CFL?

That's what happened in 1994 when Don Matthews became the head coach of the Baltimore franchise. The team was initially called the "CFLs" because the NFL held the rights to the name "Colts," even though the Colts had abandoned Baltimore for Indianapolis. In 1995, the team became the Baltimore Stallions. Also joining the CFL that year were the Shreveport Pirates as well as the Las Vegas Posse, with an exciting rookie quarterback named Anthony Calvillo. In 1995, the Sacramento team moved to San Antonio, and franchises were granted to Birmingham and Memphis.

Given Matthews' coaching expertise, it was not surprising that Baltimore was the first expansion team to challenge for the Grey Cup. After going 5–4 during the first half of the season, Baltimore went 7–2 the rest of the way, finishing second in the Eastern Division, two points behind Winnipeg. The Baltimore Stallions beat Toronto 34–15 in the semifinal and edged the Blue Bombers 14–12 to go the 1994 Grey Cup against the BC Lions in Vancouver.

The Lion theme song in 1994 was "Do You Believe in Miracles?" When training camp opened, the Leos, led by Lion tamer Dave Ritchie, were strong offensively with Kent Austin and Danny McManus at quarterback, Cory Philpot and Sean Millington in the backfield and receivers Darren Flutie (Doug's brother), Yo Murphy, Matt Clark and Ray Alexander.

But BC's secondary needed to be rebuilt. Personnel guy Bill Quinter signed veterans Less Browne, James

Jefferson, Enis Jackson and Barry Wilburn. The defence was second best in the league.

The Lions finished third with a record of 11–6–1.

Although the Grey Cup was played at BC Place, the Lions first had to face the difficult task of winning two playoff games on the road in Alberta to get there. They fashioned a dramatic comeback in the fourth quarter to knock off the defending champion Eskimos 24–23. Then it was on to Calgary.

The Stampeders hadn't lost a playoff game to BC in 30 years. To make matters worse, the Lions were in no shape to play anybody. Kent Austin had a separated shoulder, Danny McManus had a torn thigh muscle, Less Browne a cartilage injury and Barry Wilburn a broken rib.

The Lions matched the Stamps play for play in the Western final. Calgary was leading 36–31 with a minute left when they drove into BC's end and tried a field goal. It was blocked. Stampeder kicker Mark McLoughlin explained what happened. "Apparently Ray Alexander pyramided. The ball was hit well, but he made a great play." It was the first time in his CFL career he'd had a kick blocked.

Not to worry. With less than a minute to play, the Lions would have to move the ball 64 yards and score a touchdown to win. With Kent Austin sidelined, it was up to Danny McManus. After barely missing one to Alexander, he connected in the flat to Matt Clark and Yo Murphy. Darren Flutie caught one at the Calgary four. And then it was McManus again to Flutie, for the winning touchdown. Final score: BC 37, Calgary 36.

McLoughlin had a simple explanation for losing the Western final. "No matter how you look at it, everything strange that could happen in the fourth quarter did happen."

Because national pride was at stake, the 1994 Grey Cup was special. It was Canada versus the United States. The Lions were determined to prove that Canadians were just as good as Americans. It was up to a battered bunch of BC Lions to prevent the Holy Grail of Canadian football from falling into American hands.

Even the Americans on the team were caught up in the nationalistic fervour. Danny McManus, an American citizen, said, "I don't know if it was confidence or what, but we just had a feeling we needed to represent Canada in the right way and keep the Grey Cup in Canada. We didn't want to be the first team to let the Grey Cup go south of the border."

BC's Lui Passaglia said, "When they played the national anthem of both countries before the game, you could see it in some of the players' eyes, in their reaction to the anthems, that this was more than a Grey Cup game. There was an extra incentive to play harder than you normally would."

Baltimore was the jewel in the expansion crown. Mike Pringle had set records for rushing with 1972 yards and 2414 total yards from scrimmage. Tackle Shar Pourdanesh had won the Outstanding Offensive Lineman Award, and linebacker Matt Goodwin had been named top rookie. Don Matthews won his second Coach of the Year Award.

Baltimore's offensive line of Pourdanesh, Guy Earle, John Earle, Nick Sabis and Neal Fort averaged 306 pounds. They faced three Canadians—Doug Peterson, Dave Chaytors and Andrew Stewart—who each averaged 35 pounds less. If football games are won in the trenches, Baltimore had the advantage. They also had Tracy Ham at quarterback, at the top of his game because Don Matthews knew how to use him. Defensively, Baltimore ranked third in the 12-team league.

The Lions' 13th man was the 55,097 fans in attendance, many carrying Canadian flags. A full BC Place is incredibly noisy and hot, both factors working very much in the home team's favour. The crowd kept up a steady roar from the opening kickoff to the thrilling end. It was one of the best Grey Cups ever played.

BC struck first. After returning the opening kickoff to their 32, Kent Austin, playing with a separated shoulder, marched the Lions to the 40, where Passaglia kicked a 47-yard field goal.

On Baltimore's first play, Tracy Ham was picked off by James Jefferson. Coach Dave Ritchie explained, "When we played them in Baltimore, on the very first play, they completed a pass over by James Jefferson. In the Grey Cup, they threw the same pass, and Jefferson intercepted."

Returning the favour, Austin was intercepted three plays later by Karl Anthony. The opening quarter ended with the Lions leading 3–0.

The fireworks began with less than seven minutes left in the half. Ham led his team to the BC six. The Lions were called for interference in the end zone on Chris Armstrong, and Ham scored from the one.

BC returned the kickoff to the 35. Austin was picked off by Ken Watson, who lateralled to Karl Anthony who ran 36 yards for a touchdown. Baltimore 14, BC 3. Two Baltimore majors were scored in 35 seconds.

Kent Austin moved his team from the 35 to the enemy 46. Passaglia punted them in deep. On second down at the seven-yard line, Ham was picked off by Charles Gordon, who ran 17 yards to the end zone. The visitors closed out first-half scoring with a field goal.

With 52 seconds left in the first half, Austin's shoulder injury caught up with him when Watson made the second interception. "I had pressure," said Austin. "That was one I probably shouldn't have thrown. I couldn't step into the ball because I was getting hit on the play. I wanted to help the team, but if it had been anything but the Grey Cup, I wouldn't have been playing, I'm sure." After 30 minutes, Baltimore led 17–10.

The Americans had reason to be optimistic going into the second half. They were getting lots of opportunities, and the Lions had lost their starting quarterback.

The injured Danny McManus stepped into the breach.

Early in the third quarter, it looked like Baltimore was going to pull away. They began the half with a nine-play drive culminating in a field goal and a 10-point lead. It was then the Lions started to implement their strategy, partly to compensate for McManus' injury. "We want to run the football," Dave Ritchie said.

First down at their 35, Cory Philpot ran for 10 and then 8 yards. Canadian Sean Millington rumbled 32 yards to

Baltimore's 25. Philpot for two. Then McManus was sacked by O.J. Brigance, the only sack Baltimore got that day. Lui Passaglia came on for a 34-yard field-goal try.

It was a fake! Holder Darren Flutie raced around the right end for 18 crucial yards and a first down at the nine. Three plays later, McManus scored. After a drive that consumed over 5:05, the Lions trailed by three.

"We worked on that field-goal fake," said Ritchie. "We had noticed that they brought seven guys off the edge on the one side whenever they lined up. So we wanted to run a fake, and Jody Allen, the special teams coach, came up to me and said, 'Do you think this is the time?' I said, 'Let's do it.' That really changed the momentum."

On BC's next possession, after running every first down in the quarter, McManus threw to Ray Alexander for 42 yards, setting up a Passaglia 42-yard field goal. The teams were tied at 20 when the third stanza came to a close.

At 3:09 of the final frame, Passaglia booted the Lions into a three-point lead. But the Yanks weren't done. Tracy Ham hit Joe Washington on a 55-yarder to get to the enemy 10. After an incompletion, Ham headed for the end zone. At the one-yard line, he reached out with the ball to get it over the goal line. Tony Collier thanked him kindly and relieved him of it. With a facemask penalty tacked on, the Lions scrimmaged at their 23.

But Baltimore wouldn't quit. On their next possession, set up by a great punt return and a 21-yard run by Ham, the visitors evened the score with a 29-yard field goal.

The ball changed hands four times before the Lions started from their 37 with 1:40 left in regulation time. Again, the big play was a pass to Alexander, bringing the ball to Baltimore's 36. Millington lost two, Philpot gained eight. Third down at the 30, and Passaglia missed from 37 yards out.

Don Matthews liked to run the ball out. In 1996, the strategy would help him win the Grey Cup, but in 1994, it proved disastrous when Mike Pringle got it out to the two. Three plays later, Baltimore had to punt. With 28 seconds left, BC had a first down at the Baltimore 34. Said McManus, "All we did was try to run the clock down and let Lui come on for the last play. I knew he wouldn't miss two in a row."

He didn't. The game ended BC 26, Baltimore 23.

Don Matthews considered Passaglia's miss a blessing in disguise for BC:

> *No question. That was one of those plays where we got caught up in the moment. We had a return call on, and Passaglia kicked it to the side of our return. When we do a field-goal return, we figure anything short of 40 yards means we didn't do a good enough job.*
>
> *Instead of us jamming their guys on the line, three of our guys turned to see if the kick was going to be good or not. Their guys, released free, made the play. Had my players done their jobs, we would have had the ball out to the 30–35 yard line.*

Most observers were astonished at how the underdog Canadians dominated the line of scrimmage.

Said Dave Ritchie, "The game was won in the line. Our Canadian kids stood tall, I tell you, they stood tall."

Added Danny McManus, "We got caught up in hearing how the American players had better coaching. I think that's what fired up our Canadian offensive linemen. It was a real battle of pride for those guys. They just stepped up to the challenge."

Less Browne offered another reason for victory. "When we went to Baltimore, they kicked the crap out of us. Being outside on grass benefitted their huge linemen. But the Grey Cup was inside where a lot of people have a hard time breathing. It was warm. After awhile it took its toll."

Matthews, who would never win a Grey Cup at BC Place, said, "It took me over six months before I was able to watch the film of that game. I was very, very disappointed that we lost. I thought for sure we'd win that game."

Lui Passaglia observed, "We won two key playoff championship games and the Grey Cup on virtually the last play. That rarely happens. There's one thing about our team: it had guts and true grit."

The symbol of Canadian football supremacy was safe for another year—but Baltimore would be back.

Grey Cup 1995

Calgary got off to a fast start in 1995, winning their first seven games. In game eight on August 18, at home to the Birmingham Barracudas, disaster struck. After breaking the 30,000 career passing-yards mark, Doug Flutie injured his elbow and was unable to answer the bell for the third quarter.

Jeff Garcia stepped in. The Barracudas went on to win 31–28, ending Calgary's record-setting 27 home-game winning streak. Flutie had surgery the following week. His doctor said he was out for the season. Surely, the Stampeders were doomed.

When Garcia replaced Flutie in the third quarter of the game, sports writers scrambled to find out something about this red-headed kid from California. No one had given a second thought to the second-string quarterback because Flutie had never missed a game in his CFL career. After returning from his injury, he wouldn't miss another.

Showing the self-assurance of an old veteran, Garcia proceeded to win six games in a row, including the Labour Day Classic against Edmonton when he threw six touchdown passes, equalling the record held by Peter Liske and Flutie. Calgary's newest hero took it all in stride.

"Today was just a dream come true," said Garcia. "I know it's a big game for the province, but I've been through big games in college, games where we were highly overmatched. But in this situation, we were not overmatched. I'm surrounded by a great supporting cast. We just get out there and play ball."

Knowing how good Flutie was, it must have been frustrating for Garcia to sit on the bench behind Flutie.

"Was I content with that? Not really," said Garcia. "But I was in a situation where I was backing up the best quarterback in the league. I was learning and growing within the system. I pretty much felt that I was just going to wait out my remaining years on my contract. I never really saw what was coming, but I was prepared for it."

Calgary finished at 15–3 to top the Northern Division. In three years, Calgary's regular-season record was 45–9, the best streak in CFL history in terms of wins. Dave Sapunjis won his second Most Outstanding Canadian Player Award, and the Stamps dominated most statistical categories.

So what? It was playoff time. This time, Calgary left nothing to chance. In the new playoff format to accommodate American expansion, all the Canadian teams were in one division. Calgary faced Hamilton in the semifinal. Against all odds, Flutie was back, but he turned the ball over five times before being booed off the field at halftime. Garcia returned, winning a surprisingly close game, 18–15. Was the horse collar getting tight?

Edmonton had been thoroughly whipped by the Stamps during the Labour Day games, 51–24 and 33–17. The Eskimos didn't lose after that, including their playoff win over BC 26–15. For the fifth time in six years, the Alberta teams contested the division final. This time, Calgary kicked King Kong off its back, winning 37–4.

The Stampeders scored on every first-half possession. Flutie played the game of his life. He threw short over the middle to Vince Danielson, Sapunjis and Allan Pitts. Flutie went long to Terry Vaughn and Tyrone Williams. He ran with the ball, putting moves on defenders that would make a bullfighter green with envy. He was magnificent.

The competitive fire burns deeply in this man. He was stung by the booing the week before. He was hurt by suggestions that Calgary lost the final in 1993 because he couldn't handle the cold. He looked forward to vindication in Regina against Don Matthews' Baltimore Stallions.

They proved to be a formidable opponent.

The Stallions also finished at 15–3 that season. They were led by running back Mike Pringle, who found a home in Baltimore after being cut by Edmonton and traded by Sacramento. When he retired, he was Baltimore's all-time leading rusher.

In 1995, Pringle was rushing champion again with 1791 yards. He beat out Dave "Sponge" Sapunjis for the Outstanding Player Award. Sponge caught 111 passes for 1655 yards and 12 touchdowns, winning the Outstanding Canadian Award. Baltimore also had Chris Wright, who picked up 2450 all-purpose yards.

The Stampeder strategy for the Grey Cup was to box in Tracy Ham and force him to throw, the belief being that Ham wasn't a good passer but was a dangerous runner. Coach Wally Buono overlooked the fact that Ham had the third-highest career-percentage completion rate in CFL history.

After leading the team into the playoffs, Jeff Garcia was the odd man out. "Hopefully I'll get an opportunity to play in Sunday's game. I'm preparing like it's any other game, not trying to overemphasize it, even though I know it's for all the marbles." Garcia didn't play a down.

To say Grey Cup day in Regina was windy would be an enormous understatement. The theme for Grey Cup '95 was "Huddle Up in Saskatchewan." The cold weather never materialized, Grey Cup week being unseasonably balmy. Early Sunday morning, a ferocious wind blew in.

Linebacker Matt Finlay had said they had to stop Mike Pringle and at least match Baltimore's special teams. Pringle picked up 137 yards rushing, and the special teams were a disaster.

On Calgary's first possession, after four plays, Tony Martino punted 43 yards to Chris Wright at the Baltimore 28. He returned the ball 82 yards for a touchdown, a record. With 2:26 gone, it was 7–0 for Baltimore.

The Stallions had an opportunity to add to their lead when Andrew Stewart fumbled the kickoff, recovered by Tracey Gravely at the Calgary 47. Three plays later, a field-goal attempt went awry when Dan Crowley fumbled the snap. Flutie then engineered two field goals. At the end of 15 minutes, the score was Baltimore 7, Calgary 6.

On the first play of the second quarter, Ham threw a screen pass behind Gerald Alphin. Will Johnson picked it up and raced to the enemy three. Flutie fooled everyone in the ballpark by throwing to linebacker Marvin Pope for a touchdown.

The Stallions replied with a 30-yard Carlos Huerta field goal. Then disaster struck.

Set to punt five minutes later, the Stampeders, in total confusion, were looking at each other and throwing up their hands. Sure enough, O.J. Brigance blocked the punt. Alvin Watson picked up the ball and ran to the end zone. Baltimore 17, Calgary 13, both touchdowns coming on special-team breakdowns. The Americans added a brace of field goals to lead 23–13 at the half, one of them, a 53-yarder, is still the longest Grey Cup field goal ever.

The third quarter was pivotal. Baltimore had the wind in the third quarter. Miller kicked an 80-yard single. Then Flutie went to work. Flutie for nine, Stewart 10 and two. To Allan Pitts for 10. Stewart five, to Sponge for seven, to Vaughn for 22. Flutie took it the rest of the way on three plays. The 65-yard drive ate up six and a half minutes into the wind. The score was Baltimore 24, Calgary 20.

Then it was Tracy Ham's turn. Starting at the 18, he completed passes to Robert Clark and Gerald Alphin. Will Johnson batted down a pass at the Stallion 52. Ham then threw to Peter Tuipulotu for nine. Third-and-one, quarterback sneak. Ham was awarded the first down over the strenuous objections of the Stampeders. Four plays later, Ham eluded a fierce pass rush and ran in for a touchdown. Baltimore 31, Calgary 20.

Even with the wind at their backs, Calgary was shut out in the final quarter while Huerta added two field goals. Mike Pringle sealed the Stamps' fate by picking up 90 of his 137 yards in that quarter. The final score was Baltimore 37, Calgary 20. Canada's Grey Cup had fallen into American hands.

Tracy Ham completed 17 of 29 for 213 yards, ran for 24 and was named Grey Cup MVP. Dave Sapunjis, eight for 113 yards, was the Canadian Player of the Game for the third time.

For Sapunjis, Chris Wright's punt return for a touchdown was déjà vu all over again. "It was just like that play in

1991 where Rocket returned it all the way, and the guys on the sideline were trying to get going and all of a sudden they break a big play and our emotional level dropped and it hurt us. [The years] 1995 and 1991 were similar in the fact that the other team's special team dominated."

Defensive end Will Johnson disagreed with the strategy to contain Ham. "The plan was to box him in and let him throw out of the pocket," said Johnson. "They didn't want to let him run. But any quarterback, no matter how lousy he is, if he stays in the pocket for a long time, is gonna pick you apart."

Johnson thought they should be going after Ham. Why didn't he?

> I did later on, but the other guys—they are more coach conscious whereas I'm more win oriented, doing what it takes. I've been in the league a long time so I do what I think it takes to win.
>
> If you're pushing a guy back into the quarterback on almost every play and bumping him, then you've got him. If you're not getting any push up the middle, it's useless. So I've got to pass rush. I've got to get off what the coach is saying and do what it is going to take to win this thing. I've had my battles with Tracy Ham. When I first came into the league, we had our battles, and I ended up winning because he ended up leaving Edmonton, and we ended up beating them often.

Don Matthews agreed with Johnson. "It is a surprise when anyone uses that strategy. Tracy Ham or any scrambling quarterback hurts you when you get conservative on your pass rush. That's when he's dangerous. Tracy's very bright. He's a remarkable talent and a quality guy. If you say 'Keep Tracy in the pocket and make him throw, he'll kill you.' You've got to go get him."

When the observation was made that Ham had a lot of time to throw, Wally Buono said:

That was part of our plan for keeping Tracy boxed in. The defensive line was doing pretty much what we asked them to do, push the pocket, try to stay in front. Overall, the majority of time, we did keep him in the pocket. There were times he did have the time to throw, but I don't think his throwing really hurt us. The key factors were the two special team plays and out inability to catch the football and keep drives alive.

We let them score in the third quarter. We were trying to get momentum, and it was critical for our defence not to give up any points in the third quarter. We did, which neutralized the touchdown we got. We wanted to win the third quarter and put our offence in a position to get points in the fourth. But they put the ball in the end zone, which was a big demoralizer.

But there was a play before that. It was third down, they went for it and made it by an inch, and they could easily not have made it by an inch on the spot. If they don't make it, we not only had momentum because we just scored, now we have the momentum because we had just taken it away from them. They get the first down, they go in and we're right behind the eight ball again.

Grey Cup 1996

In 1996, Cleveland Browns owner Art Modell moved his team to Baltimore, thus ending the life of the one bright spot in CFL expansion south of the border. The other U.S. teams folded. Stallions owner Jim Speros moved the team to Montréal, but Don Matthews couldn't see much of a future for the CFL in Montréal and therefore signed with Toronto.

In the West, Calgary Stampeder owner Larry Ryckman was bankrupt. He hadn't paid Doug Flutie all year, rendering his contract null and void. Jeff Garcia filled the void. Not only was Garcia successful, but he also played for $900,000 less.

Flutie was available, wanted to be closer to his Massachusetts home, wanted the big bucks and so signed with Toronto. Don Matthews cleaned house. Seventeen of the starting 25 players in 1996 (including the kicker) were new to Toronto. The fit was perfect.

The Argos offence was spectacular with Jimmy "The Jet" Cunningham leading the league with 2638 yards. Second in all-purpose yards was Michael "Pinball" Clemons, with 2626 yards, including 286 rushing, 1268 receiving, 145 on punt returns, 883 on kickoff returns and 44 on missed field-goal returns, moving him into fifth place on the all-time list. Pinball led the league with 116 receptions, fourth best ever, though he did not make the All-Star team. Flutie completed 434 of 677 passes for 5720 yards and 29 touchdowns.

Toronto won 15 games and finished first in the Eastern Division, advancing to the Grey Cup after eliminating Montréal 43–7. Although the Stampeders finished first for the fifth year in a row, the Eskimos upset them 15–12 in the Western final.

The 1996 Grey Cup was hosted by Hamilton for the first time since 1972. Alas, for the Tiger-Cats, Hamilton was the only host to lose money on the Grey Cup. Capacity at Ivor Wynne was 40,000, and 38,595 tickets were sold, including 4500 end-zone seats bought by Tim Hortons the day before the game. They sold those $100 tickets at their Hamilton area stores for $25 per.

The organizing committee hadn't accurately gauged the depth of Torontonians' indifference to their fine football team. Despite the fact they were less than 70 kilometres away and the weather was good that week, less than 6000 tickets were sold in Toronto.

Perhaps there was another reason for the poor ticket sales in Toronto. It would be an understatement to say that Grey Cuppers new to Hamilton were taken aback by the degree of animosity displayed by the locals for Toronto. It was hard to find a Hamiltonian cheering for the Argos.

The most common button displayed during the Grey Cup read "Argos Suck." Doug Flutie in particular was offended by it, especially when asked for an autograph by a "fan" sporting the button.

This "Argos Suck" attitude had a double-barrelled effect on ticket sales. Torontonians were loathe to come to

Hamilton, and many Hamiltonians were loathe to fork over more than $100 to watch the hated Argonauts.

Edmonton's offensive stars were receivers Darren Flutie (86 catches for 1362 yards) and Eddie Brown (70 receptions for 1325 yards). They also had wily veteran Jim Sandusky, who left the sidelines as special teams coach to return to action.

The other stars of the Eskimo show were Eric Blount (1091 yards rushing, 275 receiving, 277 on kickoff returns) and Danny McManus, who won the Grey Cup for BC in 1994.

Toronto was the better team offensively.

Defensively, they were much closer: Toronto surrendered 359 points, Edmonton 354. The Argos gave up 5636 yards to Edmonton's 5046, a difference of about eight yards per quarter. The Esks had the better pass defence.

Despite the Esk presence of Henry "Gizmo" Williams, the greatest punt-returner of all time, Toronto had the edge on special teams with Cunningham and Clemons. Edmonton had the advantage in the kicking department with veterans Sean Fleming and Glenn Harper against the 26-year-old rookie Mike Vanderjagt.

As it turned out, Edmonton outperformed Toronto offensively, the Argo defence played better than that of the Eskimos and the kicking game was won by the rookie.

It started to snow about 11:00 AM on Sunday morning. As the day wore on, the wind came up. By kickoff at 6:30 PM, the temperature was −3°C, with a wind of 35–40 kilometres per hour reducing it to −11°C. The first snowstorm of the winter blew in. Despite the elements, the Argos and Eskimos put on one of the most entertaining Grey Cups ever.

In the first quarter, Toronto did not perform like a team that went 15–3 and was favoured to win. On their first play, Paul Masotti dropped a Flutie pass. With Derek McCready in his face, Flutie threw the next one away.

Edmonton's first possession was a sign of things to come—they had no trouble moving the ball. Starting at his 47, McManus moved them to the Argo 30 in five plays. Sean Fleming missed a 37-yard field-goal try; Cunningham returned it to the 19.

On first down, All-Star centre Mike Kiselak snapped the ball over his quarterback's head. Flutie conceded a safety touch. Edmonton 2, Toronto 0.

Eight minutes later, the Eskimos opened up a nine-point lead. McManus dropped back to pass from his 46-yard line. Given great protection, he hooked up with "Downtown" Eddie Brown for a 64-yard pass and run for a touchdown. Streaking toward the post, Brown caught the ball at his knees, somehow managing to maintain his balance on the slippery field.

"Eddie said he could run past the guy," said McManus, "and when I got single coverage on that side, I just threw it up, and he made a great catch."

Edmonton 9, Toronto 0. Almost three minutes remained in the quarter.

When the opening stanza ended, Flutie had the Argos on the Edmonton 15-yard line. After a holding call and a Derek McCready sack, Mike Vanderjagt kicked a 37-yard field goal.

Then the fireworks began. Through the next 13 minutes and 25 seconds in driving snow, both teams scored 41 points between them. It was an incredible show—it was Canadian football at its best.

Jimmy Cunningham ignited the explosion. After the field goal, Edmonton scrimmaged at the 35. Two plays later, Glenn Harper outkicked the coverage. Cunningham took the ball on his 30, got a devastating block from Donald Smith, burst up the middle and outraced the rest to the end zone, 80 yards for a touchdown. Toronto 10, Edmonton 9.

On the Argos' next possession at their 48, Flutie scrambled 14 yards to the Edmonton 48. He threw to Cunningham for 20. Vanderjagt was good from 32 yards out, making the score Toronto 13, Edmonton 9.

Edmonton quickly regained the lead. Danny McManus found a wide-open Jim Sandusky at the Argo 50-yard line. The great veteran went the rest of the way. Halfway through the quarter, it was Edmonton 16, Toronto 13. But not for long.

At 4:18, Flutie marched the Argos 65 yards down field in six plays to the end zone. The key was Canadian receiver Paul Masotti, who picked up 64 of his 100 yards on that drive.

On second-and-eight at the Toronto 37, Flutie connected with Masotti for 29 yards to the Eskimo 44. On the next play, Derek McCready dropped Flutie for a 10-yard loss. Flutie came right back to Masotti for 35 yards, Cunningham for 15. First-and-goal at the four, Robert Drummond ran the ball in for the touchdown. Toronto 20, Edmonton 16.

The Argos' lead lasted all of 15 seconds. Fielding the ball at the 19, Gizmo Williams electrified the crowd with a 91-yard kickoff return, the longest to date in Grey Cup history. Although Gizmo has returned 24 punts for touchdowns, this was only his second running-back kickoff. Edmonton 23, Toronto 20.

In this Grey Cup, TD returns did not demoralize the opposition like the Rocket did in 1991. Toronto came right back. Pinball Clemons returned the kickoff 30 yards to the Argo 48. The next sequence of plays was pivotal.

First down at the 48, Flutie threw toward Clemons in the flat. Darian Hagan got his hands on the ball and should have picked it off. Instead, it went incomplete. On the next play, Flutie was trapped but pitched the ball forward between two defenders to Clemons, who ran 16 yards into enemy territory. Flutie threw to Drummond for 11, then to Clemons for five. Flutie ran for 10, Drummond eight and two. After missing Cunningham on a pass, Flutie scampered 10 yards into the end zone.

Edmonton had an opportunity to close the gap, but Sean Fleming missed a 47-yard field-goal attempt. The score at halftime was Toronto 27, Edmonton 23. In terrible weather, the two teams had scored 50 points in one half of football. Incredibly, there were no turnovers. Forty-one points were scored in the second quarter and just three in the third when Vanderjagt made it 30–23 at the 4:22 mark from 16 yards out. On the next sequence, Fleming missed from the 37.

As with the other misses, the Argos didn't concede singles, returning all three into workable field position.

Esks coach Ron Lancaster explained what was wrong with the usually reliable Sean Fleming. "He got hurt in the Western final making a tackle, which probably preserved our win against Calgary, to tell you the truth. On the one field goal he missed, the guy came out, he made the tackle and hurt his leg. We missed three field goals in a Grey Cup. Sean's not going to do that. But he had the bad leg."

By the end of the third quarter, the Argo offensive line was winning the battle in the trenches. Still, the Eskimo defence stopped the enemy drive at the 21-yard line, forcing the Argos to settle for another field goal. They retaliated with a 65-yard march of their own when McManus threw twice to Marc Tobert and Eddie Brown and once to Eric Blount and Tony Burse. Blount ran the ball in from the five. The Westerners trailed by three with 6:57 left to go, an eternity in the CFL.

But Flutie was at the controls. The little guy engineered a brilliant 71-yard, 13-play drive for a field goal that used up five minutes and 23 seconds. The drive was kept alive by a controversial call at the Edmonton 24.

On first down at the 33, Flutie ran for nine yards. Drummond was stopped dead in his tracks. Flutie called a quarterback sneak on third-and-one.

As soon as he took the snap, Flutie was hammered by Willie Pless. Flutie appeared to drop the ball. Before Edmonton could recover, the play was whistled dead, giving the Argos a first down.

Head referee Jake Ireland said, "What I saw on television afterwards is that clearly he fumbled the ball before his forward progress was stopped. However, an official on the field blew the whistle and marked the forward progress. That was the end of that. There was nothing I could do about it."

"It wasn't just a fumble," Eskimo veteran centre Rod Connop argued. "It was going to be a fumble for a touchdown because we had a convoy gathering steam, and the only person who had a chance to get that ball was Robert Drummond. If you watch the replay, you'll see he dives, he misses the ball and it's behind him now."

Ron Lancaster was so incensed at the call that he ran on the field, screaming at the officials. After Vanderjagt increased the lead to six, Lancaster took to the field again and slipped and fell. Embarrassed and angry, he returned to the bench. Just over a minute remained. Months later, he looked back on the fumble that wasn't.

"You know what? It probably wasn't that important," Lancaster said. "Things happen in any athletic event at a certain time, and they seem like they're life and death, but in the overall picture, it wasn't really that important."

As to Jake Ireland's comment, the ever-gracious Lancaster said, "That's okay. I really believe that when you've sat down at the end of the game and looked at it, the referees probably make far fewer mistakes in a game than either team."

Scrimmaging at the 39, McManus, looking for Darren Flutie, threw the ball low, toward the sideline. The ball bounced off Flutie's chest into the arms of Adrian Smith, who ran 49 yards to the end zone. Toronto 43, Edmonton 30. Fifty-eight minutes and 38 seconds had gone by before the first and only turnover of the game.

Characteristically, the Eskimos weren't finished. On third-and-five at their 45, McManus hit Darren Flutie for 20 yards and Tobert for 9 and 26. After an incompletion, McManus found Tobert in the end zone for a seven-yard touchdown.

The final score was 43–37, the second highest total in Grey Cup history.

To Lancaster, the reason Toronto won was simple: Doug Flutie.

> *Basically, it was just controlling Doug Flutie. That was probably the biggest thing about the game. That's always going to be your problem when you play against him. I just like to watch the guy play. I think he's great, but playing against him is very, very difficult. You have to control him because if you don't, he'll figure a way to beat you. That was the difference in the game.*

Said Eskimo linebacker Willie Pless, "Flutie could be playing marbles, and he'd be hard to beat."

Don Matthews explained the offensive explosion in the second quarter.

> *It was a very difficult field to defend. Traction was bad. I think the advantage goes to the offence on that kind of a field. The snow was not a factor. Traction was the factor.*

We couldn't get as good a pass rush because we couldn't get traction up field and eventually they couldn't either. Quarterbacks were able to hold the ball a little bit, and then when they threw it, the DBs were having a very hard time breaking on the ball. The field was really, really difficult to defend.

What a year. The Argos went from 4–14 and 12th in a 13-team league to 15–3 and a Grey Cup.

"If this isn't the best Argo team of all time," summed up Paul Masotti, "you tell me why it isn't."

Because the 1997 team was the best of all time.

Grey Cup 1997

The slogan for the 85th Grey Cup was "Party in Your Parka." Saskatchewan fans from all over the country converged on Edmonton to have the time of their lives. Commonwealth Stadium was a sea of green. Although the Roughriders had rained on Edmonton's parade by knocking the host team out of the event, the good people of Alberta's capital became instant Saskatchewan fans. (Deep down, most of them are anyway.)

The Argos swept through the regular season with a record of 15–3 and demolished Montréal in the Eastern final. The Roughriders had finished third with a mark of 8–10. They were led by quarterback Reggie Slack, who got hot at the right time and would never reach such a level again. Saskatchewan was coached by Jim Daley, who cut his two best defensive players K.D. Williams and Lamar McGriggs in September because they accused the coaching staff of racism.

Doug Flutie with the Grey Cup in 1997 after the Toronto Argonauts win over the Saskatchewan Roughriders

The Cinderella Roughriders were one of three teams to beat the Argos during the year. Because Don Matthews had coached in Regina, he knew how hard they would play. The Riders had vanquished both the Stampeders and Eskimos, so he wasn't going to take them lightly.

Temperature at game time was a bearable −7°C with little wind. The festivities got underway with an ominous sign for Saskatchewan. The public address announcer began the introduction of the Roughrider offence by calling out the name of centre Carl Coulter. Nothing happened. No one appeared. Sensing what lay ahead, had the Roughriders decided to stay in their dressing room? *Au contraire*. After what seemed like an eternity, Coulter emerged from the tunnel, prepared to meet his doom.

And doom it was.

Toronto led 20–9 at the half on touchdown passes from Doug Flutie to Derrell Mitchell and Robert Drummond, plus two Mike Vanderjagt field goals.

The Argos were out of the dressing room early, anxious to get the second half underway. For Saskatchewan to have a chance, it was imperative they got off to a good start in the third quarter. Instead, the Argos ran a reverse on the opening kickoff and Adrian Smith ran the ball 95 yards for the winning touchdown. Game, set, match. Toronto 27, Saskatchewan 9.

On their next possession, the Argos went 73 yards in five plays for another touchdown. Three plays later, a Lester Smith interception led to a Flutie to Pinball Clemons major. At the end of the third quarter, the score was Toronto 41, Saskatchewan 9.

In the final 15 minutes, Toronto added two field goals, and the Riders scored touchdowns by Mike Saunders and Reggie Slack. The final tally—Toronto 47, Saskatchewan 23—flattered the Westerners.

Doug Flutie was proud of his back-to-back Grey Cup wins. "For those that were there last year and this year, it is something extra special because it puts you into an elite group. Now you start working towards next year."

Saskatchewan's special teams coach Cal Murphy observed, "The whole thing boils down to Doug Flutie. He's the guy who oils the engine, who gets it going. There were so many times there when you think you've got him, and he comes out of it, just like when he had Pinball Clemons in the end zone. You think you've got him, and all of a sudden, he flips the ball out to the side. It's just too much."

chapter thirteen

Go Stamps Go! 1998–2001

In the 1990s, no team won more games than the Calgary Stampeders. Between 1992 and 1996, the Stamps finished first every year. But they made it to the Grey Cup only three times, and they lost twice.

When the 1998 campaign got under way, the Stampeders were the most talented team in the country. Wally Buono had signed a contract extension as coach. Jeff Garcia and his backup, Dave Dickenson, were outstanding quarterbacks. Allan Pitts, Vince Danielson, Terry Vaughn and Travis Moore were the best receiving corps in the league. Kelvin Anderson was coming off two straight 1000-plus rushing seasons, and the offensive line of Jamie Crysdale, Rocco Romano, Fred Childress, Jay McNeil and Rohn Meyer was first-rate.

The Stamps fielded a veteran defence with a front seven of Jermaine Miles, Ray Jacobs, Bronzell Miller, Steve Anderson, Darryl Hall, Anthony McLanahan and Alondra Johnson; a secondary of corners Marvin Coleman and Willie

Hampton; defensive backs Eddie Davis and Jack Kellog and safety Greg Knox. Tony Martino and Mark McLoughlin led formidable special teams.

But in the past, having the best players in the league wasn't always enough.

"In 1997," explained Buono, "there was a lot of turmoil, which was unsettling all around, all the time. I spent a lot of time putting out fires, trying to mend fences, trying to create what really wasn't there. In 1998, the big thing we always talked about was keeping focused on the goal ahead, which was to be Grey Cup champions."

The Stamps finished first with a record of 12–6. After easily disposing of Edmonton in the Western Conference final, 33–10, the Calgary Stampeders headed for Winnipeg for the Grey Cup.

Grey Cup 1998

Calgary carried their new attitude into Grey Cup week. In 1995, in Regina, Wally Buono had imposed no curfew on the players during that Grey Cup week. On the Thursday, at about 7:00 AM when team officials were coming down to the hotel lobby for a meeting, several players were just getting in after an evening of revelry. By their own admission, they had partied too much and weren't all that focused on the game. Grey Cup 1998 was different. Buono imposed a curfew:

> *That was my idea. I talked to the captains about it. Whether that was a big issue or not, I really don't know. Just the fact that they even were willing to listen to that showed that their intentions were better. Maybe the disappointment we shared*

in the middle '90s had a lot to do with their mental framework more so than a curfew.

They came to Winnipeg wanting to win, and if that meant they had to be in a couple of nights, it wasn't going to be a big deal. A couple of them probably went out anyway after we checked. But enough of them cared. You've got to get enough to care. If you get enough to care, they will discipline themselves.

Grey Cup '98 was an intriguing match-up, another battle of Alberta, pitting the Calgary Stampeders against "Edmonton East," a.k.a. the Hamilton Tiger-Cats. The Stamps faced the dynamic duo that broke their hearts in '94 and '96—Danny McManus and Darren Flutie. Add in old nemesis Ron Lancaster as the Ti-Cat's new coach, and the cast was complete. Hamilton's defensive coordinator, Don Sutherin, formerly of Calgary, knew how to stop his old team.

The Westerners were loaded with veterans. Fifteen had played in the '95 Grey Cup, seven in '92 and six in '91. Only four Ti-Cats had been in the big game, including kicker Paul Osbaldiston. The Stamps knew what it took to win a Cup, as well as how long the offseason is when you lose.

The Stampeders wore their black uniforms in which they had never tasted defeat. Come kickoff, it was a balmy 10°C with a west wind of 28–37 kilometres per hour.

Wally Buono addressed the troops. "I told them that we had worked awfully hard to get here, and let's make the most of the opportunities. Let's not come back in here with any regrets. We talked about some of the key factors as far as field position and big plays."

In the Eastern dressing room, Ron Lancaster said:

We've probably got further than a lot of people thought. The opportunity to win a Grey Cup isn't there every year. That's basically what I tried to tell them.

You get there one year. I can remember even myself, I got there in my rookie year, and it took me six years to get there again. It is hard to do, it is hard to get to that Grey Cup game, and when you get there, you've got to take the opportunity to win it. You've worked your tail off to get here; let's finish it off right.

Calgary won the coin toss, keeping the wind in the second and fourth quarters.

The Stampeders opened the scoring at 3:02 with a single on a missed Mark McLoughlin 48-yard field-goal try. Four minutes later, Paul Osbaldiston kicked the Cats into the lead with a 24-yarder, followed soon after by a 34-yard field goal by McLoughlin. After 15 minutes, Calgary led 4–3, but they were at the Hamilton three.

In the second stanza, whatever could go wrong, did go wrong for Calgary. Kelvin Anderson capped the 86-yard, eight-play drive with a three-yard plunge into the end zone. But the snap went awry, and the convert was no good. Calgary 10, Hamilton 3. McManus replied by marching from his 24 to the enemy 13 where Osbaldiston's 20-yarder reduced Calgary's lead to four points.

Six plays later, Bobby Olive clearly fumbled Tony Martino's punt, but the referee blew the call. On second-and-11 at the Hamilton 20, Greg Frers intercepted McManus but was called for interference.

With passes to Darren Flutie, Andrew Grigg and Mike Morreale, the Cats drove to the Calgary 39. McManus then read the blitz brilliantly and hooked up with Ron Williams for a 35-yard touchdown. Hamilton 13, Calgary 10.

Calgary came back, moving the ball to the Ti-Cat 42 where they lined up for a field goal. But it was a fake! Dave Dickenson hit Kelvin Anderson right in the bread-basket, but he dropped it. When the Stamps got nowhere on their next possession and with the ball on their 24, Martino went back to punt. The snap was high; Martino rushed to get it off. The ball dribbled 23 yards, and the Stampeders were called for no yards. On the final play of the half, Osbaldiston kicked a 40-yard field goal, making the score Hamilton 16, Calgary 10.

Buono was not concerned:

The issue we addressed was the fact that when you look at it, everything really went against us—but we're only behind by six points. In my mind, six points was just one play.

There are highs and lows, there is excitement and relief. At halftime, some of the guys were getting a little bit edgy, but we calmed them all down until they just relaxed. "It's no big deal, it's just six points, and there's still 30 minutes to be played. Let's not come back in here regretting the next 30 minutes." I thought the players recaptured their focus very well.

Lancaster wasn't concerned that the Ti-Cats led only by six, considering everything went their way:

The game's going to go 60 minutes, and Calgary didn't get to the Grey Cup by lying down.

There was still 30 minutes of football to be played. In our league, three minutes is an eternity, so 30 minutes is forever.

You never make drastic changes at halftime. You take the game plan you went in with and cut it down to the things you are executing well and that you think will be good for you the second half. You go in trying to cover all situations, and each quarter you cut it down a bit. You eliminate some of your offences and defences and zero in on the things you're doing best. If you execute your game plan better than them, you'll win. If not, you're going to get beat.

Hamilton continued to have the upper hand through the first half of the third quarter but only came away with two points. On their opening drive with a third-and-five at Calgary's 52, Lancaster ordered a direct snap to Jarrett Smith who ran for 20 yards. Three plays later, Osbaldiston missed a 32-yarder.

It was two and out for Calgary. Starting at the 35, McManus moved his team to the Stamp's 46 where Ozzie hoofed a 66-yard single, making the score 18–10 Ti-Cats.

The Calgary Stampeders celebrating with the Grey Cup in 1998. Jeff Garcia is on the left and Travis Moore (number 83) on the right.

Then Jeff Garcia and Anderson went to work, marching 75 yards in 14 plays for a touchdown. Anderson picked up 25 yards on the ground and 15 through the air. Garcia took it in from the one on the final play of the third quarter. With the convert, Hamilton's lead was cut to one.

Calgary took the lead at 4:28 of the final frame when Mark McLoughlin kicked a 22-yard field goal, set up by Aldi Henry's 26-yard interception return. McLoughlin added another three points on their next possession, this one from 32 yards out. With 5:45 remaining, the Stampeders led by five.

Starting at his 35, McManus was incomplete. He then hit Andrew Grigg for 15. Incomplete again. McManus rumbled for nine. Third down on the Calgary 51, a two-yard quarterback sneak. Danny Mac then threw a short pass to Archie Amerson who took it 47 yards to the two. On third-and-goal, Ron Williams scored. The two-point conversion attempt failed. Hamilton 24, Calgary 23.

The Stamps started out at their 20-yard line with 1:57 to go. Garcia hit rookie Aubrey Cummings for 12 and Travis Moore for nine. After a two-yard quarterback sneak and a first down, Garcia completed the last pass of the game to Moore for 13 yards. First down at the Hamilton 44, 57 seconds to go. Garcia ran for eight and three, Anderson for two, Garcia three. It was third-and-five on the Ti-Cat 28 right in front of the uprights. Mark McLoughlin and Dave Dickenson took to the field.

Like all great kickers, McLoughlin lived for the moment when the big game is on the line. He went down his mental checklist and prepared to kick. "I was calm. I'd known for about the last three minutes that I'd have to make that kick."

Hamilton called a timeout. Asked what he and Dickenson talked about before the kick, McLoughlin replied, "Nothing."

The ball was snapped and put in place. McLoughlin drove it through. Calgary 26, Hamilton 24, no time left on the clock. Calgary had won its fourth Grey Cup.

For Winnipeg-native Mark McLoughlin, it was the sweetest Grey Cup of all. Referring to his father who died of a heart attack the year before, he said, "If only Dad would have been here to see. But he was here; he helped me.

Without a doubt, my dad was right by my side when I kicked it. I wish he could have been here physically to share this moment with me, but I know he was here in spirit."

The King of the Quarterbacks praised Jeff Garcia. "He took care of the ball very well on that last drive," said Lancaster. "He hit open receivers. He didn't throw into any trouble, and when it wasn't there, he ran with it. Especially when they got across mid-field, and he was getting close to field-goal range, he did a great job protecting the ball.

"They did a real good job of executing on their last drive. That's a sign of a good team. They didn't make any mistakes when things were on the table."

"I was so relaxed on that drive," Garcia said. "I didn't feel any pressure on me. All the pressure was on Hamilton's defence.

"It just feels so good, finally being on a championship team. In all my years in football from high school to college to pro, I've never been on a team that has won a championship. It was particularly great being able to do it with this team. You can't even imagine how this feels until it happens to you." Jeff Garcia would not win another.

Because of the enormous pressure to win, Grey Cup '98 was especially meaningful for Wally Buono. "For me, it was a very satisfying win for a lot of reasons. I was happy for the players, I was happy for the organization, but I was also happy for myself in a very non-selfish way. To see the city really enjoy the victory was tremendous. It is a pleasure to see people get so much joy out of touching and feeling the Cup.

Sometimes we participants don't realize what a great joy it is to the average fan."

During the offseason, Jeff Garcia, Tony Martino, Most Outstanding Offensive Lineman Fred Childress, receiver Terry Vaughn and linebacker Anthony McLanahan all moved on.

Grey Cup 1999

Overcoming injuries to the key position of quarterback was Calgary's theme for 1999. On the final play of game two, a 37–27 loss in Vancouver, Dave Dickenson dislocated his shoulder. He reinjured it the following week at home against Edmonton and was replaced by Henry Burris, who preserved a 41–37 win. After beating the Alouettes in Montréal seven days later, 36–17, Burris tore his knee ligaments on August 5, and the Stamps lost at home to BC. Burris was gone for the season. But while some football teams couldn't find a quarterback at an all-star game, the Stamps seemed to have a never-ending supply. After losing two starters, Mike McCoy entered the picture.

With limited experience in NFL training camps and the World League, McCoy was rescued from a desk job in Salt Lake City after Dickenson went down. When Burris got hurt, he stepped in and won his first three starts. McCoy also stepped in later in the season when Dickenson injured a knee. Despite the adversity they faced on the injury front, the Stamps were 12–6, including four of five wins to complete the regular season. They finished second to the Lions.

The 12–6 Stamps hosted the 6–12 Eskimos in the semifinal. With Dickenson at the top of his game, they rolled over Edmonton 30–17 and into the Western final in Vancouver. One week later, the Grey Cup was contested at BC Place so the 13–5 Lions had an extra incentive to beat Calgary on home turf.

"We had some great battles with them," recalled Dickenson.

> We played them six times. They won the season series 3–1, and we won the preseason and the playoff games.
>
> All of the games were close, and the final was tight. We were dominating them, and then I got sacked by Johnny Scott. And that's when I broke that bone, the coracoid. We were up 21–1, and I got hurt, and they came right back and took the lead. In the fourth quarter, Wally came over to me and said, "Can you play?" I said, "Yeah." I went in and got that last drive to win it.

The score for the final was Calgary 26, BC 24.

The 87th Grey Cup would be a rematch with the Hamilton Tiger-Cats.

Hamilton opened the scoring at 10:08 of the first quarter when running back Ronald Williams handled the ball six straight times and scored on a one-yard plunge. Three minutes later, Paul Osbaldiston added a field goal, then a single on the second play of quarter number two. Calgary didn't get a first down until 3:17 of the second stanza when Kelvin Anderson ran for 12. The Ti-Cats closed out first-half scoring with another field goal and a McManus to Darren Flutie touchdown. It was 21–0 for Hamilton at the half.

When play resumed, Osbaldiston made it 22–0 on the kickoff. That was when Calgary went to work. Starting at the 35, Dickenson was incomplete, then hit Cummings for nine. Third-and-one, McCoy ran for two. Then Dickenson threw 57 yards to Travis Moore and seven to Vince Danielson for the touchdown. On their next possession, Dickenson threw to Marcus Dowdell for 13, Travis Moore for 31, Allan Pitts 15. Dickenson scrambled for 10 and then found Pitts for 18 yards and a touchdown. Hamilton responded with a 21-yard field goal, making the score 25–14 for the Ti-Cats after 45 minutes of play.

McManus threw a seven-yard TD strike to Flutie to open the final quarter. The Stamps added a touchdown by Duane Forde, but that's all she wrote. Final score: Hamilton 32, Calgary 21.

Dave Dickenson analyzed the defeat. "I wasn't very sharp. I'm going to take a lot of the blame. They really played physically and were able to knock us out of our routes. What surprised me was they used a three-man rush a lot. Do the math. That's nine guys dropping back. It was tough to get open. We couldn't do enough to counteract that."

Dickenson went on to explain why the Stamps couldn't break through.

"We couldn't run a run play to the right because I couldn't hand off with my left hand. There was a broken bone in the back—the coracoid—it is part of the shoulder blade. I got this sharp pain, and I knew something was wrong."

So "Double D" had a dismal day and stunk the joint out? Not exactly. Dickenson was too hard on himself. He completed 24 of 28 passes for 321 yards, two touchdowns and one interception. That's a great performance by a completely healthy quarterback. In the shape he was in, it was unbelievable.

Danny McManus, the CFL's Most Outstanding Player in 1999, was good on 22 of 34 passes for 347 yards and two touchdowns, both to Darren Flutie, who caught six passes for 109 yards. McManus was the Grey Cup MVP, and slotback Mike Morreale was the Most Valuable Canadian.

After the game, Ron Lancaster stood outside the dressing room with a look of contentment on his face. Asked why he didn't go inside, he replied, "This is the players' time. They're the ones who did it. Let them celebrate."

The year 1999 was a disappointing one for the Grey Cup hosts. The Lions' slogan for 2000 was "The Beast Must Feast."

Grey Cup 2000

Seldom the soul of equanimity, BC coach Greg Mohns was absolutely growly during the 1999 Grey Cup festivities. With the Grey Cup in Calgary in 2000, Mohns was determined to get there and exact his revenge.

It was not to be. With the Lions at 3–4, Mohns quit over a dispute with GM Adam Rita, who turned to his old friend Steve Buratto to take over.

Buratto had been brought into the league by Don Matthews in 1983. The following year, Buratto was named head coach of the Calgary Stampeders and had a 6–10 season. Five games into the 1985 campaign, Calgary fired him. After that, he coached for Matthews in BC, Saskatchewan and Baltimore. When the Stallions folded, Matthews went to Montréal, and Buratto moved north of Seattle where he was helping a family member with his business—out of football and quite content.

Buratto, a quiet thoughtful man, was just what the doctor ordered for an uninspired Damon Allen who had grown uneasy under the heavy hand and loud mouth of Greg Mohns. Although the Lions were only 4–7 the rest of the season, they peaked at the right time. Like they had done in 1994, they marched through Alberta, edging the Eskimos 34–32 and eliminating first-place Calgary 37–23. BC moved into the Stamps dressing room to await the Montréal Alouettes for Grey Cup 2000.

Since 1996 when the Baltimore franchise moved to Montréal, the Alouettes had two second-place finishes before topping the Eastern Division in 1999 and 2000.

The Alouettes were 61–28–1 since moving north, the best record in the CFL. They hadn't won a playoff game until 2000.

Going into the title game, Montréal had a superb offensive line that would dominate the Eastern Division throughout the first decade of the new century. They opened gaping holes for Mike Pringle who entered the game nursing a sore hamstring.

Still, Montréal's strength was defence and not turning the ball over.

BC led the league in first downs, total offence, including both yards rushing and passing. Defensively they were average.

Alouette quarterback Anthony Calvillo was considered mediocre while Damon Allen was headed to the Hall of Fame.

The 88th Grey Cup was a marvellous affair from start to finish. The weather was gorgeous all week long and throughout the entire contest.

After the opening kickoff, BC moved to the Alouette 47. Lui Passaglia picked up a single on a missed field-goal try. Three minutes later, Damon Allen plunged over from the one, and then Terry Baker notched a field goal for Montréal, making the score 8–3 for BC at the end of the first quarter.

Passaglia added four points in the second quarter while Calvillo connected with Jock Climie in the third on a one-yard TD pass. After 45 minutes, the Lions led 12–10.

Thirty-two points were scored in the final frame. First, BC running back Robert Drummond ran 44 yards for a major. Terry Baker kicked a 51-yard field goal, after which Damon Allen and Mike Pringle exchanged rushing touchdowns. Passaglia added a field goal, and with 44 seconds remaining, Calvillo and Ben Cahoon teamed up for a 59-yard pass and run for a touchdown. Final score: BC 28, Montréal 26.

In proving the Lions were the best team in the country, Buratto unleashed a running attack reminiscent of the 1994 Grey Cup when BC beat Baltimore. Sean Millington, the CFL's Most Outstanding Canadian in 2000, ran for 94 of his 99 yards in the first half. Drummond ran 16 yards through quarters

Mike Crumb of the BC Lions celebrating the Grey Cup win in 2000

one and two, 106 in the last 30 minutes. By keeping the ball on the ground, the Westerners enjoyed a seven-minute edge on the clock.

While Mike Pringle had a fine game with 115 yards on 20 carries, he wasn't able to get beyond linebackers Mike Fletcher, Kelly Lochbaum and Carl Kidd, whereas Drummond eluded the Lark linebackers all day. Pringle averaged 5.785 yards per carry, Drummond 12.2.

With a regular-season record of 8–10, the Lions became the first team with a losing record to win the Grey Cup. It would happen again the following year.

Grey Cup 2001

Wally Buono had the worst head coaching record of his career in 2001 with his Stampeders finishing 8–10. Dave Dickenson had gone to the NFL, leaving the team in the hands of Marcus Crandall. Despite the losing record, Calgary finished in second place, just one point ahead of BC. They eliminated the Lions in the semifinal 28–19 and headed to Edmonton where Crandall and his six-pack offence throttled the 9–9 Eskimos by a score of 34–16.

The Stamps were headed to Montréal to face the Winnipeg Blue Bombers for the Grey Cup.

Winnipeg had swept through the Eastern Division, winning 14, losing four. They won the division final over Hamilton 28–13. They had thrashed Calgary at McMahon Stadium in the season opener, 48–20, but Calgary managed to clinch a playoff spot on the last day of the regular season, winning in Winnipeg, 22–15.

It seemed Winnipeg only remembered the first game. They yapped incessantly all week about how good they were, which made the Stampeders even more determined to shove the ball down their collective throats.

"We felt like they were talking like they'd already won the game, and we hadn't even played yet," said Marcus Crandall. "That gave a few guys extra incentive to beat them."

Perhaps the Bombers should have focused on the last time the teams had met. Said Crandall, "The last game of the season was a confidence builder for us. A team's already in the playoffs, and they are playing their starting quarterback the whole game? That means they are trying to win the game. Khari [Jones] stayed in the whole game, and we felt they were really trying to put us out of the playoffs. They did everything they could to beat us, and they didn't succeed. That was an emotional lift for us."

After the league awards when the players mingled with the great unwashed, the Bombers made it clear that Sunday's game wouldn't even be close. While that angered the likes of Alondra Johnson, Ray Jacobs and Jamie Crysdale, Mark McLoughlin just shrugged. "It's nice to be confident," he said with a smile.

Stampeder defensive coach Jim Daley said, "I feel really good about Sunday. The guys are ready, they've worked hard, they're well prepared, and they believe they're going to win."

Said safety Greg Frers, "The whole week, I had reporters coming after me asking how we were going to stop this basically unstoppable receiving corps. We took it upon ourselves to really challenge ourselves to get the job done. We came out and proved we did have some skill."

The Bombers were heavily favoured. Winnipeg's defence gave up the fewest points, first downs and total yardage. They were second in interceptions. Calgary's offence scored the most points and was second in total offence. Winnipeg had the best giveaway-takeaway ratio at +8, Calgary the worst at −8. A couple of key statistics: Winnipeg was the most penalized team in the league, Calgary second least. And Mark McLoughlin's field-goal percentage was 73.68. His counterpart Troy Westwood's was 60. The best in the league was 78 percent.

It was 17°C on Grey Cup Sunday, the warmest day on which the game has ever been played. Not that the temperature mattered, since the contest was inside the cavernous but enclosed Olympic Stadium. The "Big O" was packed to the rafters with the second largest crowd in Grey Cup history, despite the fact that Les Alouettes were not the Eastern champions.

During the playing of "O Canada," Winnipeg veteran Bob Cameron and Stamp safety Greg Frers had tears in their eyes. The roar of the crowd reached an ear-splitting crescendo inside the great stadium. The good people of Canada's second-largest city turned out in spectacular numbers to watch two teams from Western Canada battle it out for Earl Grey's old mug. There was no doubt football was back in Montréal.

During the early going, it looked like Winnipeg could walk the talk. After returning the opening kickoff to their 36, Charles Roberts ran for 14 yards. Khari Jones hit Milt Stegall for five, ran for seven and then completed a 22-yarder to Robert Gordon. When the drive stalled at the 22, Troy Westwood kicked a field goal.

Calgary's first possession wasn't promising. Doug Brown sacked Crandall who then went incomplete. Aided by a no-yards call on Ricky Bell and a 15-yard strike to Gordon, the Bombers made it to the 31 where Westwood was wide on a field-goal try but scored a single. Two possessions later, running back Kelvin Anderson's fumble set up a Westwood 40-yarder, but it hit the post. After 15 minutes, the Easterners from the West led 4–0. Calgary was on the march when the second quarter began, all for naught, though, when McLoughlin missed from 36 yards out and Charles Roberts returned it to his 38.

On the next play, Jones completed a 33-yard pass to Stegall, which was nullified when Joe O'Reilly was called for roughing. Undeterred, Jones put together a nice march to the enemy 35. Eric Blount picked up a yard, and in a turning point in the game, Alondra Johnson sacked Jones for a 13-yard loss, forcing a punt. Instead of being hemmed in deep, Calgary started at the 25 when Lukas Shaver was called for no yards. Crandall completed five in a row, missed one and set up a successful 37-yard McLoughlin field goal. Winnipeg 4, Calgary 3.

Three and out for Winnipeg. Calgary first down on the 30, Crandall missed, then hit Marc Boerigter for 12 yards. Crandall then found Boerigter streaking down the sidelines, laid it in perfectly for a 68-yard pass and run for a touchdown and a lead the Stamps did not relinquish.

"That was one of the plays George Cortez put in the week before," explained Crandall. "We noticed that every time we ran a post pattern, the DB would turn and run after the guy. We had Boerigter run kind of a lazy pattern to the flat, and then he turned it up the field and ran down the sideline."

After the ensuing kickoff, Winnipeg went three and out. Starting at their own 22. Crandall threw to Antonio Warren for six yards, but Lamar McGriggs brought him down by the facemask, giving Calgary field position and room to manoeuvre. Mixing his plays, Crandall got them to the 28, where he completed a 10-yarder to Vince Danielson. Brian Clark was called for facemasking so it was first-and-goal at the nine.

"We flooded the zone thinking they would leave one guy open," said Crandall, "and Travis [Moore] did a great job hiding himself coming out of the backfield. They got confused with all that motion. It was up to me to find the guy who was left open, and that was Travis." Touchdown, with 54 seconds left in the quarter. Halftime score, Strong Silent Types 17, Undisciplined Big Mouths 4.

After watching Dave Ritchie peel the paint off the dressing room wall, the Bombers promptly marched 47 yards on their first possession of the second half for a touchdown—a pass from Jones to Arland Bruce III. Later, Westwood missed on a 53-yarder, scoring the single. After three quarters, Calgary 17, Winnipeg 12.

It takes all three phases to win most football games. The Stampeder defence turned the game around in the second quarter. Crandall was on fire, and Boerigter and Moore scored a brace of majors before the half. Time for special teams to make a contribution. On Winnipeg's second possession of the final 15, Bob Cameron dropped back to punt. Aldi Henry roared in and blocked it. Willie Fells picked the ball up and ran for the touchdown. Calgary 24, Winnipeg 12. The Bombers added a touchdown and Calgary a field goal to make the final score Stampeders 27, Blue Bombers 19. Coming off their worst record of the Wally Buono era, Calgary had won their most unlikely Grey Cup, the fifth in the team's history.

Marcus Crandall was voted MVP, going 18 for 35, 309 yards, no interceptions and two touchdowns.

Aldi Henry was the outstanding Canadian. The award was particularly gratifying for Modest Marcus.

"Yes it was, yes it was, considering everything I'd been through to get there, finally becoming a starter in the CFL, overcoming years of disappointments, it definitely was a great feeling to win the Cup and the award."

Despite the loss, the Bombers were unrepentant. "They remained mouthy," recalled Greg Frers, "even when the game was over. They never showed any respect for the ability we had. They were a very confident bunch who won a lot of games, and they were a very good team, but obviously you don't play with your mouth."

After a losing season in 2002, new Stamps owner Michael Feterick made it clear he wanted Wally Buono gone so that a more compliant coach would start his son Kevin at quarterback. The BC Lions were delighted to sign Buono. One Wally Buono era was over, but another was about to begin.

chapter fourteen

Saint Anthony and Ben, 2002–12

Between 2002 and 2010, the Montréal Alouettes were in the Grey Cup seven times. They won three. Well coached by Don Matthews, Jim Popp and Marc Trestman, the Als were led by quarterback Anthony Calvillo and his favourite receiver, Ben Cahoon, both shoo-ins for the Hall of Fame.

In 2011, Calvillo became the all-time pro-football passing leader with 73,412 yards. He became the CFL leader in touchdown passes (418) and completions (5444). He has won the Most Outstanding Player Award three times.

The Los Angeles native began his career with the expansion Las Vegas Posse in 1994, beating out 12 veterans for the job. When the Posse folded, he spent three frustrating years in Hamilton, and in 1998, Calvillo moved to Montréal.

After I was released by Hamilton, there were two teams that were interested in me and offered me a contract, Montréal and Saskatchewan. I felt I wanted to learn from an experienced quarterback and go to a winning organization. Montréal at that time was very successful, and they had a great quarterback in Tracy Ham. They had a lot of talent.

Saskatchewan had Reggie Slack, and I felt if I went there, I could compete with Reggie for the starter's job, but what concerned me was if I did start there and I had another bad year, my career would be over.

Calvillo arrived in Montréal in 1998 as a struggling backup, and in 2011, the mayor presented him with the Key to the City.

Said Calvillo when Don Matthews arrived in 2002, "He sat me down and said, 'Listen, we're going to change to a passing system, and we're going to build it around you.' It was very comforting for me to know the head coach had the confidence in me to do that."

That same year, Ben Cahoon won his first of back-to-back Outstanding Canadian awards. Born in Utah and raised in Canada, the Brigham Young graduate holds the all-time record for receptions with 1017. He has four Grey Cup records.

Between 2002 and 2011, eight Alouettes won league awards.

After Ron Lancaster left the Igloo for Hamilton following the 1997 season, Hugh Campbell hired Kay Stephenson who finished second with a record of 9–9. Campbell then dumped Stephenson and turned back to the Eskimo family, convincing his old friend and colleague Don Matthews to leave Toronto and take over the Eskimos.

In 1999, Matthews experienced the only losing season of his head coaching career, finishing 6–12, in third place and bowing to Calgary in the semifinal, 30–17. In the first season of the new millennium, he did slightly better, moving up to second place at 10–8. Again he lost the semifinal, this time to BC 34–32.

During his third training camp in Edmonton, Campbell took the incredible step of firing his friend, ostensibly for missing practices and generally neglecting his duties. Matthews was devastated. He said he had a thyroid problem and had been forgetting to take his medication. That December, Larry Smith and another old friend Jim Popp hired Matthews to coach the Alouettes.

After finishing first with a record of 13–5 and an Eastern final victory over Toronto, Matthews prepared to return to Edmonton for the 90th playing of the Grey Cup. To say there was bad blood before the game would have been a dramatic understatement. The most successful coach in CFL history vowed revenge.

Matthews' replacement on the Eskimo bench was the team's general manager Tom Higgins. When he got the call from Campbell to replace a living legend, the only head coaching experience he had at any level was for his son's bantam team. Higgins worked hard to gain the team's respect and loyalty. They went 9–9, good enough for first place and a bye to the Conference final in 2001. They lost that game at home to the 8–10 Stampeders, 38–16.

Higgins looked forward to 2002 when Edmonton would host the Grey Cup. He had reason to be optimistic. He was high on his Western All-Star Jason Maas. When he talked about his quarterbacks before the preseason, Higgins didn't even mention Ricky Ray. But when Maas sustained a separated shoulder injury in Regina on July 19, it was Ray who stepped in and saved the day.

At 23, Ray was the youngest starting quarterback in the league.

Just before Ray signed with Edmonton on May 22, 2002, he was delivering potato chips for Frito Lay. His Fresno Frenzy Arena League coach, former CFL quarterback Rick Worman, recommended his young charge to his old friend Tom Higgins.

"I played an arena game on Saturday night," said Ray. "My coach told me I had a chance to go to Edmonton right after the game. So Sunday I went back home, packed up my stuff and flew out Monday. From the time I knew I was coming to Edmonton and arrived here was only like 36 to 48 hours. It was just one of those decisions you've got to make, and hopefully it's the right one. When you come up here, you don't know anybody, you have a new country to adjust to, it's not easy, but you stick it out."

Showing maturity beyond his years, Ray led the Esks to a 13–5 finish and first place. They won the Western final, beating the Blue Bombers 33–30. (Ottawa was back in the league, so Winnipeg returned to the Western Division).

Grey Cup 2002

The Eskimos dominated the 2002 Grey Cup statistically. They had 126 more yards in total offence and a possession differential time of 35:15 to 24:45. The Green and Gold had 25 first downs, the Als' seven. But Edmonton shot themselves in the foot. Montréal didn't so much as win the Grey Cup, 25–16, as Edmonton gave it away.

Montréal opened the scoring before a capacity crowd of 62,531 with a 68-yard Terry Baker single. At 1:58 of the second quarter, Anthony Calvillo hooked up with Pat Woodcock on a record-setting, electrifying 99-yard pass and run, making the score 8–0 for the Larks.

"We tried to isolate [Woodcock] on one of the DBs that wasn't used to his speed," Calvillo explained. "We happened to get them in zone coverage, got the ball to him and he just did the rest."

From then until the fourth quarter, the Eskimos held the Als to a field goal kicked just before the half. Montréal 11, Edmonton 0.

With the wind at his back in the third quarter, Ricky Ray completed a 38-yard strike to Jason Tucker. At the Alouette 18, he exploited a safety blitz and threw to Rick Walters for a touchdown. Minutes later, after a Calvillo fumble, Edmonton closed the gap on a 13-yard field goal. In the last minute of the quarter, Ray missed a wide-open Chris Brazzell and a sure six points. After 45 minutes, Montréal led 11–10.

Early in the final frame, linebacker Sheldon Benoit was called for roughing the passer, keeping the Alouette drive alive. On the next play, Jermaine Copeland took a Calvillo pass 47 yards to the end zone, increasing the Alouettes' lead to eight. The crunch came shortly thereafter.

Backed up on their 10-yard line, Calvillo threw two incomplete passes. Baker shanked the punt; Edmonton scrimmaged from Montréal's 36. Terry Vaughn was wide open for a major, but Ray underthrew it. Second down, incomplete. Third down, and Higgins said go for it. Incomplete again.

On Edmonton's next possession, starting at their 16-yard line, Ray engineered a 15-play drive capped off with a 17-yard touchdown pass to Ed Hervey with 19 seconds left. The two-point conversion failed. When Edmonton tried the short kickoff, Copeland returned it 47 yards to the end zone. The final score was 25–16, even though the Eskimos held Montréal to a single first down in the second quarter, none in the third and just three in the fourth.

Afterwards, Ray said, "It's one of those games when you can think back and there are so many opportunities where it could have been different."

Grey Cup 2003

Saskatchewan hosted the 2003 Grey Cup. The Eskimos' sole focus and goal from the moment the 2002 Cup ended was to be in Regina on November 16. Among only four players to crack the starting line-up was running back Mike Pringle. Discarded by the Alouettes, he was second in the CFL in rushing in 2003 with 1376 yards and made All-Canadian.

After splitting their first six games, Edmonton won 10 of their last 12, including six in a row after Labour Day to finish first at 12–6. They defeated the Roughriders 30–23 in the

Western final and went on to Regina to face their nemesis, Don Matthews and the Alouettes.

Tom Higgins was quietly ecstatic. "It is not easy getting back to the Grey Cup. They've been focused all year. It has been a really fun, fun journey, and now the journey takes its final step, which is the Grey Cup. The bottom line is one team is going to be happy on Sunday, and the other will focus on next year. We like our chances."

When reminded that in three years he had gone from coaching his son's bantam team to his second berth in the Grey Cup, Higgins laughed and replied, "We actually won a provincial championship with these little bantam kids. A championship is a championship. When you have a chance to be the best in Canada and put your name on a Grey Cup, that's pretty special."

Mike Pringle was almost at a loss for words. "I can't even explain how badly I wanted to get to the Grey Cup. I've got a couple of rings, and I know what it feels like to hoist that Cup. What brings me the most pleasure is that so many people, so-called experts said that Mike Pringle is done. I know how hard I work. I know how hard I pray."

Because not a single Eskimo was up for a league award, Ricky Ray was determined to prove the selectors wrong. "Certainly the best team in the West didn't have any final nominees. It just shows that we have a lot of good players on the team and nobody really stands out. Everybody just plays their role and goes out and does their job." His teammates thought Ray should have been the league MVP, not Anthony Calvillo.

Most pundits believed the game was too close to call, although Las Vegas made the Eskimos 3.5 point favourites. It would be an intriguing match-up.

"Alas, my love, you do me wrong to treat me so discourteously," goes the old song. For Don "Captain Ahab" Matthews, the Eskimos had become his personal white whale. Rejected in favour of bad boy Lawrence Phillips by Matthews in Montréal, Mike Pringle was determined to script the final act and play the starring role. Alouette quarterback Anthony Calvillo wanted postseason respect to go along with his Most Outstanding Player Award. Ricky Ray wanted a ring on his résumé before trying for the NFL the following spring.

Matthews made a critical mistake before the game even began. He sent a videotape to the league office that detailed the Eskimo secondary's indiscretions. By doing so, he accused the referees of letting Edmonton get away with murder, a view shared by the fans in every other CFL city. The move backfired big time.

Matthews also benched veteran corners Wayne Shaw and Omar Evans because they had not played well in the Eastern final, replacing them with rookies D.J. Johnson and Brandon Williams.

After prime-minister-in-waiting Paul Martin supervised the coin toss, Regina native Matt Kellett kicked off for the Alouettes.

Ricky Ray struck early, going after the rookie corners right away. On the fifth play of the game, Ray threw 43 yards to Ed Hervey who was covered by D.J. Johnson. That made it first-and-goal at the four. Mike Pringle took it the rest of the way. Edmonton 7, Montréal 0.

"Getting off to a good start like that really pumps a team up," Ray said later. "It set the tone for the game. We wanted to keep them back on their heels, and we did."

Edmonton opened the second quarter with a first down at their 40-yard line. Pringle gained two before Ray passed to Troy Mills for 29 yards. Three plays later, Ray threw 41 yards to Jason Tucker for a touchdown. Edmonton, 14, Montréal 0.

Were the Eskimos picking on the rookie corners? Tucker laughed. "I'm a happy guy, smiling all the time. When I saw two young guys on the corners, I smiled a little more and went 'Whoo!' He started backing off once I beat him. I noticed that."

Coaches and quarterbacks usually vehemently deny going after a particular defender. Tom Higgins, incapable of deceit, acknowledged that it was part of the game plan to exploit the Montréal rookies. "Absolutely. That's why we went after them right away. We were going to test them, but we knew that our challenge was going to be whether we could afford our quarterback time to actually throw the ball to the receivers."

Just when it looked like the rout was on, Anthony Calvillo mounted a 71-yard, six-play drive ending with a bit of razzle-dazzle. Calvillo handed off to Deonce Whitaker who threw a pass to the wide-open Pat Woodcock in the end zone. Three plays later, Kevin Johnson recovered a Mike Pringle fumble at the Eskimo 32. Calvillo cashed in on the next play with a pass-and-run touchdown to Sylvain Girard. Tie ball game.

Three plays after the kickoff, Alouette return man Keith Stokes fumbled Sean Fleming's punt on the 40-yard line. Ray quickly converted the turnover into a Jason Tucker touchdown. Edmonton 21, Montréal 14. The Tucker touchdown was set up when the Eskimo receiver literally threw Brandon Williams out of the way. In a travesty of officiating, possibly a response to Don Matthews' tape, Williams was the one called for interference on the 16-yard line.

Continuing the scoring spree, Montréal marched 65 yards in five plays with Ben Cahoon making a sensational catch for the major. Later, he was named the 2003 Grey Cup Outstanding Canadian. The game was tied once again at 21.

Edmonton wasn't finished. Forced to punt three plays after the Montréal kickoff, Keith Stokes coughed up the ball again, recovered by Donny Brady at the Alouette 20. Sean Fleming kicked a field goal, giving the Esks a 24–21 lead at the half. The two teams had combined for a record 38 points in the second quarter. After enjoying Bryan Adams during halftime, the 50,909 fans expected more fireworks in the remaining 30 minutes.

They didn't get it. Montréal scored a single in the third quarter, the Eskimos a Ray touchdown and Fleming field goal in the fourth. Edmonton had their 12th Grey Cup, 34–22.

Tom Higgins praised the Grey Cup MVP Jason Tucker. "One of the most unselfish players on this team is Jason Tucker because he played in the shadow of Terry Vaughn and Ed Hervey. But we knew when we asked him to make plays, he would do so." Tucker had seven receptions for 132 yards and two touchdowns.

Don Matthews responded to the criticism of his decision to go with the rookie corners. "It's pretty obvious that penalties and turnovers were the difference—they were all on our side. Our rookie corners were not the reason why we lost the football game. We made enough mistakes, but I don't care if we had Superman on the field for Tucker's touchdown, that was a perfectly thrown pass that couldn't have been stopped."

"I really couldn't be happier for the Edmonton Eskimo organization," said Tom Higgins. "It doesn't get any sweeter than when you finally win the last game of the year."

Was Higgins a classy guy with a classy organization? Pretty much. You couldn't meet a finer man than Tom Higgins. The Eskimos? Not so much. After doing Hugh Campbell a favour by leaving the security of the front office to replace a living legend, finishing first for three straight years, appearing in two Grey Cups and winning one, Higgins was fired when the club slipped to second in 2004 and lost the semifinal 14–6 to Saskatchewan

Grey Cup 2004

In 2004, with Wally Buono in charge, the BC Lions romped home in first place with a record of 13–5. It was an incredible accomplishment considering his starting quarterback Dave Dickenson missed 10 games with a shoulder injury. All his replacement rookie, Casey Printers, did was lead the team into the Grey Cup and win the CFL Most Outstanding Player Award along the way.

The Alouettes had an even better record, 14–4, with Anthony Calvillo passing for a career high of 6041 yards. But with Montréal leading Toronto 10–9 in the third quarter of the Eastern final, Calvillo was knocked out of the game with a shoulder injury. The Argos went on to win 26–18.

On to Ottawa for the 92nd Grey Cup.

The Boatmen were led by the Michael "Pinball" Clemons. At 39, he was the youngest head coach in the CFL. His quarterback Damon Allen was the oldest player in the league at 41. While wearing Argo double blue, he became the most prolific passer in CFL history. He led his team to the Eastern final in 2003, bowing out in the first quarter with an injured hand. On August 12, 2004, Allen went down with a broken leg, certainly out for the season, likely the end of his career. Not Old Man River though. He made a miraculous recovery, coming back to lead his team into the Grey Cup.

Damon Allen was the Rodney Dangerfield of Canadian football, never getting the respect he deserved. Despite all the records he set, he never made All-Canadian nor was he ever nominated by his division for the Most Outstanding Player Award. At family reunions, the limelight was always on his older brother Marcus, a running back who had been inducted into the NFL Hall of Fame. Damon did have a Grey Cup pedigree, however, winning two titles in four tries, both times named Grey Cup MVP.

Shortly after Wally Buono arrived in BC in 2003, he signed incumbent Damon Allen to a long-term contract. But when his former Calgary quarterback Dave Dickenson was cut from the NFL, Buono signed him up and shipped Allen to Toronto.

Dickenson rode the pine for most of the 2004 season because Casey Printers was doing such a great job. Then Buono stunned the football world by benching Printers in the playoffs. The Grey Cup would be a match-up between the oft-injured University of Montana Grizzly Dave Dickenson and the grizzled CFL veteran Damon Allen.

BC could turn to the League's Most Outstanding Player if Dickenson couldn't get the job done. Both teams had solid special teams, offences and defences. Wally Buono had coached three Grey Cup winners in Calgary; Pinball Clemons had won no Grey Cups as a coach, but he and his offensive coordinator had never lost a Cup as players. Clemons was the first black head coach ever involved in a professional football championship on either side of the border. While he never played the race card as a motivator, his players knew how much the win would mean to him.

BC was favoured. The only way Toronto would win was if BC made a lot of mistakes and if the only grandfather playing pro football took advantage. That's exactly what happened.

When Toronto lost the coin toss, BC elected to receive and promptly marched 72 yards in seven plays for a touchdown, coming on a 12-yard strike to Jason Clermont in the end zone. Dickenson completed his first nine passes, six on the opening drive. He ended the first quarter nine of 11 and 101 yards while Allen was two for 17 yards. BC had 1345 yards total offence to Toronto's 30. Then the Argo defence stiffened, and Damon Allen woke up.

On their third possession of the second quarter, scrimmaging at their own 36, Toronto drove down to the Lions 20 where Noel Prefontaine kicked a 27-yard field goal.

After a BC two and out, Allen capped a 70-yard drive with a quarterback sneak for a touchdown, the key play was Da'Shann Austin being called for interference on Arland Bruce III in the end zone. Toronto 10, BC 7.

BC came right back to tie the game with a 42-yard field goal. With 1:47 left in the half, Allen marched his team 63 yards into a lead they wouldn't relinquish, the touchdown scored on a 23-yard pass and run to Robert Baker. At the half, the underdogs were ahead 17–10.

Allen was good on 15 of 23 passes for 197 yards and a touchdown. Dickenson completed 13 of 17 passes for 148 yards and a major. The Lions led in most categories, including time of possession, first downs and rushing. A key statistic: Noel Prefontaine was out-kicking BC's Duncan O'Mahony 43 yards to 22.8, allowing Toronto to win the field position battle.

To start the second half, Wally Buono opted for the short kickoff. It worked, but the Lions were offside. Bruce returned the ensuing kickoff to the Lions 54, from where Allen completed four straight passes, bringing the ball to the Lions 11. John Avery took it to the one. Allen scored his second major of the game. Toronto 24, BC 10.

BC added a 37-yard field goal in the third. The Argos returned the kickoff to their own 33. Allen ran for 10 yards before being tackled by Carl Kidd. Not only was the gain nullified by a holding call, but Allen was also hurt. With the old warrior on the bench, the Lions had new life.

BC opened the last quarter with the ball at their 13-yard line. Dickenson engineered a brilliant 98-yard drive, featuring two long passes to Lyle Green, followed by Antonio Warren runs of 36 and 15 yards to bring the ball to the enemy seven. At 6:06, Dickenson ran into the end zone. Typical of Lion mistakes throughout the game was their two-point convert attempt. Twice they were guilty of time-count violations before O'Mahony was wide right. Toronto 25, BC 19.

As the Argos scrimmaged at their 49, a great roar went up from the crowd. Old Man River was back behind centre Chad Folk. The defence had held the fort the 10 minutes he was gone.

Hanging on to their five-point lead, the Boatmen had an anxious moment halfway through the quarter when Dave Dickenson put a long bomb on Geroy Simon's outstretched fingers, but he dropped it. A few plays later, Noel Prefontaine iced the game with a field goal. Final score: Toronto 27, BC 19.

It was a strange game in many ways. Antonio Warren's 160 yards rushing was the second best performance in Grey Cup history. The usually dependable Duncan O'Mahony averaged just 27.9 yards punting. A well-disciplined team during the regular season, the Lions, said Dave Dickenson, "had aggression penalties, nothing against the referees, they were good calls on stupid penalties."

Said Wally Buono, "The bad penalties, bad kicking, bad decisions hurt us. You can't make those kind of mistakes against a good team."

And the Argos were a good team, led by a quarterback who showed why he is one of the greatest athletes the CFL ever saw. Damon Allen had just won his fourth ring and his second Grey Cup MVP Award.

After it was all over, the man of the hour said, "It is satisfying when all year they talk about how old you are. It's a beautiful thing because I had the opportunity to show that I can still play on a given day in a Grey Cup game. Through history, great players always perform in big games. If you want to be a great player, the championship is the ultimate game."

Grey Cup 2005

Entering the 2005 campaign, Edmonton had made the playoffs 33 years in a row. They made it 34 when the Eskimos finished 11–7, tied with Calgary who finished second. After dispatching the Stampeders 33–26, they got by the Lions 28–23 and moved into the BC dressing room for the 2005 Grey Cup. For the third time in four years and 11th time overall, Edmonton's opponent would be Montréal. The rookie head coach Danny Maciocia versus "the Don" Matthews.

To get to the big game, the Eskimos relied on Jason Maas to come on in relief. Ricky Ray had not thrown a touchdown pass in seven weeks, and eyebrows were raised when Maciocia opted to start Ray rather than Maas.

Anthony Calvillo and Ricky Ray were the men of the hour for the third time in four years.

At 3:49 of the first quarter of the Grey Cup, Eskimo linebacker A.J. Gass recovered a Terry Vaughn fumble at the Alouette 41-yard line. Completing six in a row, Ray moved to the enemy 11 where the drive stalled. Sean Fleming kicked an 18-yard field goal. With 18 seconds left in the quarter, the Easterners tallied a single when Damon Duval kicked a 56-yard single. Edmonton 3, Montréal 1.

On the last play of the opening quarter, Ray missed on a pass to Derrell Mitchell. He opened quarter number two with a 12-yard run, followed by completions to Mitchell for 19 yards and Mike Maurer for six. Montréal was called for roughing the passer, which moved the ball to the 10. Troy Davis picked up a yard, and then Ray threw his first touchdown pass in eight games, to Ed Hervey. The convert was good. Edmonton 10, Montréal 1.

Midway through the quarter, Montréal moved from their 28 to the Eskimo 26 from where Shannon Garrett picked off Anthony Calvillo at the six-yard line. The score remained 10–1 at the half in favour of Edmonton.

After 30 minutes of play, Ricky Ray was good on 18 of 24 passes for 171 yards and one touchdown. Calvillo completed 14 of 20 for 161 yards but had that costly interception. The Eskimos held the Als to one-yard rushing through two quarters.

Calvillo got rolling in the first drive of the second half, moving 71 yards in seven plays for a touchdown. The big play was a 34-yard pass to Ben Cahoon. Éric Lapointe crashed over from the one.

Edmonton came right back, Ray completing seven straight passes, going from his own 14 to the Montréal 30. He then overthrew Ed Hervey and hit Troy Davis for two yards.

Fleming kicked his second field goal of the game, a 35-yarder to give his team a 13–8 lead.

Ezra Landry gave the Alouettes instant field position, returning the kickoff 39 yards, to the Eskimo 49. Calvillo promptly completed a pass and run to Sylvain Girard for 43 yards. A strike to Ben Cahoon brought it to the one. Lapointe gave the Larks their first lead of the game. Montréal 15, Edmonton 13.

On their following possession, Troy Davis fumbled on his 34-yard line. Matthieu Proulx returned it to the 12. Shawn Garrett knocked away a Calvillo pass. Cahoon caught one for six; Duval kicked a 13-yard field goal. Montréal 18, Edmonton 13.

But a great kick return can change a game in the blink of an eye. Following the Montréal field goal, Tony Tompkins fielded the kickoff at his 14-yard line and blazed untouched to the opposite end zone, his 96-yard return a Grey Cup record that still stands.

After 45 minutes of play, it was Edmonton 20, Montréal 18. A slow first half was turning into one of the most exciting Grey Cups ever played.

Early in the fourth quarter, Ray fumbled on his own 28, Ed Philion recovering. Four plays later, Calvillo scored from the one. Montréal 25, Edmonton 20.

With about five minutes left in regulation time, Ray set out from his 54. Mitchell caught one for six yards. Second down, incomplete. Danny Maciocia decided to gamble on third-and-four at the Montréal 50. Ray found Mitchell open on the 15-yard line. Interference calls on Duane Butler and

Kelly Malveaux put the ball on the one. Ray took it in and passed to Jason Tucker for the two-point convert.

Montréal wasn't done. After another sterling kickoff return by Landry, Calvillo drove from his 52 down to the Eskimo 20. With no time on the clock, Duval sent the game into overtime with a 27-yard field goal. Edmonton 28, Montréal 28.

The Eastern champions went first in overtime. From the 35-yard line, Calvillo threw to Cahoon for 13 yards. Steve Charbonneau nailed the Als quarterback for an eight-yard loss, the only sack of the game. On the second down, Calvillo found Dave Stala in the end zone. Montréal 35, Edmonton 28.

The Eskimos had to match the touchdown or lose. No problem. It was Ray to Mitchell for 21 yards, Davis for three. Jason Tucker caught the 11-yard throw for the score. Edmonton 35, Montréal 35.

Three plays later, Sean Fleming extended Edmonton's lead to three with a 36-yard field goal.

A Montréal field goal would keep the overtime going, a touchdown would win it. Calvillo went back to pass at the 35. His throw was batted at the line right back into his hands. He then hit Kerry Watkins in the end zone, but he dropped it. It didn't matter because the Als were penalized for throwing two passes on the same play. On first down and 20 at the 45, Calvillo was sacked by Charles Alston. Two plays later, it was over. Edmonton had won its 13th Grey Cup 38–35.

Yanked in both Western playoff games in favour of Jason Maas, Grey Cup MVP Ricky Ray was subdued but happy. "The biggest game of the year, and you want to go out and play your best game. Fortunately, I was able, along with my teammates, to make some good plays. I just feel lucky. Most guys don't get a chance to play in a Grey Cup or with a team like this."

It was Anthony Calvillo's third Cup loss in three tries. "Losing hurts," he said. "When you lose in overtime, it hurts even more."

Although Ricky Ray never again represented Edmonton in the Grey Cup, Anthony Calvillo contested four of the next five.

Grey Cup 2006

Montréal began the 2006 season with seven straight wins, followed by six straight losses. They were 3–2 the rest of the way, finishing first with a record of 10–8, tied for first with Toronto. But in the first week of October, the big story out of Montréal was the sudden resignation of Don Matthews, the most successful coach in CFL history.

Alouette president Larry Smith reported that Matthews told him a month earlier he was having health problems, including chronic fatigue, anxiety attacks and stress so bad that he might not be able to continue coaching. Matthews' condition was serious enough that he was afraid to leave his house. He was 67 when he stepped down.

Anthony Calvillo said, "I was very surprised. Nobody expected it whatsoever. It was very hard for him when he came into that locker room and pretty much faced the whole team. He was only there for a couple of minutes, and you could just see the emotion in his face and hear it in his voice. It was tough for him."

Matthews was succeeded by GM Jim Popp.

Montréal's opponent in the 2006 Grey Cup would be BC, led by the man who would overtake Matthews as the coach with the most wins in CFL history, Wally Buono. Since moving to the West Coast in 2003, Buono guided his team to three straight first-place finishes and boasted a record of 38–16. In 2005, his Lions ran off 11 straight wins to open the season and then won but a single game the rest of the way. They lost the final to Edmonton at home.

BC finished atop the Western Division with a record of 13–5. They knocked off Saskatchewan 45–18 in the final and left for Winnipeg.

Lion Dave Dickenson was determined to win a Grey Cup ring of his own. He'd played second fiddle to Jeff Garcia when Calgary won in 1998. He lost in 1999 because of an injured shoulder. In the 2004 Grey Cup, he performed brilliantly in a losing cause. During his career, he had two concussions, a dislocated and broken shoulder, torn knee ligaments and a broken wrist. He was 33 years old; it was time to get it done.

It wouldn't be easy. The Als were appearing in their fifth final in seven years. If anyone could find the weakness in BC's dominant defence, it was Anthony Calvillo. Although hurt much of the season, Ben Cahoon had caught 99 passes for 1190 yards. Kerry Watkins hauled in 86 for 1153 yards. Robert Edwards rushed for 1155 yards.

Montréal had good special teams but was below average defensively.

It was a –1°C at kickoff. Lion Paul McCallum accounted for all the scoring in the first 15 minutes with three field goals. He added another in the second stanza, as well as converting Ian White's touchdown. Damon Duval replied with a 43-yard field goal for the Alouettes. The score at the half was BC 19, Montréal 3.

Montréal tallied a safety and a Ron Edwards converted touchdown in quarter number three, reducing the Lions lead to seven. In the final frame, BC rang up two more field goals and conceded a safety to win the 94th Grey Cup Championship, 25–14.

Dave Dickenson and his offence put in an honest day's work to earn the team's fifth championship. He completed 18 of 29 passes for 184 yards. He was brilliant in the first half, going 13 of 19 for 146 yards.

A good quarterback takes what the defence gives him. The Alouette secondary shut down slotback Jason Clermont and held CFL Most Outstanding Player Geroy Simon to 41 yards. So Dave Dickenson found Paris Jackson five times for 65 yards and Ryan Thelwell the same number for 45 yards. It was a masterful quarterbacking performance that earned Dickenson the Grey Cup MVP Award.

Calvillo completed 20 out of 41 passes for 234 yards, no TDs, no interceptions.

It was a great day for Paul McCallum who was named the game's Most Valuable Canadian. His six field goals tied him with Don Sweet, Paul Osbaldiston and Sean Fleming for most three-pointers in a Grey Cup game.

After the win, McCallum said his feelings were indescribable, just as they were in a bad way when he missed an overtime try against BC in the 2004 Western final, an error that caused so much fan rage in Saskatchewan that an idiot dumped manure on Paul's neighbour's lawn, by mistake. At the end of 2005, Rider GM Roy Shivers offered him a take-it-or-leave-it 30 percent pay cut, and McCallum answered Wally Buono's call to the Lions' den, located in McCallum's hometown of Surrey.

The Alouettes took solace in the fact that Calvillo set a record for passing yardage and that Ben Cahoon, the best player on the field that day, broke Hal Patterson's Grey Cup career reception mark.

Grey Cup 2007

Halfway through the 2006 season, Saskatchewan fired GM Roy Shivers and brought in Eric Tillman. The Roughriders hadn't finished first for an incredible 30 years and hadn't hosted a playoff game since 1988.

Tillman was about to change all that.

He fired coach Danny Barrett at season's end. Tillman replaced him with the man Rider fans ran out of town, Kent Austin, who worked with Tillman in Ottawa as the quarterback coach in 2003. Austin's quarterback in the nation's capital was Kerry Joseph. The following year, Austin signed on as Toronto's offensive coordinator, helping them win the Grey Cup. When the Argos stumbled out of the gate in 2006, Austin was made the scapegoat and was fired.

A hallmark of the Barrett years was undisciplined behaviour and a litany of excuses when opportunities were missed. Austin would bring a long overdue approach to the dressing room.

"This is professional football," Austin said. "We expect it to mean something to be a professional athlete and wear this uniform. It needs to matter to them to be a good person and a great player.

"We're not here to make excuses. We're going to have players that believe the same thing and who will buy into that philosophy. It is really that simple. You play to be a champion and to be the best."

It is no coincidence that the two times the Roughriders won the Grey Cup, they had outstanding quarterbacks, Ron Lancaster and Kent Austin. There were four quarterbacks in camp: veterans Kerry Joseph and Marcus Crandall and rookies Darian Durant and Drew Tate. Austin kept them all.

Saskatchewan opened the 2007 season in Montréal, traditionally a graveyard for Rider hopes. They won 16–7 when the defence intercepted three Anthony Calvillo passes and sacked him eight times. The Roughriders followed that up with a 49–8 win in Calgary with Joseph throwing for four touchdown passes and Wes Cates running for two. In the home opener against the Lions, a dreadful performance by Joseph ended with a 42–12 defeat. Next up were back-to back games with the hated Eskimos, the first a 21–20 loss in the Igloo and a 54–4 thumping of the visitors at Mosaic Stadium. Saskatchewan then avenged their loss to the Lions, 21–9, and beat Toronto 24–13 and Edmonton 39–32. They also beat the Bombers on the Labour Day weekend to move into first place with a record of 7–2.

The Roughriders then dropped three in a row to Winnipeg, Calgary and BC. Health care facilities in Saskatchewan were stretched to the limit treating the broken ankles of fans who jumped off the Roughrider bandwagon.

Said Austin, "We lack maturity right now. We don't have the level of maturity we need because we don't have leadership throughout the team. We need to mature as a team, we need players to quit looking around and looking for someone else to make a play."

His boys responded by running the table, including the last five regular-season games and three postseason contests. Finishing second at 12–6, the Riders hosted their first playoff game in 19 seasons, a 26–24 win over Calgary.

Saskatchewan headed to the Lions' den for the Western final. They were never behind, winning 26–17. They would meet the Winnipeg Blue Bombers in the 95th Grey Cup in Toronto, Kent Austin returning to the scene of his greatest triumph.

The team overcame a number of obstacles to get there. They lost receiver Matt Dominguez on September 9. His replacement Mike Washington went down with an injury in October. D.J. Flick played the Western final with a pulled groin. Running back Wes Cates was playing on a broken foot. Fullback Chris Szarkas played with a layer of gauze on his fingertips, which had been sewn back on after a run-in with a table saw.

Player for player, the Riders weren't the best team in the league, but their whole was much greater than the sum of their parts. No group was better as a team. Only Kerry Joseph and centre Jeremy O'Day made All-Canadian in 2007. But Kent Austin was named Coach of the Year, and Kerry Joseph won the most Outstanding Player Award, beating out Winnipeg's quarterback Kevin Glenn. Unfortunately for the Blue Bombers, Glenn broke his hand in the Eastern final. He was replaced by sophomore Ryan Dinwiddie who was making his first pro start.

Canada's largest city hadn't hosted the big game in 125 years, and officials were worried about how the people of Toronto would respond. The natives embraced the classic, and a huge contingent of Roughrider fans made sure staid old Hogtown was stood on its ear. The festivities turned out to be more entertaining than the game.

The Rider offence struggled the entire game with a pumped-up Joseph overthrowing receivers, or receivers dropping catchable balls. The Bomber front four manhandled the Roughrider offensive line and smashed Joseph to the ground at every opportunity.

Winnipeg opened the scoring with a Westwood field goal following a 61-yard, seven-play drive. The Riders conceded two safeties in the second quarter as the Bomber defence stopped everything thrown at them.

Late in the half, James Johnson picked off Dinwiddie and returned the ball 30 yards for a touchdown. Luca Congi added a field goal at the end of the quarter. Saskatchewan went to the dressing room leading 10–7.

On the second play of the third quarter, John Chick forced a Dinwiddie fumble, recovered by Scott Schultz on the

Bomber 10. The Riders settled for a 17-yard Congi field goal. Saskatchewan 13, Winnipeg 7.

The Blue Bombers replied on their next possession, a 60-yard pass to Derick Armstrong for a touchdown, giving the Eastern champions a one-point lead. Congi put the Riders back in front with a field goal, set up by Johnson's second interception.

Soon afterward, Kerry Joseph marched his team 78 yards in six plays for a touchdown, putting the Riders ahead to stay, 23–14. Winnipeg added a safety and a field goal. Saskatchewan's 23–19 Grey Cup victory was preserved when a last-minute drive was snuffed out by James Johnson's third interception. He was the Grey Cup MVP, Andy Fantuz copping the Canadian award.

After the game, Kent Austin met the media. "Our guys believed they could do it all year. They went through a lot of turmoil like all teams do, and they bonded closer together as a result. That's what won the day for us. The turnover battle went our way, and that was the difference in the ball game."

Asked if he realistically believed he could win the Cup in his first year, Austin replied:

You have to believe that, or what is the point in playing? If you believe you are going to win, you walk differently, talk differently, you do what it takes to back up your belief and win.

This isn't about me. I didn't play a down this year. It's about the players, my staff, Eric Tillman, Jim Hopson, everyone in the organization.

I know what it takes to win a Grey Cup in Saskatchewan. I guess I'm just meant to win the Grey Cup as a Roughrider.

One of the reasons I wanted to come back is because there is no greater place in the CFL to win a championship than Saskatchewan.

And then Kent Austin was gone. Early in 2008, he accepted an assistant's position at his alma mater, Ole Miss. Considering what happened to every successful coach and quarterback in Saskatchewan, except Eagle Keys, it was probably a wise decision.

Grey Cup 2008

After the 2007 season, Calgary fired coach Tom Higgins and brought in former Stamp quarterback John Hufnagel.

Wally Buono's offensive coordinator in the 1990s, Hufnagel, was a head coach in the Arena League for two years. Hufnagel left there to seek fame and fortune in the NFL, first as quarterback coach in Cleveland, Indianapolis, Jacksonville and New England (his prize pupils Peyton Manning, Mark Brunell and Tom Brady). He was the offensive coordinator for the Giants, 2004–06, playing a leading role in the maturation of Eli Manning. When the Giants didn't meet the owner's expectations in '06, Hufnagel took the fall. Insiders knew that he deserved a lot of the credit for New York's subsequent Super Bowl victory. Proving you can go home again, Hufnagel returned to Calgary.

"I was very interested in having another opportunity to be a head coach, and when I had my year off, I gave a lot of thought to the direction I wanted to take. I knew the CFL would be looking for head coaches before the NFL would be. I spent a lot of time thinking about it, realized the direction I wanted to go if a possibility came up, when it did, I jumped at the situation."

His first priority was fixing a Stamp defence that ranked at or near the bottom in most categories. He hired former Alouette Chris Jones to solve the problem.

"When I took the job and watched some film," said Hufnagel, "I wanted to change the style of defence. Chris Jones' name came up, so I watched a lot of Montréal's film. I enjoyed how he played his defence. He'll make the players better, and he'll make his assistant coaches better."

The 2008 Stampeder defence was first or second in most categories, including points. The 2007 team had the most penalties and worst giveaway/take-away ratio (−20) in the league.

"You can do a lot of good things on offence and then just throw the game away because you're not taking care of the football," said Hufnagel. "We need to have more poise on both sides of the ball and play within the rules because you can't be killing yourself each week with penalties."

What about turnovers? "We gave a lot away and created very few," replied Hufnagel. "We need to raise some havoc defensively to create turnovers. I want us to be faster, bigger and more physical."

The 2008 team had the best turnover/take-away ratio at +20. The Stamps reduced the number of penalties but were still second worst in the league.

With 16 new faces in the line-up, the Stampeders opened at home against the Lions, winning 28–18. Next up was a 23–19 win at Montréal. Henry Burris was brilliant, completing 28 of 37 passes, one touchdown and no interceptions. Calgary followed that with another strong performance at home against Hamilton, winning 43–16. Ken Yon Rambo caught six for 127 yards, Nik Lewis nine for 125 yards and two touchdowns. After that, the Stamps were maddeningly inconsistent. They were 5–3 going into Labour Day.

In the Battle of Alberta, Calgary finally moved into the lead against the Eskimos, 16–12, at 4:18 of the third quarter. But that was it. Edmonton won 37–16. This time the Stamps' problem wasn't turnovers and penalties. They couldn't move the ball.

After the game, Hufnagel was despondent. "I told them all they had accomplished through nine games was lost. We have to go right back to square one and start all over again."

The team responded, winning eight of their last nine games. Henry Burris was in a league of his own down the stretch, moving up the record book to second place behind Doug Flutie.

"That's huge," said Burris. "It's a compliment to the guys I'm working with here. It's great to have your name up there with the best, but there is one thing they have that I don't have, and that's a championship. I won't be satisfied until I get that ring."

Key to the Stampeders' season was responding to the Labour Day loss with a win in Edmonton four days later.

They concluded their schedule by beating BC 41–30 with a lot of second stringers, a game the Lions wanted to win to finish second. The Stamps were first at 13–5.

"I'll be back in two weeks," vowed coach Buono. And so he was, the Lions winning the semifinal in Regina 33–12.

But the win was to no avail as Calgary won the Western final over BC, 22–18. The Stamps were off to Montréal to face the Alouettes.

The Alouettes' veteran offence was up against a rookie-laden defence that was fast and tough and played a lot of man-to-man.

Montréal had the great Anthony Calvillo, one of the finest passers of all time. The receivers were Ben Cahoon, Kerry Watkins, Brian Bratton and Jamal Richardson. Avon Cobourne had 950 yards rushing. Their offensive line surrendered the fewest sacks. The Als were first in total offence and points. They took the fewest penalties—none at all in the Eastern final. Their Achilles heel was defence, where they ranked sixth or worse in most categories.

This would be Henry Burris' first Grey Cup as a starter, having backed up Jeff Garcia and Dave Dickenson earlier. Burris was under pressure to win the big one. So were Lark veterans Calvillo, Cahoon, Bryon Chiu and Scott Flory. Time was running out for them.

John Hufnagel and Marc Trestman were rookie head coaches in the CFL. Both were exceptionally thorough in their preparation, and both created a good feeling in the dressing room. It was a Grey Cup between two classy organizations with men of excellent character.

Stampeder determination was heightened by Burris losing the Most Outstanding Player Award to Calvillo, and kicker Sandro DeAngelis was bested by return man Dominic Dorsey in the Special Teams award category. Neither was a gracious loser.

When the hostilities ended, would the winner be singing "Dance With Me Henry" or "Alouette, gentille Alouette"?

After a rousing pep talk by Hufnagel who said, "We're playing on the road, we're playing in a dome in front of 65,000 fans, men, we've got them right where we want them!" the Stampeders took the field at the Big O before the second largest crowd in Grey Cup history (66,308), most of them loud and proud for the home team.

Montréal opened the scoring on their first possession with a 14-yard David Duval field goal. The key play in the drive was a 50-yard Calvillo completion to Jamal Richardson and two nine-yard strikes to Cahoon. Shortly after, Burris, starting at his seven, marched 66 yards in 10 plays, completing passes to Jermaine Copeland, Joffrey Reynolds and Ken Yon Rambo. With the ball on the enemy 30, Burris threw to Reynolds for eight, but Nik Lewis took a roughing penalty that put the ball back on the 37. DeAngelis tied the game with a 44-yarder.

After two and out by Montréal, Burris was picked off by Reggie Hunt. Five plays later, Avon Cobourne scored, making it Montréal 10, Calgary 3.

The ball on the 35, Burris seemed rattled by the crowd noise and took a time-count violation. Burke Dales punted, and Larry Taylor returned it 44 yards to the Calgary 43. Duval completed the drive with a 19-yard field goal.

Then Burris took control. On first down, he ran for 11 yards. "After Hunt's interception, I saw they were dropping back and not paying any attention to me." It was then 12 to Lewis, incomplete, 18 to Lewis, Reynolds three, 12 yards to Reynolds and 20 to Brett Ralph in the end zone. At halftime, it was Montréal 13, Calgary 10.

Burris had a great first half, completing 11 straight. He was 15 of 20 for 166 yards, a pick and a touchdown. Calvillo was 16 for 20, 199 yards.

On Calgary's second possession after the break, Burris began on his 13-yard line with a 30-yard strike to Lewis. Joffrey Reynolds lost three, Burris to Lewis for 14. At centre field, Reynolds picked up two, Henry ran for 14 and 29 yards to the Alouette 10. Three plays later, DeAngelis tied the game. After Montréal replied with a single, Burris marched his team 61 yards for another three points. At the end of three quarters, Calgary led for the first time, 16–14.

On the first play of the fourth quarter, Dwight Anderson intercepted. The Stamps moved 35 yards into field-goal range, Calgary 19, Montréal 14.

The same Anderson took a dumb objectionable conduct call, allowing Calvillo to move into good field position. He got to the Calgary 36 on a 22-yard pass to Cahoon, was sacked by Mike Labinjo for eight and struck for 22 to Richardson. With the ball on the 22, Calvillo threw into the end zone to Brian Bratton. Shannon James came up with a game-saving interception. DeAngelis iced the cake with a 50-yard field goal. The final score: Calgary 22, Montréal 14. The Stampeders had won their sixth Grey Cup.

Burris was named Grey Cup MVP, and DeAngelis was awarded top Canadian for his five field goals. Not a gracious winner, DeAngelis berated the media after the game for giving the Outstanding Special Teams Award to Dominic Dorsey.

Calgary won because of Hufnagel's coaching, a defence that held Montréal's high-flying offence to one point in the second half and a quarterback who proved he could win the big one.

Coaching? Calvillo had a quick release. Rather than try harder to get to him, Calgary decided to distract him by waving their hands in the air to block his vision and knock down or tip passes. "They did a great job getting their hands up and knocking the ball down," said the dejected Montréal quarterback. "They played more zone than we thought they would."

Indeed, the Stamps had trouble with Cahoon and Richardson who each had five first-half receptions. Richardson had 101 yards in 30 minutes. So Chris Jones switched from man to zone, a gutsy move, changing your strategy in the middle of the most important game of your career.

After the game, Burris was ecstatic.

Montréal's a tough team. We knew it wasn't going to be a cakewalk, and they played their hearts out in front of their fans. This team is resilient; we were truly on a mission and it showed.

It's all about managing the game. That's one thing I've learned from watching Anthony Calvillo over the years, Dave Dickenson, also.

If you were told you could win the Cup and only score one touchdown? Wow. I wouldn't have believed it because of the firepower both teams have. I believed in our defence. As long as we could keep Calvillo off the field and win the battle of possession like we did in the second half, that gave us the opportunity to just score one touchdown and give DeAngelis the chance to kick the ball through the uprights time and time again.

The heart of the Stamps' defence was Mike Labinjo. Down with the flu, in the second half he sacked Calvillo and knocked down three passes.

Sixty years to the day after the Stampeders won their first Grey Cup, the city and team celebrated in front of City Hall, a glorious end to a glorious season.

Grey Cup 2009

The Canadian football world was rocked in early 2009 when general manager Eric Tillman was charged with the sexual assault of a 16-year-old babysitter. He was eventually given a conditional discharge, but his career was effectively over in Saskatchewan.

With the salary cap system, teams become victims of their success. The Roughriders weren't immune, losing all-star linebackers Maurice Lloyd and Anton Mackenzie to Edmonton and BC, respectively. Safety Scott Gordon signed with the Eskimos. James Johnson, 2007 Grey Cup MVP, went to Winnipeg. Still, at the beginning of the 2009 season, Roughrider CEO Jim Hopson proclaimed, "The roster is the best I've seen in my memory, especially Canadian talent."

Added Kent Austin's successor Ken Miller, "We are going to be strong in all areas."

They were right.

With Darian Durant at the controls, the Riders battled the defending champion Stampeders all season long for first place. In the end, both teams were tied at 10–7–1 with Saskatchewan taking the top spot by beating Calgary twice, even without their injured star receiver Weston Dressler. The other game was a 44–44 thriller. For the first time in 33 years, Saskatchewan would host the Western final.

Durant was third in passing behind Ricky Ray and Henry Burris. Although he was the only Rider quarterback to get the team to first place since Ron Lancaster, when asked about the most difficult thing for him to adjust to, Durant replied, "Dealing with the scrutiny around here. It's pretty tough. You hear everything that comes out because the media will let you know how the fans feel. There was a time this year I got kind of comfortable and felt I was getting settled in, and then we lose a game and they want to run me out of town."

The Roughriders continued their dominance of the Stampeders in the final, winning 27–17. Durant was good on 18 of 25 passes for 204 yards and three touchdowns. The victory was sweeter because they deprived the Stampeders of the opportunity to defend their 2008 title at home.

Saskatchewan's opponent in the Grey Cup at McMahon Stadium was the Montréal Alouettes, who beat Saskatchewan twice during the season.

The Als dominated the East with a record of 15–3. This was their seventh Grey Cup appearance during the decade, all losses but one.

The dynamic duo of quarterback Anthony Calvillo and receiver Ben Cahoon were at the top of their game. Statistically, les Larks led the league in both offence and defence. Four of the six league awards went to Alouettes, including Most Outstanding, won by Calvillo. John Chick won for defence. Montréal was the prohibitive favourite to win the 97th Grey Cup before a crowd that was 90-plus percent cheering for Saskatchewan.

Confounding the experts, the Roughriders didn't let them down, marching to Montréal's 35- and 33-yard lines on their first possessions. Congi missed the first field goal and made the second one.

The teams exchanged punts. Montréal scrimmaged at their 25 when Marcus Adams forced Calvillo to fumble. It was returned 11 yards by Keith Shologan. First-and-goal at the eight, Durant found Andy Fantuz in the end zone for a touchdown. At the end of the first 15 minutes, it was Saskatchewan 10, Montréal 0.

The Alouettes opened second-quarter scoring with a 28-yard field goal. They drove deep into Rider territory soon after. Calvillo threw to Kerry Carter at the Rider 17, but middle linebacker Renauld Williams knocked the ball loose. It was recovered by Chris McKenzie.

Near the end of the half, Damon Duval shanked a seven-yard punt out of bounds at his 44. Three plays later, Congi kicked a 45-yard field goal and scored a single on the kickoff. Saskatchewan got the ball back with 1:01 on the clock at their own 46. It was Cates for five, Durant to Fantuz for 10 and Gerran Walker for eight. Durant ran for 11. Fantuz made an acrobatic catch at the Montréal two. With two seconds left, Congi nailed a nine-yard field goal. Halftime score: Saskatchewan 17, Montréal 3.

The Als began their comeback with a nine-play, 74-yard drive culminating in a Calvillo to Jamal Richardson touchdown at 7:01 of the third quarter. Six minutes later, Durant was intercepted deep in Als territory by Billy Parker. The defence forced them to punt from their own end zone. The Riders took advantage to record a 23-yard Congi field goal. At the end of 45 minutes, Saskatchewan led 20–10.

Montréal recorded a single when Duval missed a 51-yard field goal early in the final quarter. Starting at his 35, Durant threw to Fantuz for 11. Cates picked up 17 yards. Gerran Walker ran for 18, Cates for 19, bringing the ball to the enemy 10 from where Durant ran into the end zone. With 10 minutes and 52 seconds left, Saskatchewan was in control, leading 27–11.

The never-say-die Alouettes roared back with a six-play, 71-yard drive for a TD scored by Avon Cobourne. The two-point conversion was good.

On Saskatchewan's ensuing possession, with second down at his 33-yard line, Durant threw an interception. Montréal went 85 yards in eight plays, capped off with a Calvillo to

Cahoon major. The two point convert failed. Saskatchewan 27, Montréal 25.

Saskatchewan went three and out on their last possession. Starting at their 34, Montréal moved to the Rider 36-yard line. With no time left, Duval attempted 43-yard field goal try. It was wide. But wait! Saskatchewan was penalized for having too many men on the field. Ten yards closer, Duval lined up again. As the ball sailed through the uprights, all the wind was sucked out of the stadium, and there was an eerie silence. Over 40,000 Roughrider fans sat stunned in their seats and then quietly filed out to the parking lots.

Final score: Montréal 28, Saskatchewan 27.

Except for muffled sobs and a few players throwing up, the Roughrider dressing room was like a morgue. Coach Ken Miller wandered out into the night beside the dressing room door, sadly shaking his head. A few minutes later, he said, "We had 13 men on the field. We had a lack of communication. We had what we called a 'beef block' go on the field. One of the men who should have run off, stayed on. We made a critical error and permitted them to win. I'm just so disappointed by the loss. It will affect each one of us as long as we're on the planet. We should have won the football game."

The following spring, Miller said, "There isn't a man who was part of that team who would ever want to experience that day ever again. Coming back here, walking across the field to greet our fans empty-handed after such a terrible loss. For those of us who were involved, it compares to losing a job or you've had a relationship that failed, something like that. When you think about it, it's always with you."

Special teams coach Kavis Reed took responsibility for the error and accepted that his coaching days in Saskatchewan were over. But it wasn't his fault. Nobody owned up to the error, letting a fine man and coach take the fall. There seems little doubt that the culprit was linebacker Sean Lucas. It doesn't really matter.

The fact is, Saskatchewan blew a 16-point lead in 10 minutes. If Duval had made the first attempt, the game would have been remembered as an epic comeback engineered by a great quarterback.

Compared to other gridiron disasters, Saskatchewan fans got over the 13th man rather quickly and looked forward to the upcoming season.

Grey Cup 2010

The year 2010 was the Saskatchewan Roughriders' 100th birthday of the storied franchise. Every game was a sell-out. With Darian Durant and the Canadian air force of Andy Fantuz, Chris Getzlaf and Rob Bagg plus North Dakotan Weston Dressler, the Roughriders were entertaining and competitive.

There were plenty of fireworks at Mosaic Stadium on Canada Day 2010 when Saskatchewan defeated Montréal 54–51 in overtime. Fantuz and Dressler caught TD passes in OT. Durant threw for 478 yards and five majors.

The Roughriders followed that up with wins over BC and Edmonton before dropping a 40–20 decision in Calgary. At the halfway mark, they were 6–3, in second place, four points behind Calgary. Darian Durant led the league in passing.

From then on, Calgary was 5–4, Saskatchewan was 4–5, with losses in four of their last five games. BC came to Regina for the semifinal on a roll. To make matters worse, Luca Congi was knocked out for the season during the October 17 loss to the Stampeders.

The Western semifinal was a shootout with the teams matching score for score. After regulation time, BC and Saskatchewan were tied at 27.

First, Wes Cates tallied a touchdown in overtime, then BC quarterback Travis Lulay. In the second overtime period, Paul McCallum put the Lions in front with a field goal. Darian Durant responded with a pass to former Leo Jason Clermont in the end zone for the winning score. Saskatchewan 41, BC 38.

Although Calgary won the season series with the Riders, the Green and White always felt comfortable playing in Calgary, which they considered their home away from home. They also knew Henry Burris had never won a playoff game against them. The Western final was no different.

Usually, Calgary-Saskatchewan games were shootouts. Not this time. Saskatchewan 20, Calgary 16.

The Roughriders were in their third Grey Cup in four years, this time in Edmonton.

The Alouettes once again dominated the East, finishing first at 12–6 and demolishing Toronto 48–17 in the division final.

The 2010 Grey Cup was a plodding affair on a cold day. Montréal scrimmaged on the Rider 38 on their second possession because of a no-yards penalty. Calvillo surprised everyone by running for eight yards. Avon Cobourne carried for 13, and Jamal Richardson took a 15-yard pass to the two. Cobourne scored. Montréal 7, Saskatchewan 0. Wes Cates concluded an eight-play, 75-yard drive with a one-yard plunge for the TD. Montréal got a single and led 8–7 at the end of the first quarter. The Riders added a field goal in the second stanza, giving them an 11–8 lead at the half.

After the break, the often-gambling Ken Miller retreated into a conservative shell while the usually conservative Alouette coach Marc Trestman gambled. In addition, the great Calvillo staged a quarterbacking clinic, relieving the pass-rush pressure with short stuff.

Saskatchewan took the kickoff to start the second half and moved to the Als' 38. They punted, rather than letting rookie Warren Kean try a field goal. Starting at the 12, the Als picked up a first down to the 33 and eight yards more. On third-and-two, Trestman called for a fake and blocker Eric Deslauriers ran for a first down at the 51. When the drive stalled at the Saskatchewan 15, Damon Duval tied the game with a field goal. The Als went ahead with another three-pointer at 1:37 of the final frame before adding a Cobourne touchdown to lead 21–11 halfway through the fourth quarter.

Four minutes later, Saskatchewan benefitted from a no-yards call and started their drive at the Montréal 32. Durant threw to Fantuz at the one. He then found right guard/tight end Marc Parenteau in the end zone for the score. With three minutes left, Saskatchewan trailed 21–18.

Calvillo took his team from his 40-yard line to the Rider 33. Showing shades of 2009, Duval missed a 40-yard field-goal try, and Weston Dressler ran the ball out. But that was it. Durant threw a desperation pass at his 25, which was intercepted. The final, Montréal 21, Saskatchewan 18.

Four times during the game, the Riders had a yard or two for a first down and elected to punt. Twice they punted rather than have their punter Eddie Johnson try a field goal. During the regular season, Weston Dressler had picked up 323 receiving yards against Montréal. In the Grey Cup, he was two for 11 yards, and his number was never called in the second half. Darian Durant was the leading quarterback rusher in the league, yet he ran but once for eight yards. The immobile Calvillo ran twice for 16 yards.

Although the Alouettes were the better team, once again the Rider Nation believed they lost a Grey Cup they should have won.

Anthony Calvillo had chalked his second straight Grey Cup win, Jamal Richardson was the game MVP and Saskatchewan's Keith Shologan the Outstanding Canadian.

Grey Cup 2011

While the 99th Grey Cup game between BC and Winnipeg was a tame affair, that couldn't be said for the off-field action during Grey Cup week. BC first appeared in the big game in 1963 at home to Hamilton, a game remembered for Angela Mosca's late hit on Willie Fleming that knocked him out of the game, which the Ti-Cats went on to win. Lion quarterback Joe Kapp was so incensed he wouldn't shake hands with "Mosca the Meanie." On Friday of Grey Cup week in Vancouver, at the CFL alumni luncheon, Kapp sarcastically presented flowers to Mosca who responded by clubbing Kapp with his cane. Kapp then punched Mosca senseless and kicked him when he was down.

It was that kind of year.

Wally Buono, the most successful coach in CFL history, had just gone through consecutive 8–10 seasons, a first for him. He approached 2011 with cautious optimism, talking about transitioning his Lions for a new era.

"I definitely believe the transition is on target," he said that May, "but obviously the young guys have to take another step in the right direction. Travis Lulay, Solomon Elimimian and other veterans have to be better." They were, but they took their own sweet time about it.

The Lions went 0–5 to start the season. After Labour Day, they were 3–6 and lost only one more game thereafter. It is no coincidence the turnaround began soon after Buono acquired receiver Arland Bruce III from Hamilton in August for draft picks.

"He's a pro," enthused Buono. "He comes to work every day. He's dependable. He brings a winning attitude. He's good to be around. We started to get on a roll when he arrived. He's just one guy being positive and encouraging, and then everybody is doing it. He has been very, very good for us."

Along with the great Geroy Simon and rookies Shawn Gore and Akeem Foster, the Leo offence was so alive that quarterback Travis Lulay won the league's Most Outstanding Player Award.

Defensively, with the likes of linebacker Solomon Elimimian, linemen Brent Johnson, Aaron Hunt, Keron

Williams and Khalif Mitchell, along with DBs Dante Marsh, Ryan Phillips and Korey Banks, BC was able to stop everything thrown at them. And they had the great Paul McCallum to do the kicking.

BC's opponent for the Grey Cup would be Winnipeg who tied with Montréal for first. Without the injured Anthony Calvillo, the Als lost the semifinal 52–44 to Hamilton who were in turn vanquished by the Bombers 19–3 in the final. During the season, Calvillo became the leading passer in pro-football history.

The Bombers went from worst in 2010 (4–14) to first in 2011 (0–8) on the strength of a defence led by the great Canadian lineman Doug Brown.

For Grey Cup 2011, it would be Bomber Paul LaPolice in his second year as a head coach versus the Lion of Autumn Wally Buono who was taking part in his 14th Grey Cup, nine as a head coach, four as a player. He had six Grey Cup rings, four as a coach, two as a player.

It would be Lion-reject Buck Pierce quarterbacking the Bombers with the ascendant star Travis Lulay on the other side.

The hometown team opened the scoring on their second possession. Tim Brown ran a punt back to the Bomber 45. Lulay completed 13-yard passes to Foster and Paris Jackson. Rookie running back Andrew Harris ran it in from the nine-yard line.

It was two and out for the Bombers. BC promptly moved into field-goal range with McCallum kicking it through from 22 yards out. He added a single three minutes later to make the score at the end of the opening quarter, BC 11, Winnipeg 0.

Second-quarter scoring consisted of three field goals, two by the Bombers. At the half, it was 14–6 for BC.

Despite strong defensive play by the Bombers, the Lions put the game away with 10 third-quarter points on a 22-yard McCallum field goal and a 44-yard strike from Lulay to Kierre Johnson at the 14:40 mark. Winnipeg had a field goal to narrow the score to 24–9 after 45 minutes of play.

In the final frame, Lulay combined with Arland Bruce III for a touchdown and a BC 31–9 lead. The Bombers scored two majors, but it was too late. Add in another McCallum field goal, and the final score was BC 34, Winnipeg 23.

It would have been a runway in the first half if BC's Travis Lulay hadn't been overthrowing receivers. He began to hit them in the third quarter, especially Bruce, who had five catches for 73 yards and a touchdown.

Lulay, named Grey Cup MVP, was good on 21 of 37 passes for 320 yards. He was intercepted twice. Andrew Harris picked up 65 yards rushing and the Outstanding Canadian honour.

Bomber Buck Pierce was 19 of 37 for 250 yards, one TD, two interceptions. Jovon Johnson who won the CFL's Most Outstanding Defensive Player Award, the first time a member of the secondary has been so honoured, was the best bomber on the field. He consistently put his team in good field position with great runbacks. He made three key knockdowns of Lulay passes.

It looked like Paul LaPolice and his young team would have a bright future. But he didn't last until Labour Day in 2012, fired when the club started the season at 2–6.

For Wally Buono, now tied with Lew Hayman, Hugh Campbell and Don Matthews with the most Grey Cup victories at five, it was time to leave the sideline and concentrate on the front office. Buono relinquished the coaching reins to long-time assistant Mike Benevides.

Grey Cup 100

The 100th Anniversary of the Grey Cup marks a major milestone in Canadian football history. As this book goes to press, the outcome of the game is unknown, but other aspects of the celebration are quite predictable. We know that over 54,000 football fans will yell themselves hoarse when the winners of the East and West divisions meet on November 25, 2012, at the Rogers Centre in Toronto in a battle to claim the 100th Cup. We know that they, and thousands more Canadians, will have partied royally in a 10-day, 11-night celebration storming Toronto—at the Fan Zone in the Toronto Metro Centre; the Adrenaline Zone, for those with a taste for adventure; at Nathan Phillips Square; at the Family Zone at Yonge-Dundas Square; and at the Street Festival, where tail-gating is not only allowed but is also encouraged.

We also know that the historic trophy itself will have criss-crossed Canada on a train called the Grey Cup Special, drawing many of the young and young-at-heart who won't physically be able to make it to the game itself.

Of course, the game's the thing, with all the hoopla just a warm-up to the main event. We don't know which two powerhouse teams will face each other across the line of scrimmage. At press time, it was just too close to call. In the east, it could be the Montréal Alouettes with quarterback Anthony Calvillo, at the age of 40, enjoying one of his best seasons. Or it could be the Toronto Argonauts, with former Eskimo pivot Ricky Ray at the helm. The BC Lions have led the West most of the season, but the Calgary Stampeders are close behind with Canadian running back Jon Cornish enjoying a blockbuster season. And Saskatchewan and Hamilton are coming on strong.

Finally, back to something we do know for certain. No matter which team has the honour of hoisting high the 100th Grey Cup, the thrill of the game will carry the CFL well into the next 100 years.

Happy 100th Birthday, Grey Cup!

Notes on Sources

Calgary Herald, Regina Leader-Post and *The Albertan*, various editions, 1909–2011.

Canadian Football Hall of Fame. www.cfhof.ca

Canadian Football League: Facts, Figures and Records. Canadian Football League Publication, 2011.

CFL Media Guide, 1976–2011.

Kelly, Graham. *The Grey Cup: A History.* Calgary: Johnson Gorman, 1999.

Kelly, Graham. *Green Grit: The Story of the Saskatchewan Roughriders.* Toronto: HarperCollins, 2001.

Kelly, Graham. *Grey Cup Glory.* Calgary: Johnson Gorman, 2003.

Kelly, Graham. *Greatest Grey Cups: The Best of Canadian Football.* Canmore: Altitude Publishing, 2005.

Kelly, Graham. *Go Stamps Go: The Story of the Calgary Stampeders.* Calgary: Panorama Press, 2010.

Kelly, Graham. *Saskatchewan Roughriders: The Players, the History & the Fans.* Edmonton: Folklore Publishing, 2012.

Saskatchewan Sports Hall of Fame. www.sshfm.com

Walker, Gordon. *Grey Cup Tradition.* Toronto: ESP Marketing and Communication, 1987.

Graham Kelly

GRAHAM KELLY has covered 37 Grey Cups in a career that landed him in the Canadian Football Hall of Fame's media section. The author of *The Grey Cup History*, *Greatest Grey Cups* and *Saskatchewan Roughriders*, Graham was the Roughrider waterboy in 1956–57. He covered the Riders for United Press International from 1963 to 1968 and has covered the CFL for the *Medicine Hat News* since 1972.